The British Poets, Including Translations
by British Poets

Address:
HardPress
8345 NW 66TH ST #2561
MIAMI FL 33166-2626
USA
Email: info@hardpress.net

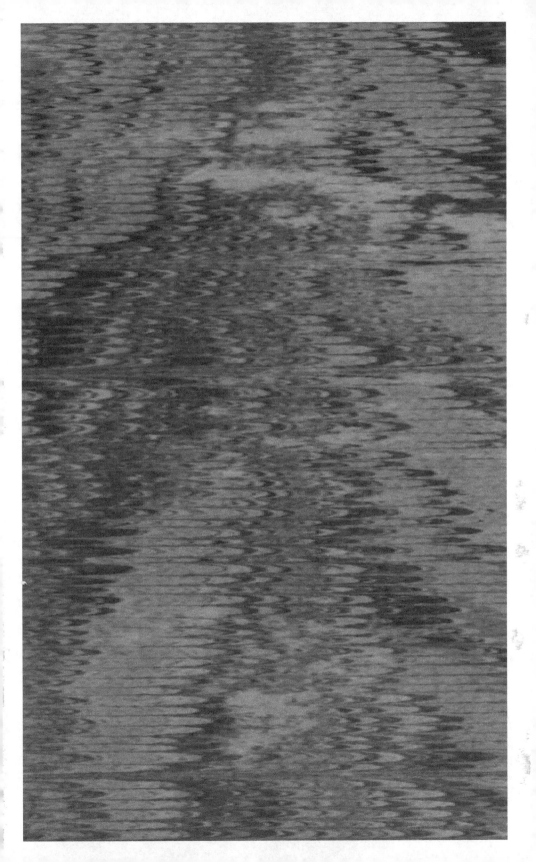

THE
BRITISH POETS.

One Hundred Volumes.

VOL. XCI.

THE

BRITISH POETS.

INCLUDING

TRANSLATIONS.

———

IN ONE HUNDRED VOLUMES.

XCI.

APOLLONIUS RHODIUS, VOL. II.

═══════

CHISWICK:

𝔓rinted by ℭ. 𝔚hittingham,

COLLEGE HOUSE;

FOR J. CARPENTER, J. BOOKER, RODWELL AND MARTIN,
G. AND W. B. WHITTAKER, R. TRIPHOOK, J. EBERS,
TAYLOR AND HESSEY, R. JENNINGS, G. COWIE AND CO.
N. HAILES, J. PORTER, B. E. LLOYD AND SON,
C. SMITH, AND C. WHITTINGHAM.

———

1822.

THE

ARGONAUTICS

OF

APOLLONIUS RHODIUS.

TRANSLATED;

WITH

Notes and Observations,

CRITICAL, HISTORICAL, AND EXPLANATORY,

BY

W. PRESTON, ESQ. M. R. I. A.

VOL. II.

Chiswick:

FROM THE PRESS OF C. WHITTINGHAM,

COLLEGE HOUSE.

CONTENTS.

THE

ARGONAUTICS

OF

APOLLONIUS RHODIUS.

BOOK III.

The Argument.

Juno and Minerva, having consulted together how they may best aid the Argonauts in their enterprise, resolve to apply to Venus.—They persuade her to send Cupid to inspire Medea with love for Jason. That hero, with the sons of Phryxus, presenting himself before Æetes, demands of him the golden fleece.—The monarch, enraged at this bold application, propounds tremendous, and, as he thought, impracticable tasks, as the means of obtaining the fleece.—These were, to yoke the bulls breathing fire.—To sow the dragon's teeth, and reap the harvest of armed men.—In the mean time, Venus finds Cupid playing at dice with Ganymede.—She bribes her son with a couple of golden balls, to cooperate in the design of inflaming Medea with love.—The passion and mental conflicts of that princess are described.—She resigns herself wholly to the dominion of love; and, under the influence of that emotion, determines to assist Jason in his enterprise.—She has an interview with the young hero at the temple of Hecate.—She furnishes him with a certain medicament, composed of enchanted herbs and drugs; by which he should be enabled to endure the fiery breath of the bulls.—And instructs him how he is to conduct himself, so as to avoid the fury of the

earthborn brothers, who were to spring up from the dragon's
teeth.—The fatal day arrives.—Jason, duly instructed and
prepared, enters on his task with alacrity.—Description of
his yoking the bulls, compelling them to work, and sowing
the dragon's teeth.—The harvest of armed men springs up.
—Jason, as he had been previously instructed, throws a
stone among them.—They begin to fight, and destroy each
other.—Jason exterminates the survivors.—Æetes beholds
the scene with rage and despair.

COME, Erato[1], sweet parent of the song,
That tell'st the feelings of the' enamour'd throng.
Relate how Jason, from that Colchian shore,
The fleecy treasure to Thessalia bore:
While artful Love to Pallas lent his aid,
And gentle phrensy fired the royal maid.
The tender wars of Venus are thy care,
Thy melting numbers sooth the virgin fair;
O soft historian of the lover's flame,   [name.
Hence are thy songs, and hence the' endearing
   Yet undetermined on their future way,   11
The Grecian band conceal'd in sedges lay.
Meantime the daughter and the wife of Jove
Consult, sequester'd from the powers above;
When to their fragrant chamber they repair'd,
Not Jove himself their sacred counsels shared;
The converse first from royal Juno moved,
Anxious to learn what wisdom's power approved.
   'Daughter of Jove, what purpose fills thy mind?
Say, what expedient can thy wisdom find?   20
What soothing speech from stern Æëtes gains
The fleece of gold? what stratagem obtains?

[1] The muse who presided over love and poetry, so called
from the Greek word, *erao.*

Fierce as he is, much labour it will ask,
But shall immortals shun an arduous task?'
   She ceased, and Pallas thus—' Revolving thought
Already with the favourite theme is fraught.
From scheme to scheme I turn my doubtful mind,
Yet none propitious to the Greeks I find.'
   She paused; and both upon the pavement keep
Their glances fix'd, in meditation deep.   30
Then Juno—' Let us seek the queen of charms,
And gain her son to lend his powerful arms;
Let him inflame the fair Medea's heart;
Philtres she knows, and many a magic art.
His gentle weapons shall invade her rest,
And love for Jason fill the' enamour'd breast;
The slave of fond desire, she may unfold
Expedients, that shall win the fleece of gold.'
   Minerva with the prudent speech accords,
And thus replies, in soft and gentle words— 40
' My sire produced me, of impassive kind;
Love's fond artillery never touch'd my mind.
Unskill'd I am, in amorous hopes and fears;
Yet if this engine of such force appears,
Let knowledge still o'er inexperience sway;
I freely follow where you point the way.'
They sought the palace of the Cyprian queen;
A spacious pile, where Vulcan's hand was seen.
The beauteous bride when sovereign Jove bestow'd,
His choicest skill the' impassion'd workman show'd   50
The courts they pass'd, and found the portals closed,
Where the fond spouse his bridal bed disposed.
With fairest hands the goddess deck'd the bed;
To wonted labours while her husband sped.

His forge, his anvil, and the' erratic isle,
Invite him early to the scene of toil,
Where all the wonders of his art he made,
Recesses deep, that cavern'd fires pervade.
    Full opposite the portal, on a throne
That circled round, the goddess sat alone.   60
Her tresses floated on her shoulders fair,
A comb of gold adjusts her radiant hair.
The queen of beauty then her cares bestow'd,
In braids prolix to weave her locks, that flow'd
Like streaming sunshine.   When her guests she
          view'd,
The pleasing labour she no more pursued.
She bade them enter, and with courteous grace,
Sprang from her seat to give the strangers place.
Reclined, the heavenly visitants beside,   69
Her careless tresses in a knot she tied.   [heart,
Then with soft smiles that search the throbbing
And gentle stings, and secret wishes dart—
'Say, honour'd goddesses, what counsel springs?
After long absence what occasion brings,
Unwonted favour, to the queen of love,
The first and chief of deities above?'   [art
    'We feel the sarcasm, though conceal'd with
(Juno replied), but grief invades the heart.
In Phasis' stream the ship of Jason lies,   79
Allured by hopes to make that fleece his prize.
From Grecian shores he leads a gallant band;
Unequal conflicts the bold youths demand.
For all I fear, for Æson's offspring most;
O shall the flower of warlike hope be lost?
No, should the youth to Stygian glooms descend,
My care should follow, and my arm defend.
E'en should he try to loose from bands of steel
That wretch Ixion, he my aid should feel.

Shall haughty Pelias mark, with impious scorn,
My frustrate vengeance, and my shrine forlorn?
And shall not, then, the' atrocious tyrant dread
The fate impending o'er his guilty head?   92
Not from caprice my care of Jason flows;
His piety thy stream, Anaurus, knows.
Returning from the chase, when all around
The snows lay white on every rising ground,
And roaring torrents, from the mountain roll'd,
O'erspread the plain, in shape deform'd and old,
With helpless seeming, and with piteous strain,
I proved his feeling heart, nor proved in vain. 100
He bow'd his shoulders to my weight, and bore
Safe through the deluge and the torrent's roar.
O deed humane! recorded in my mind,
No common recompense it claims to find.
But punishment and recompense demand
Alike concurrence from thy gentle hand.'
    She ceased.   The novel language and request
Fill'd with amazement Cytherea's breast;
And veneration mix'd with secret shame,
While regal Juno used the suppliant's name. 110
    ' Goddess revered (she said, in accents kind),
Depraved and reprobate were Venus' mind,
Dare she presume thy wishes to despise,
For word or act that in her province lies.
Poor, poor auxiliaries are hands so weak;
But task them freely.   No return I seek.'
    With prudent answer Juno then proceeds—
' Nor strength nor force our present purpose needs.
A peaceful influence with thy son employ,
That mighty arbiter of pain and joy.   120
At thy persuasion let him wing the dart,
And love and Jason touch Medea's heart.

Thus may the Minyæ find a powerful aid;
For artful wiles endow the royal maid.
Thus may they safely reach Iolcus' shore,
And gain the fleece that shines with golden ore.
    Then Venus to the Goddesses replied—
' Your influence sooner would that urchin guide;
For, shameless though he is, and unconfined,
Some touch of reverence might affect his mind.
Of me regardless, with reluctant scorn   131
A mother's rule the wayward imp has borne.
In bitterness of grief, and passion's glow,
Oft have I thought to break his shafts and bow.
For, swoln with pride, at chastisement he spurns;
And menaces to reprimand returns.'
    With smiles the Goddesses her plaint attend,
And meaning glances on each other bend.
    In mournful notes resumed the queen of love—
' I find my sorrows your derision move.   140
Why weary others with my plaintive tone?
No; let me weep in silence and alone.
Though secret anguish on my bosom prey,
Yet, where I can, your wishes I obey.
When softest blandishments assail his breast,
My son may grant a parent's fond request.'
    Then Juno press'd her soft and polish'd hand,
And spake with soothing smiles and language
            bland—
' Perform the' appointed task with gentle art;
Nor let contention agitate thy heart.   150
Indulge thy son.   A parent's wish will find
Short opposition from his playful mind.'
    The Goddess ceased, and from her seat arose.
With her returning, virgin Pallas goes;
While o'er Olympus, and the realms above,
Fair Venus seeks the fleeting power of love.

Sacred to Jove where spread the flowery ground,
The little deity his mother found.
Nor found alone—the Phrygian boy ' was there,
Whom Jove translated to the starry sphere, 160
Struck with his beauty.   Them, as suited boys,
At golden dice the careless hour employs.
Minion of fortune, in exulting mood,
On tiptoe raised, the wanton tyrant stood.
His left hand grasp'd the winnings which he
His wealth securing to his ivory breast. [press'd,
Delirious sweetness from his glances flow'd,
And o'er his cheeks translucent colour glow'd.
Near him with bending knee the' opponent stands,
Two dice alone remain within his hands.   170
His heart the conqueror's mirthful triumph stung;
His drooping head in silent grief he hung.
Now the two dice, that of his store remain'd,
That urchin god, by lucky chance, has gain'd.
With empty hands in deep despairing trance,
He turn'd, nor saw the queen of charms advance.
She stood before her son—she press'd his cheeks;
And thus, with sweet insinuation, speaks—
   ' Why, wayward urchin, that malicious smile ?
What thoughtless victim does thy craft beguile ?
Thy mother brings thee an appropriate task ;
Nor yet, without reward, thine aid I ask.   182
Indulge thy mother; and I give my boy,
What once to Jove belong'd, a beauteous toy.
To him an infant in the' Idæan cave,
His nurse, Adrasté ³, the bright plaything gave,
A polish'd sphere.   And never, from the flame,
Or skill of Vulcan, sweeter trinket came.

  ² Ganymede.
  ³ Adraste or Adrastea, together with Ida, was the nurse of
Jove in Crete.

The various circles are of burnish'd gold;   189
Two swelling curvatures round each are roll'd.
The joinings are conceal'd with skill profound,
And over each is pale green ivy bound.
Launch'd from thy hand, in fields of ether bright,
That starlike orb will draw the train of light.
The prize is thine, if thy successful art
With love for Jason fills Medea's heart.
Send forth thine arrows, let her feel thy sway;
Nor be the favour lessen'd by delay.'   198
    The goddess paused; the boy, with ravish'd ears,
The task proposed and promised payment hears.
The gather'd playthings from his grasp he flung,
Then to her robe with both his hands he clung.
Her knees he clasp'd, and sprang from side to side,
While every art of blandishment he tried.
' I pine, I languish, for a toy so fair;
This instant grant it to my ardent prayer.'
But Venus slily parries the demand,
With artful words, and with caresses bland.
She stroked his cheeks, she kiss'd him, and she
            press'd,   209
And, gently smiling, thus her speech address'd—
    ' Thy dearest head be witness, and my own,
Here no deceit by Venus shall be shown.
The gift is thine; it shall not be delay'd;
But first thy shafts must touch the royal maid.'
    She spake.   The wily urchin, in a trice,
Collected from the ground his scatter'd dice.
He counted, one by one, the shining hoard;
And all in Venus' radiant bosom stored.
His quiver, leaning 'gainst a tree reclined,
He seized, and in the golden belt confined.   220
He snatch'd his bow; he traced the realms above,
Etherial, all-productive plains of Jove.

Then through the portals of Olympus tends,
Where sloping the celestial path descends;
There the two poles of the celestial sphere,
To meet the heavens, their lofty summits rear;
The highest points of earth, where first upborne
The blushing sun unfolds the rays of morn.
The foodful earth appear'd within his ken,
And cities, fair abodes of polish'd men;   230
With verdant banks, where sacred rivers flow,
And cloud-capp'd mountains lift the' aerial brow,
In prospect wide the vast of ocean lies,
And seems to mingle with surrounding skies.

The ship was moor'd beside the rushy bank;
The crew the benches fill'd in many a rank;
Tall spiry reeds that in the marshes grew,
Their ambush'd numbers hid from hostile view.
Each, in his place, in silent order sate;   239
While Jason thus commenced the deep debate—
  ' Hear, gallant friends, what present thoughts
          suggest,
And then decide as suits the' occasion best.
Our common dangers common counsels need;
From free discussion safety must proceed.
That man whose thoughts a guilty silence veils,
Of glory and of Greece defrauds our sails.
In arms your station at the ship retain,
While I the palace of Æëtes gain.
The sons of Phryxus shall with me along,
And two beside selected from the throng.   250
I mean to try the power of peaceful words;
If chance the king that fleece of gold accords,
'Tis well.   If, trusting to his strength of hand,
He treat with insolence a stranger band;
We then the worst of our condition know, [show,
And thoughts matured our future course may

Whether we shall depend on open force,
Or find in stratagem some safe resource.
Injurious 'twere to seize the prize in arms,
Ere soft persuasion has applied her charms. 260
With soothing words persuasion can prevail,
While brutal force and rageful menace fail.
When blameless Phryxus fled his stepdame's [4] ire,
And murderous rites of a misguided sire [5],
His mild demeanour rising pity bred,
And stern Æëtes spared his gentle head.
The laws of hospitable Jove, confess'd
In every clime, pervade the rudest breast.'
    The band assented with a loud acclaim;
Nor one the counsel could in secret blame. 270
The hero's steps the sons of Phryxus guide,
With Telamon Augeas guards his side.
He bears the staff of Hermes [6] in his hand,
And through the reeds and waters hastes to land.
    They reach'd an eminence amid the plains;
From Circè famed the place a name retains.
Osiers, in ranks, and vines o'erspread the ground;
Where carcasses are hung with chains around.
For, still the Colchians with abhorrence view
Sepulchral rites, that other tribes pursue. 280
Nor to the flames the lifeless man they give,
Nor bid the womb of parent earth receive.
No monumental mounds their hands compose.
Crude hides of bulls the manly kind enclose;
While, to the elemental air consign'd,
From trees they welter to the parching wind,
Without their walls. But different rites await
Their females when they feel the stroke of fate.
The corse is yielded to the parent clay.
Such various customs o'er that nation sway. 290

[4] Ino.   [5] Athamas.   [6] The sign of peaceful intentions.

Propitious to their journey, Juno shrouds[7]
The Colchian city in a vale of clouds;
That safely they might reach the monarch's seat;
Nor insult from the swarming rabble meet.
Soon as the heroes pass'd the spacious plain,
The city walls and royal dome to gain;
The goddess then dispell'd the mist in air;
Wondering they stood before the palace fair.
Its ample gates their admiration call,
And stately columns rank'd along the wall. 300
On brazen chapiters projecting placed,
The roof above a marble cornice graced.
The threshold then they pass, in mute amaze;
There her broad leaves the paly vine displays.
Beneath the shade four springs perennial flow'd,
Where Vulcan's hand had wondrous skill bestow'd;
One milk dispensed, and one the grape's red blood;
One fragrant oil, and one the crystal flood.
Hence, when the Pleiades forsake the skies,
With boiling heat the gushing waters rise;   310
When the fair stars returning radiance show,
With icy coldness from the rock they flow.
Such wonders in the Colchian palace shine,
Eternal monuments of art divine.
And wondrous bulls from Vulcan's labour came,
With brazen hoof, and mouths disgorging flame:
For these a plough he form'd, of structure rare,
And temper'd adamant composed the share;
A grateful offering to the god[8], whose car
Received him faint from the Phlegræan war. 320

[7] Imitated from the fourth book of the Odyssey, where Pallas draws a veil of thick air round Ulysses.   See also Virgil, lib. i.

[8] Phœbus.

Amid the court the stately palace rose.
Compacted valves each spacious entrance close.
In ample range the sumptuous chambers stand.
A portico projects on either hand.
Oblique a lofty building closed each wing.
Here, with his spouse, abode the Colchian king,
Within the turret, that in height excell'd.
The' inferior tower his son Abyrtus held.
Him, earliest object of the monarch's care,
Caucasean nymph, Asterodea, bare.   330
Ere yet the bands of nuptial faith were tied,
That mark'd Idya⁹ for his virgin bride,
This youngest offspring of the hoary wave
To parent ocean matron Tethys gave.
The graceful youth shone so supremely bright,
The Colchians named him, from the source of light,
Fair Phaeton.   The chambers that remain'd
The' attendant virgins of the queen obtain'd.
Chalciopé—Medea there abode,
Offspring by marriage on the king bestow'd. 340
    That morning, to salute her sister bent,
The fair Medea from her chamber went;
For Juno's care confined the nymph at home,
Unusual chance, within the splendid dome.
Priestess of Hecaté, within the shrine
Day after day she pass'd in rites divine.
Soon as she view'd the strangers, in surprise,
Mingled with fear, she utter'd piercing cries;
Full soon the piercing cries her sister hears; 349
Full soon they reach the' attendant virgins' ears.
They cast their webs and distaffs to the ground,
And all, with hurried wonder, crowded round.
With them Chalciopé beheld her sons;
Through all her veins a thrilling pleasure runs.

⁹ The queen of Æëtes.

With eager joy her arms aloft she holds,
Each grateful youth his parent then enfolds,
With fond caresses, to his gentle breast;
While plaintive sounds the matron's cares ex-
  press'd.
' In vain, regardless of a mother's pain,
Ye left me here, to tempt the dangerous main,
Fate has repell'd you.   What unstay'd desire?
What cruel mandate of a dying sire, 362
O wretched me! would leave me to deplore,
My darlings ravish'd to some distant shore?
O Phryxus, how thy last commands impart
Eternal anguish to my bursting heart!
Why seek Orchomenus? why plough the deep,
To reach the seats that fancied treasures keep?
What place is that? ah, whither would you go?
Can sons delight to see their mother's woe?' 370

 Roused by her plaints, Idya, royal dame,
And last Æëtes, from the palace came.
The startling ear a mingled clamour thrill'd;
And various noises had the' enclosure fill'd.
Some of the train surround the mighty steer;
Some cleave with sharpen'd brass the billets sere.
Some, for the bath capacious caldrons boil;
Each for his lord was busied in some toil.

 Through the clear air unseen, relentless Love
Came, like the fly, that mads the youthful drove.
Through valley, and through flood, it drives them
  wild, 381
Scourge of the herd, the breeze by rustics styled.
Behind a column at the porch he stands,
And bends the' unerring bow with cruel hands.
A shaft untried he from the quiver drew,
Parent of pangs that bosom never knew.

With footsteps light the threshold then he pass'd,
And round and round his wily glances cast.
By Jason screen'd, he now contracts his size,
And to the nerve the' indented shafts applies. 390
He draws the feather'd mischief to the head;
Home to Medea's heart the shaft is sped.
Delirious trances all her powers subdue.
Back from the lofty dome that urchin flew,
A laugh malign his cruel mischief show'd.
Deep in the virgin's breast his arrow glow'd.
Like pent-up fires it raged; and from that flame,
At Jason darted, ardent flashes came.
While soft oblivion o'er the spirit flows;
With fainting throbs her bosom sunk, and rose. 400
Sensations new the melting spirit fill'd;
Through all her veins delightful anguish thrill'd.
    As when the toiling matron's frugal hand
Has heap'd the fuel round the smother'd brand;
From works of wool her scanty means are drawn;
Her wakeful toil anticipates the dawn,
And stores the hearth with lurking seeds of light,
That industry may steal an hour from night.
With gradual waste the fire in secret preys;
The billet moulders as it feeds the blaze;   410
Thus love, pernicious love, consumed the maid,
A fire unseen that on the bosom prey'd.
The various hue tumultuous passion speaks,
And pale and red alternate seize the cheeks.
    Now had the'attendants spread the festive board,
And lenient baths the weary limbs restored.
When food and wine had cheer'd the' expanding
        breast,
The king his grandsons mildly thus address'd—
' Say, gentle offspring of my daughter's love,
To Phryxus, honour'd all my guests above; 420

What to these walls returns you? choice? or force?
Say, did misfortune interrupt your course?
Might counsels built on pass'd experience sway,
Ne'er had your bark essay'd the weary way.
The space immense before your eyes I placed;
For every shore and distant gulf I traced.
Borne in the chariot, at my father's [10] side,
O'er many a clime I pass'd; in circuit wide;
What time from Colchos to Hesperia's shore,
The god of light my sister Circé bore.   430
Our wanderings ended on the Tuscan strand;
There yet she dwells, far from the Colchian land.
But why should tales of other times detain?
The' occurrence of the present hour explain.
Why from the vessel ye are present here?
And who these men that in your train appear?'

Before his brothers [11] Argus quick replies,
While prudent fears for Jason's ship arise.
In language mild he clothed his prudent thought,
For riper years had more experience taught. 440
' Our ship asunder torn by wind and wave;
Sole hope of refuge from the watery grave,
One precious plank, with anxious grasp, we keep;
That isle of Mars received us from the deep,
Buoy'd o'er the billows, by celestial care,
When shades of midnight blacken'd our despair.
No more we found the birds of Mars; erewhile,
Brooding they harbour'd in the desert isle;
But, ere we came, they fled their favourite land,
Chased by the prowess of a stranger band.   450

[10] Phœbus.

[11] Lest they might be too frank and unguarded, and compromise the safety of Jason and his companions.

That band for us, in pity, Jove detain'd;
They gave us garments, and with food sustain'd.
A tyrant's jealousy this youth expell'd,
Who all the race of Æolus excell'd.
With boundless wealth endow'd, and regal sway,
His haughty mandate none may disobey.
He bids him wander, destined to remove
A curse, impending from the wrath of Jove.
Hopeless alike, to disobey or speed,
And only sure the tyrant's hate to feed,   460
He comes, enjoin'd to purge away the stain,
Derived from Phryxus on the' Æolian train.
His efforts failing, they are doom'd to know
Inflictions dire, intolerable woe.
Nor cease their pangs, ere his return to Greece,
Means of atonement, wafts the golden fleece.
Minerva's skill the stately ship supplied;
Not like those barks that Colchian pilots guide;
Not like the bark our evil genius gave,
Sport of the winds, and scorn of every wave; 470
But, firm and tall, compact with timbers vast,
To ride the billows, and to dare the blast.
Alike contrived, with swelling sails, to fly,
And bending oars, that nervous rowers ply;
She bears collected all the prime and boast
Of youthful heroes, from the Grecian coast.
Far have they wander'd to the Colchian plain,
Through many a city, many a stormy main.
If generous thoughts the precious fleece may yield,
No force they meditate, no listed field.   480
Supreme in all things shall thy pleasure sway,
And ample gifts for the possession pay.
Their timely aid may quell the warlike kind,
Sauromatæ, that bear a rebel mind.

Wouldst thou be told from whence his lineage
The race heroic shall my tongue disclose. [flows ?
This chief, whose cause convokes the brave and
Is son of Æson, and from Cretheus sprung, [young,
The gallant Jason.   If we credit fame,
A common lineage with the chief we claim. 490
Cretheus and Athamas the vital fire
Derived from Æolus, a common sire;
Phryxus from Athamas.   His parent bright,
Augeas honours in the source of light;
And Telamon, allied to powers above,
Through glorious Æacus, descends from Jove.
The hero's followers all, of strain divine,
From deities deduce the' illustrious line.'

As Argus ended, indignation fill'd
The monarch's soul ; and storms of passion thrill'd.
Reproach and fury all the band engage;   500
His grandsons chief attract the burst of rage.
For them he censured, as the guilty cause,
That hateful visit from the strangers draws.
Beneath his brows his eyeballs darted fire.
' Hence, from my sight, ye caitiff brood, retire ;
Back, with your fables and your wiles, to Greece ;
Nor wait the fruits of Phryxus, and his fleece,
Bitter to you.   Not for the fleece ye come;
My sceptre ye would seize, and regal dome. 510
My table ye have touch'd with genial rite ;
Or direful thanks intrusion should requite ;
Tear out your tongues, and lop your arms away,
And send you forth a pageant of dismay ;
A timely check to wild attempts and lies ;
A just reward of monstrous blasphemies [12].'

[12] Lies—blasphemies: because Argus said that Telamon
was sprung from Jove, and other companions of Jason of
divine origin.

He spake infuriate; high disdain impell'd
The son of Æacus; his bosom swell'd
With indignation; and he had repaid
Reproaches with reproach; but Jason stay'd 520
The war of words; and mildly thus address'd
The haughty king—' Æëtes, calm thy breast;
Let not our armament thy fears engage,
Or fill thy bosom with tumultuous rage;
Not ours the motive painted by thy fear;
No hostile purpose to thy realm we bear.
What man would traverse such a tract of main,
To spoil, with hand unjust, a stranger's reign?
But, placed by Jove beneath a tyrant's sway,
His cruel mandate I, perforce, obey.   530
Indulge our wishes. Through the Grecian land,
Thy name and honour shall immortal stand.
Nor shall the favour meet a thankless race;
Our warlike service shall repay the grace,
Whether the proud Sauromatæ must bend;
Or other tribes the shock of arms attend.'

   Thus Jason with persuasive language wrought,
While doubtful fluctuates the tyrant's thought.
Now bent with sudden onset to destroy;
And now their strength in trials to employ.   540
With him revolving, the last thought prevails.
' Why, strangers (he replied), these long details?
If ye, indeed, a line celestial boast,
And, as our equals, seek the Colchian coast,
Lo, to your wish I grant the fleece of gold;
From valiant men I nothing can withhold.
Bear it to him, the despot of your land,
Whoe'er he is, that rules the Grecian band.
But, proved in trial, I demand to see
The daring man, who vies in force with me. 550

Now to the test; and let experience show
What tasks of peril I can undergo.
Two bulls upon the plains of Mars I tame,
With brazen hoofs, and mouths exhaling flame.
Obedient to the yoke the beasts I guide,
And plough the sacred space from side to side.
Four acres are allotted to the toil;
But rude the surface, stubborn is the soil.
No common seed is in that furrow sow'd;
No grain that Ceres erst on man bestow'd. 560
Along the furrow dragon's teeth I fling,
And hostile warriors from the tillage spring,
With mortal fury menacing around,
But soon my spear extends them on the ground.
At dawn I yoke my steers, and labour meet;
When twilight comes, I from the toil retreat.
If thou art equal to the task; this day
Home to thy king; and bear the fleece away.
But think not thou on other terms to gain;
The brave concede not to the recreant train.'

Silent the hero sat in grief profound,   571
His downcast eyes he rivets to the ground.
Much he revolved the proffer in his mind,
If thought perplex'd might some expedient find.
How shall he meet the trial? how refuse?
'Tis equal danger to reject or choose.
How shall he promise such a test to bide?
At length, with artful words, he thus replied—
 ' Just are thy sayings, king.   I feel their force;
Nor shun probation in this glorious course. 580
I claim the labour, should my death impend,
The last of ills that fates on mortals send.
Those fates subject me to a cruel lord;
His stern commands, no doubt, no choice afford.'

Thus he, while terror wrung the' astonish'd mind;
In language stern, the monarch thus rejoin'd—
'Now, get thee to thy comrades. Thou hast dared
A task of peril.   Come, with mind prepared.
Woe to thee, if I mark the signs of fear!
If but reluctance in thy looks appear;   590
If thou shouldst tremble at the fiery breed;
Or fly when warriors rise from fatal seed;
Mine be the care, in thee to teach mankind,
How dreadful 'tis to gall the nobler kind.'
He ended frowning.   Jason rose in haste,
And left the table.   Forth Augeas pass'd,
With Telamon; and separate by some space
Argus attended, with more tardy pace.
He stay'd to warn his brothers, by a sign,
Their steps within the palace to confine.   600
Thus they departed.   Mid the crowd alone,
In form and grace distinguish'd, Jason shone.
The' enraptured maiden held her veil askance,
And caught, beneath the shade, a sidelong glance.
She gazed, and gazed; while grief her soul subdued;
And thought in vain the lovely guest pursued;
As when we catch at objects in a dream,
That still beyond, yet ever near us seem.
While, sorrowing, from the palace they retire,
Chalciopé, to shun her father's ire,   610
Her inmost chamber with her children sought;
Medea follow'd, with distracted thought.
The cares of love within her bosom rise,
And absent Jason stands before her eyes,
His looks, his gestures, graved within her breast:
'Such his deportment—thus he wore his vest—
Such words he utter'd—thus, and there he sate—
Thus from the portal rush'd, unhappy fate!'

Possess'd, bewilder'd, her enamour'd mind
Finds not his parallel in humankind.   620
Still, still, in thought, his honey'd words she hears;
His tuneful accents vibrate on her ears.
Much for the youth her boding fears arise:
A ghastly corse he sinks before her eyes,
She sees him with the fiery bulls engage,
She sees him bleed beneath her father's rage.
She wept the victim, as already dead,
And piteous tears of soft compassion shed.
And mournful words to solitude she spoke;   629
While from her breast the smother'd anguish broke.
    ' What means the strange disorder of my heart?
Such tumult can a stranger's look impart?
In questionable shape, from distant climes,
Comes he a prince, or slave distain'd with crimes?
No matter.   Let a chief, or miscreant fall,
Why should the' event for wild emotions call?
Me it concerns not.   Yet, renown'd or base,
In safety let him fly this fatal place.
Daughter of Perseus, venerable power[13],
O guard the youth in that tremendous hour.
Protect him, guide him, to his native land;   641
Let him not perish on this Colchian strand!
But if the fates have destined him to fail,
And perish by the bulls that flames exhale;
Let him perceive there is a feeling heart,
That in his sufferings claims an equal part.'
    Thus anxious cares the virgin's bosom waste;
The chiefs, meantime, the crowd and city pass'd.
Back, through the plain, their journey they pursued,
And Argus thus to Jason speech renew'd—   650

[13] Hecate was daughter of Perseus, or Perses and Asteria.

'Will Æson's gallant son disdainful hear
My present counsel, as the child of fear?
Yet, in a state so doubtful and forlorn,
No trial, no resource deserves our scorn.
Hast thou not heard me of a virgin tell,
In philtres learn'd, and many a magic spell?
Daughter of Perseus, Hecaté bestow'd
The magic science; and with power endow'd.
Might we this maiden in your cause engage,
No terrors would await the monsters' rage.   660
To this my mother could dispose the maid;
Her influence great, but doubtful is her aid.
Yet will I seek her, and entreaties prove,
Our common danger may awake her love.'
   Thus he benevolent.   The chief replied—
'If such thy sentence; be the' expedient tried.
Go, and with prayers thy parent's heart incline;
And be the powers of soft persuasion thine.
Yet feeble comfort can that hope instil,
That waves suspended from a woman's will.' 670
   Beside the marsh the social train they find;
Impatient transport fill'd the general mind.
While eager questions every tongue employ;
With words of sorrow Jason damps their joy.
   'O friends (he said), the king's indignant mind,
Relentless, stern, has dreadful tasks assign'd;
Such as nor I, nor all this gallant band,
May hope to finish with successful hand.
Two bulls upon the plain of Mars he feeds;
Brazen their hoof, flame from their mouth pro-
         ceeds.   680
Four acres are the space for tilth allow'd;
With dragon's teeth the furrow must be sow'd.
This fatal seed the tyrant's hand supplies;
Thence warriors clad in panoply arise.

The ploughman, compass'd by that hostile crew,
Must perish, or his earth-born foe subdue.
To try the toil, I boldly gave assent;
Other expedient none could thought present.'
    Their downcast eyes in consternation fall;
The task is deem'd impossible by all.   690
Then each his neighbour view'd with listless gaze,
And silent sat in anguish and amaze.
    Peleus at length, with dauntless mien and breast,
Arose; and thus the' assembled chiefs address'd—
' In deeds, not words, our safety must reside;
The moments haste our conduct to decide.
If, Jason, thou to yoke the monsters dare,
Preserve thy faith, and for the task prepare;
But if thy spirit from the conflict flies,
Go not, nor single any with thine eyes.   700
The glorious danger none from Peleus gains,
Death is the worst that fate for man ordains.'
He ceased. The soul of Telamon was stung;
Impatient for that enterprise he sprung.
The valiant Idas for the trial glows.
The gallant twins of Tyndarus arose.
Arose the son of Æneus [14], young and fair,
His cheek scarce shaded yet with golden hair;
Yet, firm in daring, ripe in Virtue's flame,
The' appalling task of mighty men to claim. 710
In silence from the trial shrunk the rest,
When Argus thus the' adventurous chiefs ad-
       dress'd—
    ' O friends, the labour that your force demands
May be the last predestined to your hands.
Yet Heaven, perhaps, may keep resources stored;
My parent's counsel may some aid afford.

[14] Meleager.

Your generous ardour for a while restrain,
Some little space within your ship remain.
Better the task of glorious danger shun,
Than, blindly rash, on 'sure destruction run.   720
A maid within the royal palace bides,
Whom Hecaté through paths of science guides,
From every drug earth, air, and sea produce,
Charms to prepare; and know their power and use.
Of wasteful flame she stays the rageful force;
She stays the torrent in its headlong course;
The sacred moon within her orbit chains;
The planets from their devious range detains.
Theme of discourse, on our returning way,
This virgin, haply, might my mother sway;   730
The toil were light.   If ye to this assent,
Back to the palace be my footsteps bent,
My prayers and influence in your cause to prove,
With Heaven to speed me, and parental love.'
    The favouring gods display'd a sign from high.
Chased by a falcon through the liquid sky,
With downward flight, a dove to Jason press'd,
And sought for shelter in the hero's breast.
Swift on the vane alights his cruel foe.
Prophetic Mopsus mark'd them from below; 740
And, conscious of the future, thus reveal'd
The sacred truths in mystic signs conceal'd—
' I read the favour of the powers divine.
The gods benevolent have sent this sign.
With soothing words, and each persuasive art,
Essay to bend the royal virgin's heart;
Secure to speed, if Phineus truly told,
That means of safety Venus should unfold.
The bird of love, her harbinger, we see,
Preserved from danger, to our leader flee.

A joyful prescience fills the' expanded breast,
Of toils successful, and of glorious rest.
But first propitiate beauty's queen with prayer;
Then to perform what Argus bids prepare.'
  He ceased—the heroes their assent express'd.
The words of Phineus dwelt in every breast.
Idas alone, of all the warriors, rose.
In accents loud the' indignant spirit flows.
' Did women then embark to lend their aid?
And must our vows at Beauty's shrine be paid? 760
Must we, forgetful of the well fought field,
Our childish thought to doves and falcons yield?
Perdition catch you! be your arms resign'd!
With words subdue the weak unwarlike kind.'
He ended, frowning, while, in murmurs low,
A numerous train disapprobation show.
He sat indignant; answer none return'd,
Till Jason's mind with deep resentment burn'd.
To meet the' injurious charge he roused his thought,
And utter'd accents by the' occasion taught. 770
  ' If such the pleasure of the general train,
No more let Argus at the ship remain.
Moor we the vessel boldly from the land;
Longer concealment would disgrace our band.
No more, in marshes hid, the combat shun;
Bold and determined on the danger run.'
  He ceased. And Argus, at the word, recalls
His steps, and hastens to the city walls. [mand,
They weigh'd their anchors at the chief's com-
And urged with oars their vessel to the land. 780
  Without the palace gate, accustom'd seat
Of council, round their king the Colchians meet.
The savage king insuperable snares,
And mortal anguish, for the Greek prepares.

Soon as the bulls the' ill-fated man should slay,
That rashly dares the dangerous task essay,
With wood, collected from the mountain's gloom,
The ship and Greeks he purposed to consume.
A dire example of impressive fear,
To bid the future visitant forbear.   790
' Æolian Phryxus, when these shores he gain'd,
No free reception at my hand obtain'd,
Gentlest of guests, with piety adorn'd.
Yet had my palace gates a stranger scorn'd,
With earnest prayers he vainly had implored
Place in my household, station at my board,
Had not the son of Maia, from above,
Reveal'd the pleasure of almighty Jove.
And shall these pirates, that invade my states,
Elude the vengeance that presumption waits? 800
Miscreants, that meditate by force and spoil
To seize the produce of another's toil !
With wild excursion through the seas they roam,
To vex the peasant, and his peaceful home.'
     The sons of Phryxus, too, his wrathful mood
Condemn'd to wash away their crime in blood.
' Returning thus, with an unhallow'd train,
Ye come (he cried) to shake my peaceful reign.
Ye come to spy the secrets of the land.
Ye come to wrest the sceptre from my hand. 810
Irreverent wretches ! but your deeds accord
With revelations of my father's word,
The' all-seeing Sun.   He taught me to beware
The homebred treason, the domestic snare.
That voice prophetic such a fear impress'd,
I yielded frankly to your wild request;
Pleased that the mandates of your dying sire
Should with the safety of my house conspire.

To distant climes ye purposed then to go,
And rid my palace of the' intestine foe,   820
Sole cause of fear.   For, from my daughters rise
No terrors.   They no treason will devise.
My child, Absyrtus, will not bear a part
In any scheme to rend a father's heart.
Chalciopé, my child, thy sons appear
Sole cause of danger; only source of fear.
Guard well the vessel.   Vengeance on my train,
If single miscreant scape the destined pain!'

    Argus return'd the while his mother sought,
And to his aim with various speeches wrought;
Intent Medea's powerful aid to prove;   83 .
No new expedient to parental love.
But decent sense of shame her tongue withheld,
And fear restrain'd while tenderness impell'd.
Scarce dares she to the virgin's ear confide
Requests, from common rule so strangely wide;
Matter so dangerous, should the maid comply;
So doubly dangerous, should the maid deny.
Well might she fear her father's savage mind!
Well might she fear some impious task behind! 840

    While on her couch she sunk, in trance profound,
Medea's sorrows soft oblivion drown'd;
Yet, fearful visions hover'd round her head,
Illusive forms, of mournful fancy bred.
The stranger seem'd, that trial to sustain,
Moved by no wish the wondrous fleece to gain;
But love and she the daring aim supplied;
He sought Medea for his virgin bride.
Greece he had left, at Beauty's powerful call,
And love allured him to her father's hall.   850
The fiery bulls she then appear'd to tame,
And yoke, uninjured by their breath of flame.

Her parents, then, their promises denied.
The labour finish'd, they withheld the bride.
Between her father and the strangers rose
A fierce debate.   The warfare to compose,
The maid was call'd, as umpire of the strife;
And soon the daughter yielded to the wife.
Her kindred for that stranger thus resign'd,
What indignation fill'd each parent's mind!   860
Vast was their anguish, loud and shrill their cries—
Scared at the din, the virgin's slumber flies.
Pale from the couch she sprang, in wild amaze,
And round the chamber cast a vacant gaze.
She pants.   Her bosom palpitates with dread.
Thought is absorb'd, and recollection fled.
  ' What forms of terror, miserable maid
(With feeble voice she cried), thy sleep invade?
Some dire misfortunes have these heroes brought.
With anxious doubts this stranger fills my thought.
Far let him fly, and wed some Grecian fair; 871
My parents and my virtue claim my care.
But why with cruelty my bosom steel?
A sister's anguish why refuse to feel?
Maternal terrors for her sons arise,
Wilt thou, relentless, mark her tears and cries?
Think, savage as thou art, 'tis thine to save,
Or doom her children to the' untimely grave.
Oh nature! no, thy sacred ties shall bind;
In grief thine energies support the mind.'   880
In wild disorder from the couch she flew,
Unfolded wide the chamber door she threw.
Unshod, and disarray'd, in eager haste,
To seek her sister, she the threshold pass'd.
By conscious shame and timid awe restrain'd,
Long time before the portal she remain'd.

Fearful of entering, to and fro she paced;
Now forward rush'd, and now her steps retraced;
Her trembling steps, uncertain where they stray'd.
Her gait the conflict in her soul betray'd.   890
Impetuous love, with wild desire impell'd,
And bashful fear and modesty withheld.
Impassion'd now her sister's door she sought;
Her chamber now with deep despondence fraught.
Thrice she proceeds, and thrice her foot recalls;
Then prone upon her couch distracted falls.

As the young bride laments her blooming spouse,
Lord of her bosom, object of her vows;
In love united, and the hallow'd bands,
Knit by fraternal and parental hands;   900
She flies the soothings of the' attendant train,
She hides the fond expressions of her pain.
With grief, at once, and virgin shame oppress'd,
Her tears fall lonely on the' enamour'd breast;
When fates relentless the dear youth remove;
Untried the joys, the tender thefts of love;
From every tongue, that might impart relief,
She dreads a censure on her amorous grief;
In avarice of anguish hoards her care,
And eyes the widow'd couch in mute despair; 910
Thus mourn'd Medea; thus the cause suppress'd,
That bathed her eyes and heaved her throbbing
Amid this conflict of desire and shame,   [breast.
A virgin from among her menials came.
Unseen she stood a while, her tears to view;
Then to Chalciopé with tidings flew.
Chalciopé amidst her children sate.
Her thoughts were centred on their future fate.
Much she revolved what motives might persuade,
What arts impel her sister to their aid.   920

Not inattentive to the maiden's tale,
She finds strange tumults in her breast prevail.
A grief so sudden fills her with surprise.
To working fancy strange surmises rise.
While doubt and wonder in her bosom wrought,
Her hasty steps Medea's chamber sought.
Sunk on her couch the' afflicted maid she found,
Tearing her cheeks, in floods of sorrow drown'd.
' Why do thy tears, Medea, sister, flow?   929
What fatal cause has plunged thy soul in woe?
Does angry Heaven thy feverish veins inflame?
Do seeds of malady pervade thy frame?
Hast thou for me, and for my sons forlorn,
The deep reproaches of our father borne?
Oh, would to Heaven, that I and mine might flee,
And never more the roof parental see!
For ever fly this city, and this shore;
And never hear the name of Colchos more!'
    Medea heard, suffused with crimson dye,
Eager to speak; yet shame forbade reply.   940
Now on her tongue the floating accents stray;
Now lost within her bosom fade away.
Her beauteous lips in act to speak appear;
But thence no murmurs reach the' attentive ear.
Long time she paused, and then replied with art,
That mighty love can teach the simplest heart.
' Thy sons my fond solicitude employ;
Lest them my father with his guests destroy.
When brief repose upon my senses crept,
The mind was wakeful though the body slept;
Terrific visions rose, a ghastly train!   951
Ye powers of mercy, make the portents vain!
Spare my loved sister such a cruel doom!
Preserve her offspring from the' untimely tomb!'

She spake, for trial of her thoughts ; to prove
The' extent and feelings of maternal love.
If anxious tenderness, her sons to shield,
To strangers aid against a sire might yield.
While pangs intolerable seized her breast,
The sister thus a mother's cares confess'd :   960
    ' Such visions oft are present to my mind ;
And oft I wish thy powerful aid to find.
But swear by Heaven above, and earth below,
To keep my secret, and thine aid bestow,
My sister, I conjure thee, at this hour ;
By thy loved self, and every blessed power ;
By joys and griefs maternal ties impart,
Ties that full soon may haply bind thy heart ;
Let not my children's dire untimely end
Torture my sight, my bleeding bosom rend.   970
I will not leave you, offspring of my love.
For good or ill one destiny we prove,
And should we perish—An avenging shade
I rise, to vex thy rest, unfeeling maid.'
    Tears coursing tears, in floods, each other
                chased.
Her sister's knees, impassion'd, she embraced.
Her glowing face within her bosom kept,
As lock'd within each other's arms they wept.
As thus they join'd their grief with mournful cries,
Through all the dome the lamentation flies.   980
    Medea first resumed the plaintive strain :
' Ill fated sister, what relief from pain ?
With imprecations why my aid demand ?
Why name the Stygian powers, tremendous band ?
Oh ! did the safety of thy sons depend
On me ; no sorrows should thy bosom rend.
Inviolable oath, that Colchians fear,
By Heaven above and earth below, I swear,

Earth, awful mother of the powers divine,
My wish, my aid, my choicest skill are thine. 990
Though things scarce possible thy tongue should
    ask,
Ne'er shall this hand be wanting to the task.'
    She ceased, and thus Chalciopé replies:
' Might not thy skill some stratagem devise,
Some art; if, yielding to the stranger's prayer,
To brave the fury of our sire we dare;
To bear him through the conflict safe and free;
And snatch from death my gentle sons and me?
Our being on the youth's success depends.
Within, my Argus thy resolve attends.   1000
To me deputed he from Jason came.
Thine aid, through me, the Grecian heroes claim.'
    Delight Medea's throbbing bosom flush'd.
The mantling crimson o'er the lily rush'd.
A trance of pleasure every sense confused.
Her swimming eyes a sudden night suffused.
' Chalciopé, thy safety and thy joy
Shall every thought and every toil employ.
Let me not view the dawn of morning fair;
Let me not breathe the gift of vital air;   1010
If object or connexion claim a part,
More dear, more inward, in Medea's heart,
Than thou and thine! the brothers of my love,
Thy sons by nature fond affection move;
And I thy love in double right demand,
Sister at once, and daughter of thy hand.
A playmate with thy children have I grown,
Thy cares parental from my childhood known;
Oft would thine arms, so has our mother told,
My weak and helpless infancy enfold.   1020
Go then.   Let silence veil my promised aid,
Till art my parent's jealous care evade;

Not light or idle are the words I speak,
At dawn the fane of Hecaté I seek;
With potent drugs prepared, and magic charms,
To save the' adventurous youth from fiery harms.'
    With joy her sister heard, with joy convey'd
Hopes to her children of the promised aid.
Medea now in solitude remain'd;   [gain'd.
And shame and fear, once more, the' ascendant
' What—for a stranger, in such tasks engage!
Impious—for him defy a father's rage!'   1032
    Now Night o'er earth her ample veil display'd [15];
And sailors, from the deep, the stars survey'd,
Orion, and the greater Bear; that guide
The nightly path of vessels through the tide.
Sleep on the weary travellers' senses crept,
E'en in the tower the careful warder slept.
Subdued by rest, the mother ceased to mourn
Her darling infants closed within their urn. 1040
The busy hum of crowded streets was still;
And still the watch-dog's larum loud and shrill.
The queen of darkness trod her awful round,
Her ears untroubled by a vagrant sound.
Medea's couch refused the soft control,
For love and Jason agonized her soul.
The bulls that breathe intolerable fire,
Forebodings mortal to her love inspire;
The plain of Mars in dismal prospect lies,
In fancy there the youthful hero dies.   1050
Distracting thought! she feels the fluttering heart
With feverish throbbings in her bosom dart.
As when, from caldron or capacious vase,
The trembling lymph reflects the solar face;
Uncertain glancing round some chamber walls,
Now here, now there, the darted radiance falls;

[15] See Virgil's Description of Night, Æneid iv.

The dazzling species plays incessant round,
Strikes on the roof, or dances o'er the ground;
With pulse irregular, that knew no rest,
Medea's heart leap'd fluttering in her breast. 1060
The streams of pity from her eyes distill'd.
Corroding pangs her inmost bosom fill'd,
Incessant anguish.   The devouring flame
Glows in each nerve, and wastes the weary frame.
It rends the heartstrings—hurries in each vein;
Fills every sense, and fires the madding brain.
Within her mind confused ideas roll,
Discordant purposes distract the soul.
Now, she determines to supply the charms
Of power, to save the youth from fiery harms; 1070
Now, to withhold; and seek in death to prove
A long oblivion of disastrous love.
Again, she hopes that reason force may give,
To sacrifice the youth, yet dare to live.
    Amid this conflict, mournful sounds express'd
The painful tumults of the' enamour'd breast.
'Ah, wretch! what end, what respite canst thou find
While choice of evil presses on the mind?
My thoughts are error, doubt, confusion all;
Certain in love alone, a wretched thrall.   1080
Oh, had the shafts of virgin Dian fled,
And early join'd me to the silent dead!
Then had I slept in peace, nor seen this band,
For my perdition, reach the Colchian land.
Nor seen, Chalciopé, in evil day,
Thy sons for Greece the' adventurous sail display.
Some god, some fury urged these strangers' course,
To rend this heart with anguish and remorse.
But let him perish, if the fates ordain
That direful exit on the martial plain.   1090

How might I scape a parent's watchful eye?
Or how my philtres and my charms apply?
What language might deceive the jealous ear?
Or what my purposes to Jason bear?
In privacy may succour be convey'd?
What arts, what stealth, the bold attempt shall aid?
In secret shall I own my fond alarms,
And boldly clasp the stranger in these arms?
Oh! were he lost—would that event bestow
A pause from love—a remedy for woe?   1100
Would not the soul, enamour'd of her grief,
Pursue his image, and disclaim relief?
Farewell, decorum! farewell every joy!
Let his existence all my thoughts employ.
Whatever destiny for me remains,
Fair youth, in safety fly where fate ordains.
Mayst thou but know, that from Medea's power
Protection follow'd in that fearful hour,
And I am satisfied.   Pursue thy fate;
Leave thy deliverer to misfortune's hate.   1110
His conflict over, death shall end my care;
Whether I perish pendulous in air,
Or rest from pain the' envenom'd potion give.
But shall not then the tale of shame survive?
Scorn and derision shall attend my fall,
And taunts resound within this peopled wall.
Each Colchian female shall her death deride,
Who, slave of passion, for a stranger died.
A wanton, heedless of her virgin fame,
Who stain'd her parents and her house with shame.
O foul offence, no language can defend!   1121
Disgrace to womanhood, that ne'er shall end!
No; better here resign this hated breath,
And fly reproach, so multiplied, in death.

This very chamber, and this very time,
Present a refuge from the monstrous crime.'
  She ceased—and rising for a coffer sought,
With potent drugs of various influence fraught;
Some genial; some, with operation dark,
Could sense perturb, and quench the vital spark.
Upon her knees the hoarded philtres rest;   1131
While tears, a ceaseless torrent, bathed her breast:
From grief and love unequal'd they descend,
While for those sufferings she prepares an end.
The friendly bane determined now to taste,
She touch'd the bands that held the coffer fast;
And thought the balm of all her cares to find,
When sudden terrors rush'd upon her mind.
She paused astonish'd. For, before her eyes
The forms of death, in all their terrors, rise. 1140
And in succession, blandishing appears,
All that allures the wish, and life endears;
Each darling child of hope and fancy bright,
That bids the senses teem with young delight;
And every joy that to the' expanded heart
The mutual wish and social hours impart.
Sudden a fairer face all nature show'd,
In streams more gay the solar radiance flow'd.
Again the coffer on her knees she placed, 1149
While various objects in her soul she traced;
For Juno's influence in her bosom wrought,
And gave the final bias to her thought.
No more she doubts, by warring motives drawn,
With settled aim she wishes for the dawn;
That Jason she might meet, gaze on his charms,
And drugs impart to guard the youth from harms.
Oft she unbarr'd her portals through the night;
And look'd, and look'd, to mark approaching light.

The morn, at length, unveil'd her welcome face,
And through the city waked the toiling race. 1160
Thy sons, Chalciopé, as Argus bade,
To watch her purpose near Medea stay'd;
The youth himself, ere yet the stars were fled,
His eager footsteps to the vessel sped.
Soon as the maid descried the morning fair,
She deck'd her golden locks with studious care,
That hung neglected; and the' enlivening red
O'er cheeks all pale with sorrow's ravage spread.
Ambrosial essences her skin bedew.   1169
O'er her bright frame a splendid robe she threw,
Confined with clasps around her slender waist.
A veil upon her radiant head she placed;
Her head, that more than mortal beauty show'd.
The snowy veil in waves translucent flow'd,
With spreading flowers of broider'd silver crown'd.
Her locks diffused ambrosial odours round.
Now, circling through the dome, with steps of air,
She trod the floor, and vanish'd every care;
Unseen those evils that around her lay[16],
And greater evils of the future day.   1180
She call'd her maidens—twelve, in youthful bloom,
Stood at the chamber doors that breathed perfume.
Alike in age, alike in beauteous frame,
Strangers to love, and the maternal name.
    Intent, great Hecaté, to seek thy fane,
Her mules she bade them harness to the wain.
The mules and car obedient they provide,
Meantime the nymph her mystic coffer tried.

[16] Either because she looks so well, or through joy, at
thoughts of meeting Jason; greater evils, when she should be
despised by Jason.

A drug she took that bears Prometheus' name,
Sovereign protection 'gainst devouring flame. 1190
Those who that drug employ, with midnight care,
Must sooth the power, revered with torches' glare;
Persephoné, sole offspring, sought in vain
By weeping Ceres o'er the' Ennæan plain:
That unguent with mysterious rite applied,
No steely weapon shall the skin divide.
With force innoxious the devouring flame
Shall spend its fury on the' enchanted frame.
No fear of peril shall the man subdue.
In fight, no faintness shall from toil ensue. 1200
Prometheus drench'd Caucasian steeps with gore,
And teeming rocks the potent herbage bore;
When the fierce vulture, delving for his food,
The reeking entrails tore, and swam in blood.
A cubit high the stately flower it rears,
Which like the crocus in its hue appears;
The stem disparting wide, sublime it shoots,
Like newly sever'd flesh appear the roots;
The juice effused descends in sable rills,
Like the dark sap that from the beech distils.
For magic uses, this her skilful hand   1211
In shells had treasured, of the Caspian strand.
Seven times she plunged in the perennial stream,
Seven times on Brimo call'd, tremendous name;
On Brimo, awful nurse of youthful might,
That, veil'd in clouds, pursues the dogs of night;
Whose power tremendous central earth pervades,
Whose power tremendous sways the Stygian
          shades;   [deep,
Ere, robed in black, through brooding darkness
That herb she cull'd along the rocky steep. 1220

She tore the plant of Titan [17] from the ground,
And earth convulsed shook from her base pro-
              found.
Then direful pangs Prometheus' bosom rent,
And screams of torture through the air he sent.
  This unguent o'er the fragrant zone was laid,
That bound the lovely bosom of the maid.
Medea, hasting from the door, ascends
The car; a virgin on each hand attends.
She caught the reins, and with the sounding thong,
Through the wide city lash'd the mules along.
Behind her, the remaining virgin train   1231
Clung to the chariot, as it roll'd amain;
Succinct, as through the spacious streets they flee,
They bind their snowy garments by the knee.
  As where Parthenius' [18] limpid currents gleam,
Or newly bathed, Amnisus [19], in thy stream,
Her golden chariot virgin Dian fills,
And swift-paced hinds transport her o'er the hills;
Call'd by the scent of hecatombs from far,
A thousand nymphs attend her rapid car;   1240
The Naiads, that in cool Amnisus lave,
With the brown Oreads from the mountain cave;
The pensive Dryads, that retirement love,
And haunt the mazes of the shady grove;   •
And, as they pass, the beasts of wood and lawn,
With murmurs bland, and gentle crouchings, fawn;
Such was the train, all-beauteous to behold:
The crowds receded as the chariot roll'd.
  Now, through the stately portals, o'er the plain,
With urgent speed Medea reach'd the fane: 1250

[17] So called because it sprung from the blood of Prome-
theus, who was of the race of Titans.
[18] A river of Paphlagonia.
[19] A city and river of Crete.

There from the car she sprang, with throbbing
    breast,
And eager thus the virgin train address'd—
' O friends! some error strange misleads my
    thought,   [brought.
And near those strangers hath our footsteps
Unwelcome visitors they seek this land,
And fill with terror all the Colchian band;
Hence all the female kind, possess'd with fear,
Their wonted confluence to the shrine forbear.
Yet, having ventured thus, since none advance,
Our sports to censure with intrusive glance, 1260
For wreaths collect we every fairest flower,
While tuneful songs deceive the fleeting hour;
Then home return.   Yet, might my counsel
    sway,
Most useful were the' excursion of this day.
My kinsman Argus—but, my friends, conceal
In trusty silence what I shall reveal.
Oh! should my father learn it—woe to all!
What direful vengeance on our heads might fall!
But Argus wearies me with urgent prayers;
And e'en my sister in his counsel shares.   1270
With mighty gifts they would my purpose bend,
By magic aid this stranger to defend;
Else he must perish.   Pity moved my heart,
Join'd to the treasures which he can impart;
My word is pledged obedient to their will,
And Jason comes the treaty to fulfil.
In secret here the treasure he divides,
And takes the philtre that my skill provides;
The strongest spell that magic can prepare.
Let all retire; and all his bounty share[20].'   1280

[20] I think I have rendered this passage in the most natural
sense, but my version has been objected to.   The passage

She ended; and her mandates all pursue,
Argus apart the son of Æson drew,   [break,
Warn'd by his brethren, that when dawn should
The fane of Hecaté the maid would seek :
Onward he led him o'er the spacious plain,
And Mopsus join'd them, of prophetic strain ;
Who traced events, with prescient ear and sight,
In voice of birds and in foreboding flight.
That hour might none amid the sons of Jove,
Amid the progeny of gods above,   1290
In youthful beauty and 'endowments rare,
With Jason, deck'd by Juno's hand, compare.
Around his face etherial radiance play'd,
And every gesture manly grace display'd.
A glad amazement his companions felt,
Such beamy charms on every feature dwelt.
The son of Ampycus²¹ with pleasure glows,
And fairest omens of the future rose.

 Beside the path that to the temple tends,
A poplar, with funereal leaf, ascends : 1300
A station meet, where clustering rooks abound,
Whose ceaseless cawing fills the air around.
One of the number claps her sable wings,
And thus the will of royal Juno sings—
' Poor shallow prophet, ignorant alone,
Of what to striplings and to girls is known !
Ah, fool unheeding, amorous parleys need
Nor babbling witnesses nor jealous heed.
Go—go thou novice in affairs of love,
A vile encumbrance from thy friend remove. 1310

may be rendered differently by reading for *spell, harms,* and
inserting these two lines :
  Far different from the promise of his thought,
  A direful purchase with perdition fraught.
    ²¹ Mopsus.

What! will the soft and timid maid explain
Her tender thoughts before a numerous train?
Oh no, their presence checks the fond desire,
The sweet unfoldings of the mutual fire.
Hence, hence, thou harbinger of ill, remove,
Go, simple novice in affairs of love;
On thee may never Cytherea smile,
Or young delights thy gloomy cares beguile.'
   Thus she reproachful. Mopsus gently smiled;
Her mission own'd, and spake in accents mild—
' Alone, O Jason, to the fane repair,   1321
There shalt thou find a virgin young and fair;
Bland smiles and kind reception shall be thine,
For Venus will her heart to love incline.
From her assistance shall thy toils await;
So Phineus has reveal'd the will of fate.
With Argus here I shall remain apart,
Expecting thy return with anxious heart.
Thou singly haste, and urge the royal maid,
In hours of danger to bestow her aid.'   1330
His prudent words their approbation find,
While thoughts congenial fill Medea's mind;
Ah, wretched maid! nor song nor sport had power
To fix attention in the sportive hour.
Sport seem'd impertinent, and harsh the strain,
Through music's varied soul pursued in vain;
The varied melodies displease alike,
No chord composure to the soul can strike.
Scarce can her train allure the wandering eye,
To different objects thought and wishes fly. 1340
Absent she sat, in meditation drown'd,
And gazed on all the distant pathways round;
Intent, with eager eyes and head reclined,
At sound of trampling foot or sighs of wind;

The fluttering heart seem'd wing'd to leave her
    breast,
And painful throbs the glowing breath suppress'd.
  He comes—the subject of her fond alarms—
He comes in all the majesty of charms;
With footsteps light, exulting o'er the plain,
And bright as Sirius rising from the main;   1350
All beauteous from the briny surge he springs,
But death and mourning to the fold he brings;
Such fatal splendour Jason's charms impart,
Joy to the sight, but sorrow to the heart:
Sad interview, from thee the maid shall know
A direful tissue of reproach and woe.
Her hurried heart within her bosom flies,
A sudden darkness veils her swimming eyes;
Her burning cheek the deepest blush suffused,
Her trembling knees to bear her frame refused.
To fly, or to proceed, vain, vain her toil;   1361
Her feet beneath are rooted to the soil.
Now quickly vanish'd all the' attendant train,
Silent the hero and the maid remain.
No limb they moved; but, in astonish'd mood,
With gaze delighted, near each other stood;
Nor sounds nor gestures animation show,
Like oaks or firs that on the mountains grow;
Whose peaceful heads " all motionless arise,
While not a breeze is stirring in the skies; 1370
But, when the tempests agitate the steep,
They wave, they bellow, as the whirlwinds sweep.
Thus stood the youthful pair, ordain'd to prove
A mighty change, beneath the storms of love;
Ordain'd that flowing eloquence to find,
That passion dictates to the' enamour'd mind.

   " Imitated by Valerius Flaccus, lib. vii. lin. 403.

The wily youth perceiv'd the heaven-born dame,
And gently thus he spared the virgin's shame—
Why, beauteous maiden, in this lonely place,
Why gaze astonish'd on a stranger's face? 1380
Think me not, like the common youthful crowd,
In thoughts capricious, and in boasting loud.
Why shouldst thou fear me? In my native land,
In ease and affluence of the heedless band;
Not mine the mood to wake a virgin's fear,
Safe slept her secret in my faithful ear.
Oh, blush no more! Whate'er thou wilt, request:
Repose thy feelings on a feeling breast.
My fairest, speak. With mutual hearts we meet;
No rash presumption fear, no foul deceit. 1390
In this most awful place, where harmful mind
And thoughts unhallow'd no reception find,
Speak uncontrol'd. Nor let soft speech evade
The flattering promise to thy sister made.
The drugs of soothing power. This aid I claim,
By sacred Hecaté, most awful name;
By soft attraction of the gentle ties.
When pleading kindred to the soul applies:
By Jove, the friend of strangers, who delights
In deed benevolent, and social rites. 1400
A twofold title to thine aid I bear,
At once a suppliant and a stranger here.
By perils compass'd, for thine aid I bend,
Sole hope in those dire conflicts that impend.
We, in return, whate'er the fates allow,
Or strangers can in climes remote bestow,
Will pay; the tribute of our thanks and praise,
And gratitude her monuments shall raise.
Their labours ended, our heroic throngs
Shall celebrate thy praise in martial songs. 1410

APOLLONIUS RHODIUS

By perils compass'd, for thine aid I bend,
Sole hope, in those dire conflicts, that impend.

Argonautics Book IV line 209

The wily youth perceived the heaven-born flame,
And gently thus he spared the virgin's shame—
Why, beauteous maiden, in this lonely place,
Why gaze astonish'd on a stranger's face? 1380
Think me not, like the common youthful crowd,
In thoughts capricious, and in boasting loud.
Why shouldst thou fear me? In my native land,
In ease and affluence of the heedless band;
Not mine the mood to wake a virgin's fear,
Safe slept her secret in my faithful ear.
Oh, blush no more! Whate'er thou wilt, request:
Repose thy feelings on a feeling breast.
My fairest, speak. With mutual hearts we meet;
No rash presumption fear, no foul deceit.   1390
In this most awful place, where fraudful mind
And thoughts unhallow'd no reception find,
Speak uncontrol'd.   Nor let soft speech evade
The flattering promise to thy sister made.
The drugs of soothing power.   This aid I claim,
By sacred Hecaté, most awful name;
By soft attraction of the gentle ties,
When pleading kindred to the soul applies;
By Jove, the friend of strangers, who delights
In deed benevolent, and social rites.   1400
A twofold title to thine aid I bear,
At once a suppliant and a stranger here.
By perils compass'd, for thine aid I bend,
Sole hope in those dire conflicts that impend.
We, in return, whate'er the fates allow,
Or strangers can in climes remote bestow,
Will pay; the tribute of our thanks and praise,
And gratitude her monuments shall raise.
Their labours ended, our heroic throngs
Shall celebrate thy praise in martial songs. 1410

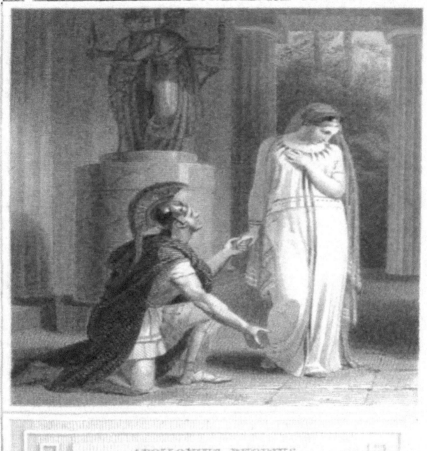

APOLLONIUS RHODIUS
By perils compass'd, for thine and I bend.
Sole hope, in those dire conflicts that impend.
Argonautics Book. III line 129.

Drawn by Rich.d Cook   Engraved by J. N. &c.

Published by Suttaby, Evance & Fox, London.
Jan.y 1819.

The Grecian fair thy merits shall rehearse,
In strain symphonious, or in measured verse;
Our wives and virgins, who with sorrow pale
Their absent loves along the shores bewail.
Grateful to thee the' exulting train shall prove,
Peace to their hearts, protection to their love;
Thus Ariadne on the Cretan shore,
Daughter of Minos, aid to Theseus bore.
Pasiphaé fill'd her veins with heavenly fire,
Derived from Phebus, her immortal sire; 1420
Though Minos purposed to destroy the train,
His daughter's pity made that purpose vain;
To share the safety that her counsels gave,
She join'd their wanderings o'er the distant wave.
Dear to the gods above, her garland bright [23]
Adorns the glittering canopy of night;
Rank'd with the beauteous host of heavenly signs,
Her crown the pledge of fame immortal shines;
So, should my friends to thee their safety owe,
The' admiring gods their favour will bestow. 1430
We read the means in that expressive face,
The fair deportment, and the beaming grace;
There our fond hopes the bright assurance find,
Of soft persuasion, and the prudent mind.'
    Thus dropp'd the dews of flattery from his tongue,
With nectar'd smiles her eyes she downward flung.
Then, fill'd with soft confusion by his praise,
Her eyes she ventured on the youth to raise;
The virgin wish'd, but tried in vain [24] to speak,
Such throng'd ideas for expression seek; 1440
A thousand thoughts at once her fancy strike,
Alike important all and apt alike.

[23] The constellation called Ariadne's Crown.
[24] See Valerius Flaccus, lib. vii. line 433,

Forth from her fragrant bosom then she drew
The potent charm, instinct with magic dew.
She placed it in the youth's delighted hand:
And, had he pleased her being to demand,
Her life, her soul, in that consenting hour
Of amorous yielding, had confess'd his power.
From Jason's form, his face, his sunny hair,
Such beams of beauty flash'd upon the fair; 1450
The sweet contagion, through the kindling eyes,
Subdued the melting heart with fond surprise.
The fumes of passion drink the hurried blood,
As shrinks within her veins the vital flood;
Their downcast eyes now spoke the timid shame;
Alternate now they darted looks of flame;
Beneath their brows sweet smiling lustre play'd,
Then hesitating, slow, rejoin'd the maid:
   ' Attentive hear me, that thou mayst derive·
The means of safety from those aids I give. 1460
With deadly purpose rankling in his heart,
The dragon's teeth my father will impart;
The fatal seed in peril thou must sow,
A crop most fertile in despair and woe.
Thou, by the march of constellations bright,
Observe the moment that divides the night.
Bathe in the current of the' unwearied flood,
Then, veil'd with sable stole in solemn mood,
A circling trench with hallow'd reverence trace,
And kill a female lamb within the space.   1470
Then rear with unpolluted hands the pyre,
And give the victim to the flames entire.
Appease the goddess in that awful hour,
Daughter of Perseus, sole begotten power.
On Hecaté libations due bestow,
Let honey'd streams from sacred goblets flow.

This ended, home return with backward pace,
Nor turn at startling noise thy heedless face;
Though hurried steps along the causeway sound,
Or mastiffs hoarsely bay, with note profound;
Shouldst thou, ill fated, rashly turn thy head,
Vain are the rites, and hopes of safety fled. 1482
Seek not thy comrades with irreverent haste,
Ere all precautions are observed and pass'd.
Soon as the morning shall illume the sky,
Dissolve this drug, and o'er thy frame apply.
Unwearied strength and courage shall be thine,
And vigour, not of men, but powers divine.
Remember too, with this same drug to smear
Thy shield, thy trenchant sword, and pointed
          spear.   [charms,
No wounds shall pierce thee through the potent
From weapons wielded e'en by giant arms. 1492
The furious bulls that roll devouring flame,
Shall breathe innoxious on the' enchanted frame.
But, oh beware! The' enchantment will not stay;
Its force is bounded by a single day.
Yet, not for this the bold emprise decline,
Some other aid in dangers shall be thine;
When with the fiery team, and potent hand,
Through all the' extent is plough'd the rugged
          land;   1500
When all the tract is sown with dragon's teeth,
An earthborn race shall spring to light beneath.
When thou shalt see the crowding warriors rise,
In secret cast a stone of ample size;
For this, as famish'd dogs for food engage,
The giant brothers will in combat rage.
Fell'd by each other as they press the ground,
Then join the fight, then deal thy blows around.

Thus, safe from Æä shalt thou bear the fleece,
Scope of thy voyage, to the shores of Greece:
But let my image dwell within thy mind,   1511
And sometimes seek these shores; but leave thy
        train behind.'   ·   [eyes;
  She paused and silent stood, with downcast
A flood of tears succeeding stormy sighs;
While she reflected he must far remove,
Death to her hopes, and torment to her love!
But now with bolder confidence endued,
She press'd his hand, and thus her speech renew'd,
With mournful tone—'Thou, on the Grecian plain,
Remember me.   Thy form I shall retain,   1520
Alas! too firmly.   But, ingenuous youth,
Disclose thy home and household gods with truth.
What course will bear thy vessel from our coasts?
Where proud Orchomenus her treasure boasts?
Or, mid the waves, will Æä's nearer isle
Allure thy wishes, and in prospect smile?
But who that virgin, theme of thy applause,
Whom ties of kindred to my father draws?
Thy words have painted her as fair and young,
Of noble lineage, from Pasiphaé sprung.'   1530
  Engender'd by her tears, pernicious guest,
Love rush'd impetuous on the hero's breast.
Ardent he answer'd—'Neither day nor night,
Shall thy bright form be absent from my sight.
If I may scape, indeed, on Colchian plains,
The dreadful conflict that thy sire ordains,
And safely reach the happy shores of Greece,
I bear thine image, with the precious fleece.
My fairest asks me where my country lies,
My heart, my tongue, are strangers to disguise;

'Tis pleasure to perform the soft request, 1541
By lips so sweet, and eyes so bright express'd.
A land there is, that lofty hills surround,
Where numerous flocks and fertile plains abound,
Sprung from Iäpetus, of heavenly fire,
There dwelt Prometheus, good Deucalion's sire.
He first by laws o'er willing subjects reign'd,
And towns for men, and fanes for gods ordain'd.
'Tis called Hæmonia [25] by the neighbouring race,
There towers Iolcus, my paternal place; 1550
And various other stately cities smile,
Nor e'en by name is known Æeä's isle.
From thence, 'tis said, the noble Minyas went,
Who drew from Æolus his proud descent,
And built Orchomenus, a town that stands
In peaceful neighbourhood with Theban bands.
But why amuse thee with this idle fame,
My natal spot, and Ariadne's name?
Daughter of Minos. Let her memory live
In that esteem benignant actions give. 1560
Her sire and lover she to friendship led,
And concord firm, with healing influence spread.
Oh might thy father hear the words of peace,
From those dear lips, and all his fury cease!'
   Thus he, with flattering words and soothing art,
While sharpest anguish wrung the virgin's heart;
Desponding looks and mournful tones express'd
The gloomy thoughts that labour'd in her breast.
   ' In Greece, perhaps, the solemn pact may bind,
And laws of honour overawe the mind; 1570
Alas, Æëtes knows no law but force,
Unlike that Minos, theme of thy discourse.

---

[25] Thessaly.

And far inferior to that maiden mild,
In charms and influence, his unhappy child!
Oh think no more of hospitable rite;
But, when Iolcus' towers rejoice thy sight,
Remember me.   Be some few sighs consign'd
To the poor victim that remains behind.
For me, no power shall tear thee from my soul,
Nor mother's voice nor father's stern control.
May fame the tidings of thy welfare bring, 1581
Some bird propitious waft them on his wing.
To bear me, might the favouring breezes rise,
And o'er the seas transport, and through the skies!
While round thee all the sports and pleasures flow,
That affluence, ease, and kindred, can bestow;
Before thee might I stand a sudden guest,
And say, through me these raptures fill thy breast?
Oh, might I soon be placed, and long remain,
A favour'd inmate with thy household train!' 1590
    Then piteous tears her lovely cheeks bedew'd;
His gentle accents thus the youth renew'd—
' Wish not, my fairest.   Fruitless wish to find
The bird of embassy, the wafting wind.
But, wouldst thou yield to seek the Grecian shore,
Our maids shall honour thee, our youths adore;
Our matrons hail thy tutelary power,
Our guardian goddess, in the' eventful hour;
Whose counsels wise and salutary charms
Return the dearest pledges to their arms.   1600
To some, the tried companions of their youth;
To some, the husbands of their plighted truth;
To this, a brother thine assistance gives,
That from thine hand a darling child receives.
Oh might I claim thee as my blooming spouse,
Sole darling object of my faithful vows;

In hallow'd league of soul with soul combined,
One wish, one love, one fortune, and one mind!
Form'd for each other, by the gods allied,　1609
Death, only death, our union should divide.'
　His words her soul with amorous softness fill;
Yet, starting, she recoils from purposed ill.
Vain were thy conflicts, most unhappy maid!
For Juno's will, with power compulsive, sway'd;
Brief was thy force, a lover to deny,
To Grecian shores thou art ordain'd to fly.
To wreak her vengeance against Pelias plann'd,
The goddess claims thee on Iolcus' strand.
　Meantime the' attendants of the royal fair
At distance watch'd her steps with jealous care;
They watch'd the progress of the wearing day,
And silent murmur'd at the long delay.　1622
The sun so forward on his journey pass'd,
Home to her parents bids Medea haste:
Yet, all unmark'd the stealing moments flow,
Such pleasure Jason's looks and words bestow.
His form, his soothing speeches so delight,
Full gladly had she linger'd there till night;
More cautious he, with watchful thought and eye,
Late and reluctant urged the nymph to fly. 1630
' The day advances.　To thy mother's arms,
A while, my fairest, I resign thy charms;
Lest evening shades our intercourse surprise,
Or stranger mark it with unfriendly eyes;
In happier moments of the' expansive heart,
Hereafter we may meet, no more to part.'
　The lovers thus in fond expressions vied,
The feelings all their eloquence supplied;
And amorous doubt essay'd with jealous art
To search the secret of the heart of heart.　1640

The youth his vessel and companions sought,
Fire in his eye, and rapture in his thought.
Medea sought her train along the land,
And soon to meet her came the' assembled band;
But all unconscious, as the group drew near,
Her thoughts were rapp'd above the starry sphere :
With limbs spontaneous the bright car she gains,
And takes the polish'd whip and flowing reins;
She lash'd the mules, with eager course they flew,
And soon the stately city rose in view.   1650

Chalciopé her sister now address'd,
With all the mother labouring in her breast.
Her sons awake the mingled hope and fear,
Much she demands, and much expects to hear.
In vain.   Her words nor thought nor organ find,
Grief and confusion fill Medea's mind.
She hears not, speaks not, such a trance possess'd
The troubled soul and every sense oppress'd.
Down on an humble seat, beside her bed,   1659
She sunk, and lean'd oblique her languid head,
Propp'd on her left hand, like a drooping flower,
While from her eyes distils the briny shower.
A gloomy cloud o'ercasts her thoughtful brow,
And self-upbraidings on the spirit flow.
A calmer moment, and a deeper heed,
In all its horrors view the promised deed.

His two attendants youthful Jason finds
Awaiting his return, with anxious minds;   1668
He join'd their steps, and hasten'd to explain
The' eventful tidings to the' assembled train;
The' assembled train, as near the ship he drew,
With glad surprise their gallant leader view.
Idas alone, from all the train apart,
In secret bitterness consumed his heart;

Nor pleasure from the common gladness felt,
For pride and envy in his spirit dwelt.
   Now night came on, and shades and silence
      brought,
And calm repose the youthful warriors sought.
But, when Aurora bade the dayspring flame,
Two from the number haste the seed to claim.
Bold Telamon of Mars the darling went,   1681
And, who from Hermes drew his proud descent,
Æthalides.   Nor was their journey vain;
For from the king the dragon's teeth they gain,
Insidious gift.   He sternly bade them take
The fatal teeth of that Aonian snake,
Whom ancient Cadmus in Ogygia slew;
When fair Europa ravish'd from his view,
His sister, by their mournful sire's [26] command,
O'er many a deep he sought, and many a land.
Before his face the fabled heifer went,   1691
Guide of his way, by prescient Phœbus sent.
At Thebes, beneath his hand the serpent fell;
With poison arm'd he kept the' Aretian well.
Pallas, who stoop'd the monster's teeth to save,
The spoil to Cadmus and Æëtes gave.
His portion Cadmus sow'd in Theban fields,
And warriors arm'd the breathing furrow yields;
Contentious brood they bathed in kindred gore;
And only they survived whom Cadmus bore,
As denizens his rising walls to fill;   1701
The parent field its earthborn children till.
The seed Æëtes to their hands consign'd,
With readiness that spoke the rancorous mind;
Though to the yoke the fiery steers should bend,
The toil, he trusts, will in their ruin end.

[26] Agenor.——See the notes on this passage at the end.

Beneath the' horizon now the sun declined,
His course where Ethiopian summits bind;
Night yoked her sable steeds.   Along the sand,
Stretch'd near their cables, slept the' heroic band.
But Jason slumber from his eye repell'd,   1711
And fix'd on heaven his anxious looks he held;
Resplendent 'mid the starry host from far,
The Bear of Helicé had turn'd her star,
No noise was heard along the watery scene,
Nor breeze nor cloud deform'd the blue serene.
'Twas now the time.   With silent, stealthy pace,
The son of Æson sought a lonely place.
He bore each requisite for solemn rite,   1719
With care collected, ere the' approach of night.
Part in the fold and dairy Argus sought;
A female lamb and tepid milk he brought.
The rest the ship supplied.   The hero found,
Far from the beaten path, a space of ground,
With streams irriguous springing fresh and clear.
He bathed his tender limbs with pious fear,
In the pure lymph; and o'er his shoulders threw
A robe from Lemnos brought of sable hue,
Gift of Hypsipylé, design'd to prove
A sad memorial of ill fated love.   1730
A cubit then in depth a trench he made,
And wood for sacrifice in order laid.
The victim bleeds extended on the pyre,
And all the hallow'd pile receives the fire;
As o'er the flames the mix'd libation falls,
On Brimo Hecaté the votary calls.
'Tremendous power, assist my future toil;'
With backward steps he slowly trod the soil.
From deep recesses, awful power, she heard,
And, rising, at the potent call appear'd: 1740

Envenom'd snakes with oaken boughs entwined,
Terrific wreath! her awful temples bind.
A mighty glare of torches flamed around,
And dogs of hell were heard with piercing sound.
The meadows trembled as she moved along;
The Naiads wail'd the lakes and rills among.
Loud shriek'd the nymphs that in the marshes lave,
Where Amarantian Phasis seeks the wave;
Amaze and fear the soul of Jason felt,   1749
Yet in his thoughts Medea's warning dwelt.
With firm resolve he backward trod the plain;
Nor turn'd him ere he reach'd the social train.
    When morn began, fair daughter of the spring,
Her beams on snowy Caucasus to fling,
Æëtes rose, and clad his giant frame
In ponderous arms; a gift from Mars they came.
When sunk Phlegrean Mimas bathed in gore,
His bloody spoils the' immortal victor tore.
The golden helmet graced the monarch's head,
A fourfold cone its bright effulgence shed, 1760
From far refulgent, like that orb of day,
When, bathed in ocean, he renews his ray.
A vast expansive shield his left hand holds,
Where thickest hides are placed in numerous folds.
His right hand grasps the' inevitable spear,
Weighty and vast, the messenger of fear;
The king excepted, in the' embattled field
Alcides only could that weapon wield.
In youthful grace fair Phaeton [27] attends,
And holds the chariot ere his sire ascends. 1770
The king ascending seized the flowing reins,
And pass'd the city gates to reach the plains,

[27] Phaeton, son to Æëtes.

Scene of the' intended trial.   O'er the road
His course he held extended long and broad.
Forth rush'd the Colchians, an unnumber'd throng,
The king, like car-borne Neptune, rode along,
When Isthmian games, divine spectator, bring
The god to Tænarus [28], or Lerna's spring.
Onchestus' hallow'd grove, Euboic seat,
Or Calaureia, his beloved retreat.   1780
He seeks, emergent from the sounding floods,
The' Æmonian rock, Gerestus clothed in woods.
     The youth, admonish'd by the royal maid,
Dissolved the drug, and on his armour laid.
Full soon the massy buckler's polish'd orb,
The spear, and trenchant blade, that charm absorb;
Around the youth his brave companions stand,
And try the polish'd arms with vigorous hand.
To bend his ponderous lance, that gallant train
Their utmost efforts prove, and prove in vain. 1790
The son of Aphareus [29] with rage beheld,
Presumption vain his haughty bosom swell'd.
His mighty falchion at the spear he aim'd,
Where nigh the point the brazen circles flamed;
On the firm anvil, as the hammer sounds,
The falchion fell, the blunted edge rebounds;
With joyful shouts the warriors rent the air,
And augur'd to their toils an issue fair.
Now Jason to his limbs that charm applied;
And matchless energy the drug supplied,   1800
Ineffable, tremendous in the fight;
Unmoved he stood, exulting in his might.

[28] For an account of the places here mentioned, the reader
is referred to the notes at the end.
[29] Idas.

Redoubled courage fill'd his ardent breast;
Redoubled strength his valiant hand possess'd;
And hope elates his heart, and brightens on his
    crest.
As when the charger of illustrious strain
The battle scents, and paws the sounding plain;
In pride of strength his haughty crest he rears;
At every sound he pricks his watchful ears;
O'er his arch'd neck the floating mane is cast;
His nostrils broad propel the' impetuous blast;
In youthful glory beautiful and strong,   1812
The son of Æson bounded mid the throng.
Swift as the lightning, in a wintry night,
From pitchy darkness vibrates sudden light;
Now here, now there, it glances through the sky,
And tells the' affrighted world a storm is nigh;
So Jason moved his polish'd shield and lance,
That quick and dazzling shot a fiery glance.
Now came that awful conflict big with fate. 1820
The band in order on their benches sate;
By sounding oars, and sinewy arms impell'd,
Their course to reach that field of Mars they held.
A space like those, that goal and barrier part,
Where rival charioteers display their art,
When prizes are proclaim'd, and lists outspread,
To honour some illustrious chieftain dead;
And horse and foot the ceremonies grace,
With speed contending in the measured space,
Divides the' imperial seat of Colchian pride,
From that domain of Mars the homicide.   1831
  Æëtes with the Colchian race they found,
The lofty rocks of Caucasus around
The crowd possess'd; beside the river hoar
The monarch stood, upon the winding shore.

The band with cables made their vessel fast,
And Jason to that arduous trial pass'd.
His shield and spear he grasp'd with eager hand,
And from the deck sprang lightly to the land:
The polish'd helmet's shining brass he took, 1840
And in its womb the serpent's teeth he shook.
Nor ponderous mail his active limbs oppress'd;
Nor scaly cuirass beam'd around his breast.
Unarm'd he stood, half like the god of war,
Half like the lord of the diurnal car,
And golden brand.   His eyes around he threw,
The brazen yoke was laid within his view;
And near the plough with adamantine share,
The crisis bids him for the toil prepare.   1849
The youth approach'd, advancing o'er the ground,
And planted deep the spear with ringlets bound.
Weighty and strong, erect it stood in earth;
Near lay the teeth of that envenom'd birth,
Within the helmet.   Cover'd by his shield,
To seek the bulls he march'd along the field.
When sudden, from the stalls beneath the ground,
Dark clouds of smoke diffused their volumes round.
Seen through the blackness by the lurid glare,
Disgorging fire, up-rush'd the fatal pair.   1759
That object struck with fear the' heroic bands;
To meet the rageful monsters Jason stands,
Striding unmoved, as rocks within the deep,
When mountain billows break, and torrents sweep.
His shield opposed to meet their wrath he bore,
With level'd horns they came and furious roar.
In vain their fury the brave youth assail'd;
Nor force immense nor volley'd fire prevail'd.
On the red furnace, where the metals glow,
Through many an orifice, as founders blow,

And now the bellows urge the raging fire,   1870
And pausing now the' enfeebled flames retire,
Loud and impetuous roars the blast beneath,
At intervals; the bulls with fiery breath
Now pause—and now, the flamy volumes drive,
Quick, noxious, as the cloud when lightnings rive,
With sound tremendous. But they smote unharm'd
The dauntless youth, with magic influence arm'd.
Now by the horns, with such commanding might,
He seized the bull that stood upon his right;
Superior force his dangerous captive held,   1880
And to the yoke the struggling beast compell'd.
His foot the brazen hoof, with nimble stroke,
Supplants, and brings him kneeling to the yoke.
An equal fate his fierce companion found,
The youthful hero brought him to the ground;
His ample buckler on the plain he cast,
And firmly striding grasp'd the monsters fast.
Outstretch'd at length, with broad and nervous
            breast,
The struggling bulls incumbent he oppress'd;
Smoke wreath'd around him, darted flames were
            roll'd;   1890
With hand intrepid he retain'd his hold.
The savage monarch with amaze survey'd
The force and courage by the youth display'd.
Nor then regardless were the gallant pair,
The sons of Tyndarus and Leda fair:
Appointed service, near the yokes they stand,
They raise from earth, they give to Jason's hand.
These o'er each monster's neck he firmly braced,
Then fair between the brazen pole he placed; 1899
And threw the ring that from the extreme depends
O'er the sharp hook that from the yoke extends.

Back from the noxious glare and scorching heat,
The' illustrious brothers to their ship retreat.
In haste from earth the hero caught his shield,
And o'er his shoulders cast its orbed field;
His polish'd helm he seized, no common weight,
Replete with dragon's teeth, tremendous freight!
His ponderous javelin by the midst he held.
The biting point the' indignant beasts impell'd;
Like the sharp goad by rustic hands applied, 1910
Deep in their flanks the polish'd brass he dyed.
He guides the plough-tail with unerring hand,
Compacted firm in adamantine band:
The toiling monsters roar'd with fruitless ire,
And darted from their mouths redoubled fire;
Loud and impetuous was their stormy breath,
As blasts that menace mariners with death,
When mountain high devouring waves prevail,
And fearful hands contract the shivering sail.
Not long they moved obedient to the spear, 1920
Ere the rude earth was open'd in the rear;
The ploughman stout and potent steers combined,
Ample and broad the furrow traced behind.
O dire the crash! the sound was heard afar,
From all the broken clods, that teem'd with war.
The youth pursuing with intrepid breast,
And footsteps firm, the path of danger press'd.
With hand unsparing, onward as he pass'd,
O'er the plough'd land the dragon's teeth he cast;
And oft he turn'd, oft anxious eyed the soil, 1930
Lest giant harvests should prevent his toil,
While pressing onward, o'er the stubborn plain,
The brazen footed bulls their toil sustain.
When three full portions of the time were spent,
From dawn of morning to the sun's descent;

And gladsome now their weary task to leave,
The workmen hail the sweet approach of eve;
The' unwearied ploughman triumph'd in his toil,
O'er all the large allotted space of soil.
Four acres lay upturn'd, the share beneath, 1940
All fully saturate with dragon's teeth.
The fiery monsters from the yoke he freed,
And drove them terrified along the mead.
He gazed around.   The furrows still remain
A blank, unpeopled by the giant train.
The ship he sought, and join'd the gallant crew,
Then in his helm the cooling beverage drew;
Gladly the youth indulged in transient rest;
With words of hope his comrades cheer'd his
        breast.
His heart expanded with increasing might, 1950
Like the fierce boar impatient for the fight,
Who whets his tusks, and musters all his wrath,
And foaming waits the hunter in his path.
    But now the land its horrid harvest brings:
A giant arm'd from every furrow springs;
And helms, and shields, and lances, all around,
Like bearded corn rose bristling o'er the ground,
The sacred space of Mars, the scourge of man.
To heaven's high vaults the gleaming splendours
        ran.   [flow,
When wintry storms, surcharged with vapours,
And heap along the ground the drifted snow, 1961
The clouds disperse, and through the gloom of night
The starry train emerge in dazzling light;
Thus sudden brightness shot along the land.
Admonish'd by the virgin's wise command,
A circling stone, of mighty weight and size,
A disk for dreadful Mars, the youth espies;

Scarce could four men the' enormous mass sustain,
With ease the hero raised it from the plain;
Then rushing forward, with a sudden bound, 1970
Aloft in air he hurl'd it round and round.
Distant it fell amid the' embattled field;
The youth collected shrunk behind his shield,
Yet with intrepid heart.   The Colchians roar,
Like billows when they lash the rocky shore.
With mute and blank amaze their king beheld,
What force stupendous the huge disk impell'd.
In combat loud, as barking dogs engage,
Those earth-born brothers round that discus rage,
With hideous din, and by each other's hand, 1980
Pierced through with spears, they sunk along the
        land.
Like oaks uprooted by the whirlwind's sway,
Or mountain pines o'erturn'd in ranks, they lay.
As shoots a star portentous to mankind,
And falling draws a train of light behind;
So bright at once, and terrible to view,
The youthful warrior on the giants flew.
The naked falchion lighten'd in his hand,
And wounds promiscuous fell'd the rising band.
Some half ascended into life he found;   1990
Some to the breast yet struggling in the ground;
Some newly freed stood upright on the soil;
Some forward rush'd, to claim the martial toil.
As when a land becomes the seat of war,
The farmer marks the foe's approach from far;
And lest the spoilers should possess the grain,
Anticipates the harvest of the plain;
The curving sickle newly edged he bears,
And o'er the furrows fall the' unripen'd ears;

He bears the corn with fearful haste away, 2000
Ere yet its tinge bespeaks the solar ray;
Dire harvest, Jason reap'd that earth-born brood;
And all the' o'erflowing furrows boil'd with blood.
Swell'd by continual rains, as torrents spread
Despise their banks and inundate the mead,
In various postures they resign'd their breath,
And grim and diverse were the forms of death.
Some bit the' empurpled earth, and prostrate lay;
Some backward fell, and breathed their souls away;
Some lean'd half raised, and panted to the wind;
Some sidelong writhed, in agonies reclined, 2011
Then sunk, extended in eternal sleep;
Like mighty whales, that slumber o'er the deep.
Entangled some, fast rooted in the ground,
With head inclining droop'd beneath the wound;
High as erewhile to heaven they rear'd the crest,
So low they sunk with damps of death oppress'd;
Thus youthful plants, surcharged with storm and
          rain,
Hang their moist heads, and languish to the plain,
Bent from the roots; the gardener, in despair, 2020
Surveys the prostrate offspring of his care,
And weeps his toils defrauded of their scope,
The pride of Autumn lost, Pomona's ravish'd hope.
Such grief and rage the monarch's bosom knew,
As o'er the' expiring train he cast his view.
He sought the city with the Colchian throng,
Resolving vengeance as he moved along.
The second conflict with the day was closed,
The sun declined, and all the train reposed.

The Argument.

Æetes begins to suspect that his daughters, particularly Medea, must have had some share in the unexpected success of Jason.—He calls a council of his confidential friends, by night.—Medea is alarmed, and dreads the vengeance of her father.—Her first thoughts on the occasion lead her to end her life by poison.—Through the influence of Juno she resolves, after a conflict between love and fear, and the sense of duty, to fly from Colchos with the Argonauts.—She leaves the city by night, and joins Jason and his companions at the ship.—Their meeting described.—The fleece of gold.—The dragon that guarded it described.—Jason is aided by Medea, lulls the latter to rest, and gains possession of the former.—Medea sails with the adventurers for Greece.—Æetes pursues them.—The Argonauts, having crossed the Euxine sea, sail up the Ister.—Absyrtus, the brother of Medea, is murdered, through the contrivance of that princess and the treachery of Jason.—The pollution, induced by this act of cruelty, is expiated by Circe, at whose island the Minyæ land.—Thetis and her nymphs conduct the vessel through the straits of Scylla and Charybdis.—The Argonauts sail past the islands of the Syrens, from whose enchantments they are preserved by Orpheus.—At Corcyra they encounter the Colchians, who pursued them through the Symplegades.—The Colchians importune Alcinoüs, king of the island, to deliver up Medea to them, that they may restore her to her father.—The monarch consents to send her back to her father, provided she is yet unmarried; declaring at the same time, that, if she is already united to Jason, he will not part man and wife: by

the contrivance of Arete, wife to Aloinoüs, the nuptials of
Medea and Jason are immediately celebrated; and Aloi-
noüs protects the lovers.—The Argonauts again put to sea,
and are driven on the quicksands of Africa; where they
are in danger of perishing.—They are extricated from the
present distress by the tutelary deities of the country.—
The Minyæ bear the vessel on their shoulders to the lake
Tritonis.—The Hesperides, whom they find bewailing the
loss of their dragon, slain the preceding day by Hercules,
give them some tidings of that hero.—Fruitless attempt to
overtake him.—Death of Canthus, and of Mopsus.—Triton
appears.—His figure particularly described.—He gives the
heroes information and directions respecting the remainder
of their voyage.—The Argonauts pass near Crete.—Mar-
vellous adventure and death of Talus.—At Hipparis, the
adventurers sacrifice to Phœbus, who, standing on the top
of a hill, enlightens their way.—A clod of earth, which has
been given to Euphemus by Triton, is thrown into the sea,
and becomes an island, named Calliste.—The Minyæ an-
chor at the island of Ægina, where they water, and loosing
from thence, arrive without further interruption on the
coast of Thessaly.

YET once again I court the Muses' aid.
The toils, the counsels of the Colchian maid
Demand the song.   O virgin child of Jove,
Doubt and confusion from my soul remove,
Decide the theme—what ills from fate she bore,
Her flight immodest from the native shore,
And kindred people.   Mid the gloom of night,
With thirst of vengeance fill'd and stern despite,
The king convoked the chieftains of his land,
Within the palace, an afflicted band.   10
His meditations on the conflicts dwell,
And black suspicions on his daughters fell.
Then Juno struck the royal maid with fear [1];
She trembled, like the young and timid deer,

[1] That she might visit Greece, and execute the vengeance
of Juno.

Which opening hounds with loud alarm o'ertake
In deep recesses of the tangled brake.
She deems the secret to her father known,
And every shape of misery her own.
Her conscious maidens wake foreboding fears;
Fire fill'd her eyes, and tingling sounds her ears. 20
Dire were the shrieks of anguish and despair;
She smote her breast, she rent her flowing hair.
In poison had she sought relief from pain,
And render'd the designs of Juno vain;
But power divine her changeful purpose bore,
With Phryxus' offspring to forsake the shore.
A dawning hope her rapid thoughts embraced.
Drawn from the casket, in her breast she placed
The magic hoard of drugs.   She kiss'd her bed,
And parting tears with eager passion shed.   30
Her fond embraces both the doorposts clasp'd,
And all around the' accustom'd walls she grasp'd;
A token then, to the maternal fair,
Tore from her beauteous head a tress of hair,
Sad, sad memorial of her virgin hours,
Offering to duty's violated powers.
  She calls her mother's name with heartfelt sighs:
' And oh! farewell, my parent dear (she cries),
Far when I fly, may health and peace be thine;
This lock alone remain of what was mine.   40
Farewell, my sister; farewell, household train;
Farewell, the parent walls, the native plain.
Had billows circled o'er that stranger's head,
Ere to these shores in evil hour he sped!
Bane of my virtue!'—Thus her grief she told,
While bursting tears in ceaseless torrents roll'd.
  When cruel fate bids some fair captive roam,
Reluctant slow she leaves her splendid home:

To grief unbroken, new to pain and toil,
She goes to meet them on a distant soil: 50
In soft indulgence nursed the darling child,
Of pride parental, and affection mild;
Sad change! to prove on some ungenial land,
The task degrading, and the stern command;
Thus, driven by tyrant love and fortune's hate,
The royal virgin goes to meet her fate.
  The bolts and bars obey the magic song,
And ope spontaneous as she pass'd along.
The' expanded barriers own'd enchanted sway,
Through narrow paths she took her stealthy way. 60
Her feet are naked, on her gracious brows,
And blooming cheek, the veil her left hand throws;
The border of her robe the right sustains.
With darkling pace the city wall she gains.
Through the vast city borne in wild affright,
No warder from the turrets mark'd her flight;
To seek the fane her eager thoughts were bent,
By paths frequented oft with dire intent.   68
Where slept the dead within the heaving ground,
And noxious herbs, and potent drugs, were found.
Here had she sought materials for her charms,
And torn the lingering roots replete with harms.
As now she wander'd through the confines drear,
Her conscious bosom throbb'd with guilty fear.
The goddess of the silver crescent rose,
And look'd complacent on her frantic woes,
An object meet to justify her love.
' What though (she said) to Latmian ² caves I rove;
Not unexampled in my wild desire,
I seek Endymion with incessant fire.   80

  ² The caves of Mount Latmus, where she was fabled to
have met Endymion.

Thou too, enchantress, of undaunted breast,
Thou bold intruder on Diana's rest,
Whose guilty tongue renew'd the' insidious strain,
To wake the feelings of my amorous pain,
That Cynthia might withdraw her sacred light,
And free to magic leave the murky night,
That mutter'd spells might uncontrol'd prevail,
And corses rise beneath the glimpses pale;
Wretch, thou hast proved the' inevitable hour;
Thy harden'd nature bows to Cupid's power; 90
The god, the god has wing'd his burning dart,
And Jason's image revels in thy heart.
Go, dexterous as thou art in spells and charms,
Redeem thy soul from these delicious harms.
Go, if thou canst, the fatal pangs avoid,
That gods torment, and mortals have destroy'd.'
   Each nerve in flight meantime the virgin strain'd;
Oh, with what joy the river's bank she gain'd!
Led by the fires, that through the festive night
Gleam'd clear in honour of the prosperous fight. 100
As round the flame the gallant train rejoice,
Roll'd through the gloom, they hear a plaintive
        voice.
For as Medea climb'd the rising ground,
On Phrontis' name she call'd, with shrilly sound,
Of Phryxus youngest born; through darkness
        drear,
The well known accents vibrate on his ear.
His brothers knew the voice, and Jason knew;
Then silent wonder seized the youthful crew.
Thrice call'd the princess. Urged by all the crowd,
The son of Phryxus answer'd thrice aloud. 110
Nor yet their halsers on the bank were laid;
With eager oars they press to reach the maid.

From the high deck the youthful leader darts,
With all the fire that sanguine hope imparts;
With Argus Phrontis, springing to the shore,
The kindred mourner through the gloom explore.
   The brothers stood the' afflicted maid beside.
She clasp'd their knees, and supplicating cried—
' Save me, loved youths, preserve yourselves and
     me
From stern Æëtes and perdition free;   120
All is betray'd.   No hope for us remains,
Save in some vessel, and the watery plains.
Swift let us fly ere he ascends his car,
With rapid steeds to chase us from afar;
The golden fleece, fruit of my bounty, take;
My philtres shall subdue that watchful snake.
But, stranger, raise to heaven thy pious hand,
And join the gods to this assembled band;
Call them in witness of thy plighted word,
Bid them thy oaths, thy promises record.   130
Should I for thee forsake my friends and home,
For thee to distant climes an exile roam,
Swear thou wilt not such confidence betray;
Thou wilt not leave me to contempt a prey;
Swear that of kindred, home, and friends bereft,
I shall not be a wretched outcast left.'
   Plaintive she spoke, while piteous tears distill'd;
But secret joy the soul of Jason fill'd.
He gently raised her as his knees she grasp'd,
And soothing mild, in fond embraces clasp'd: 140
' Hear me, my fairest.   In this awful hour
I call on Jove, and every heavenly power;
On Juno chief, the spouse of ruling Jove,
The sacred arbitress of wedded love.
Within my native home thou shalt preside;
Queen of my heart, my darling, and my bride.'

Then for assurance of the mutual brèast,
The virgin's hand with plighted hand he press'd.
　Now were the train admonish'd by the maid,
To ply their oars, and gain the sacred shade; 150
And thence by nightly stealth the fleece convey
Ere stern Æëtes should their course delay.
The train obey, by hopes and fears impell'd:
Their ship they enter'd, and their oars they held.
They push'd from land incumbent on their oars,
Their clamours echoed through the winding shores.
　Then turning towards the plain, the' afflicted fair
Stretch'd forth her beauteous hands in mute de-
Now had she rush'd a watery death to find, [spair.
But Jason sooth'd her agonizing mind;　　　160
And gentle force her frantic will restrain'd;
And now the ship the' appointed station gain'd.
　What time the wakeful hunters ope their eyes,
And call their dogs, and to the chase arise;
Whose early-sports anticipate the morn,
And rouse the covert with the hound and horn;
Ere from the dewy ground the solar ray
Drinks the light traces, and the scent away;
The youthful leader with his virgin gnide,
Debark'd upon the river's grassy side.　　　170
There where the fabled ram, with toil oppress'd,
First reach'd the strand, and bending sunk to rest,
When o'er the sounding waves from shore to shore
The wandering son of Athamas he bore.
And near, with smoky base, an altar stood,
That Phryxus rear'd retiring from the flood,
To Jove [3] the stranger's friend, whose guardian
Protects the suffering exile in his flight; [might
And there, obedient to what Hermes told,
He offer'd up the ram with fleece of gold.　　180

[3] He was worshiped under the name of Jupiter Pbyxias.

By Argus warn'd, the social band withdrew;
The' adventurous path the chief and maid pursue.
Along that path the sacred grove they sought,
Where tower'd the beech, with fleecy treasure
　　　fraught,
They see the plant its giant arms unfold,
And bright between appears the pendent gold,
Like flaming clouds, with curling radiance bright,
That blush illumined by the dawning light.'
The watchful dragon, that the fleece defends,
A length immense his waving neck extends. 190
Onward the lovers move : his eyeballs flame,
And direful hissings their advance proclaim.
Baleful and shrill was that ill omen'd sound;
The' extended shores reecho'd all around.
They heard, who, far from the Titanian strand,
Plough the wide limits of the Colchian land;
Where Lycus from Araxes loud divides,
And joys, with Phasis mix'd, to roll his sacred
　　　tides.
Scared by the noise, the mothers start from rest,
And press their new-born infants to the breast. 200
From burning woods ascending to the pole,
As globes of smoke in fiery volumes roll,
Cloud urges cloud, the' incessant vapours rise,
Enormous wreaths, and whirl along the skies;
The monster huge impell'd his countless spires,
O'erlaid with scales, that shone like distant fires.
Onward he labour'd with tremendous sway;
The maid advanced, and stood athwart his way.
With softest sweetest notes she call'd a power,
Bland, but sufficient in that dangerous hour;   210
With warbled strain she call'd the god of sleep,
In Lethe's dew those watchful eyes to steep:

Yet more she summons from beneath the ground,
The queen revered in shades of night profound.
' Rise, awful Hecaté, propitious power,
Aid the bold purpose of this fatal hour !'
Brave as he was, and oft in perils tried,
With faltering steps the youth pursued his guide.
   Now wrought the mystic charm with potent
       sway.   219
Entranced, dissolved the dreadful monster lay,
With spine relax'd, extended o'er the plain,
In orbs diffuse uncoil'd his scaly train.
When breezes fill the' expansive sail no more,
And not a wave is heard to lash the shore,
In placid silence thus the billows sleep,
And languid curls are spread along the deep.
Yet still aloft his horrid head he rear'd,
And still in act to close his jaws appear'd
With dreadful menace. But the nymph display'd
A mystic bough, cut from the sacred shade, 230
A branch of juniper in drugs bedew'd,
With potency by magic spell imbued.
Melodious charm her tuneful voice applies ;
She waves her opiate o'er the monster's eyes.
Diffused around narcotic vapour flows ;
The dragon sinks subdued in deep repose,
Unmoving, harmless as the silent dead ;
His gaping jaws were fix'd, he hung his head ;
And spreading like some vast meandering flood,
His powerless volumes stretch'd along the wood.
Exhorted by the maid, without delay,   241
The youth approach'd the tree to seize the prey ;
While, near the dragon fix'd, the' intrepid maid
O'er his dire head the flattering unction laid.
She waited thus unmoved and unappall'd,
Till to the ship the youth her steps recall'd,

APOLLONIUS RHODIUS.

Exhausted by the toil, without delay
The youth approach'd the tree to seize the prey.
Argonautics Bk. 4.

Drawn by Rich.d Cook.

Engraved by T.Engleheart.

Published by Suttaby, Evance & Fox, London.
Oct.30.1811.

When now departing from the sacred grove,
He gave the sign of safety and of love.
   As when, exulting in reflected light,   249
The full-orb'd moon displays the torch of night;
Some maid delighted sees the splendour fall
On the high ceiling, or the chamber wall;
Around she sees the circling lustre dance,
And spreads her veil to catch the' illusive glance;
So joy'd the youthful hero, to behold
The light reflected from the fleece of gold;
While as he bore the glorious prize on high,
The ruddy splendours lighten'd to the sky.
O'er his fresh cheek the fiery lustre beams,
The radiance on his front, of ivory streams.   260
That fleece was ample as an heifer's hide,
Or skin of hinds, that in Achaia bide;
So large it spread with the metallic freight,
Of golden locks that curl'd, enormous weight.
The rays were darted round so bright and strong,
The path seem'd gilded as he strode along.
O'er his broad shoulders now the treasure flung,
Descending ponderous to his footsteps hung;
Now in his hands the precious fleece he holds,
And turns with anxious care the shining folds; 270
While round his eyes are glanced with jealous fear,
Lest god or mortal should the conquest bear.
   Now rose Aurora, blushing, from the main.
The youthful lovers join'd the social train.
In mute amaze that gallant band survey
The fleece refulgent with a fiery ray;
As bright, as flaming as the bolt of Jove,
And all to touch the sacred burden strove.
The youth forbade, and from their sight withdrew.
A new-wrought mantle o'er the fleece he threw.

Then near the helm he placed the royal maid, 281
And, turning to his brave companions, said—
  ' No more despondence shall afflict this band;
Despair no longer of your native land;
The vast emprise, that most allured and grieved,
Hope of our toil and perils, is achieved.
Behold this lovely maid with grateful hearts,
Ascribe your safety to her prosperous arts.
Her to my home a virgin bride I bear,
Alike from gratitude and beauty dear.   290
If charms, if benefits may claim your aid,
My friends will guard our tutelary maid,
Whose hand beneficent bestows the fleece,
And home conducts you to your loves in Greece.
But think not yet our labours at an end;
What art obtain'd your valour must defend;
Æëtes soon with savage throngs will sweep,
To bar our exit to the friendly deep.
Some urge the vessel from these dangerous shores,
Set man to man alternate at your oars: 300
Half grasp the shield compact of many a hide;
And be the foes in open fight defied.
Each in that hour will feel upon his hand
Loves, children, parents, friends, his native land,
All that, possess'd, delights the human heart;
All, all that lost affliction can impart.
This moment calls us to renown or shame.'
He ceased.   His arms around the hero flame.
  Loud shouts of ardour burst from all the crew,
Their leader from the sheath his falchion drew;
Nor weak nor erring hand the halser smote, 311
And free from land he sees the vessel float.
Then near Ancæus, while the helm he sway'd,
In arms he stood beside the plighted maid.

Urged by the' exertions of that vigorous throng,
To pass the flood the vessel shot along.
   Now from the meanest Colchian to the throne,
Medea's love and deeds by all were known.
In armour clad the crowds to council haste,
Numerous as billows with the wintry blast;   320
Numerous as leaves in forests strew the ground,
When chiding autumn bids her gale resound;
Thus countless they, in many a crowded rank,
With noise and fury fill'd the river's bank.
With steeds illustrious, and his polish'd car,
Amid the crowd Æëtes shone from far;
The steeds, donation of his sire the sun,
Were swift as winds, or flying sounds, to run.
While in the left his circling shield he took,
A branch of flaming pine his right hand shook:
Beside him lay his spear's enormous length,   331
Of weight prodigious, and resistless strength.
With dexterous hand Absyrtus held the reins.
Meantime the welcome deep the vessel gains,
Driven, by the force combined of youthful arms
And prosperous currents, from that land of harms.
   Æëtes view'd, with anguish and dismay—
To Jove appealing and the solar ray,
With hands upraised : ' Ye gods, to whom belongs,
All-seeing powers, the punishment of wrongs,
Receive my vows, my direful curses hear!   341
And you, my subjects, if my wrath ye fear,
O'ertake these traitors, if the land they keep;
O'ertake their vessel, if she ploughs the deep;
Regain that wanton from the miscreant band;
Bring her to feel a wrathful father's hand.
Let vengeance swiftly seize the caitiff crew;
In combat quell them, or in flight pursue.'

He ceased.   That very day, with active care,
Their ships and stores the Colchian band prepare;
That very day their vessels plough'd the wave,
And sails unnumber'd to the breezes gave.   352
Not ships but feather'd flocks the vessels seem,
That urge their flight with many a shrilly scream.

Meantime the Grecian vessel wing'd her path,
Charged with the messenger [4] of heavenly wrath;
The breezes, that with Juno's will conspire,
To Pelias waft the creature of her ire.
When the third morning came, the Grecian band
Their vessel moor'd on Paphlagonia's strand;
Where sounding Halys rushes to the deep   361
They land, the rites of Hecaté to keep;
So bids the maid.   No conscious heart shall know
Those mystic rites, no rhymes irreverent show;
Be far from such attempt my pious song;
To night and awful silence they belong.
Yet still the structure crowns the sounding shore,
Raised by those heroes in the times of yore.

Now Jason calls to mind the prescient strain,
Alike remember'd by the social train :   370
How Phineus sung, that, having won the fleece,
A different course should lead them home to
          Greece ;
But what the destined course in doubt remain'd,
Till Argus thus the latent truth explain'd—

' To reach Orchomenus, we trace the way
Described by Phineus in prophetic lay,
That mariners a varying track may hold
The sacred ministers of Heaven unfold;
They who the worship of the gods attend,
Where Thebes [5] beholds Tritonian towers ascend.

----

[4] Medea.   See notes at the end, and the text ante.
[5] In Egypt.

Oldest of mortals they who peopled earth,   381
Ere yet in heaven the radiant signs had birth.
The Danai, sacred race, were then unknown;
The' Arcadians held the plains of Greece alone,
On acorns wont, in silvan wilds, to feed,
Ere men the lunar wanderings learn'd to read;
Ere yet the heroes of Deucalion's blood
Pelasgia peopled with a glorious brood.
The fertile plains of Egypt flourish'd then,
Productive cradle of the first of men.   390
There Triton, beauteous stream, irriguous flows,
And o'er the' expanse fertility bestows.
No rains from heaven bedew the farmer's toil,
But inundations bathe the pregnant soil;
From thence, 'tis said, o'er many a distant land
A valiant chieftain led his hardy band.
Heroic guide of heroes to the fight,
With Europe, Asia bow'd beneath his might.
Yet not to ravage o'er the land he spread,
For walls he raised, and colonies he led;   400
A thousand states his conquering arms assail'd,
A favour'd few o'er war and time prevail'd;
Of most nor trace nor memory appears,
For ever swallow'd in the' abyss of years;
But, firm through ages, Æa's walls remain,
Firm the descendants of that martial train
Whom to that station first the warrior drew,
When o'er the land his conquering myriads flew,
Still they preserve, with reverential awe,
Sacred memorials of their ancient law;   410
And tablets, sculptured in the times of old,
The paths and bounds of earth and seas unfold;
What course the deeps to mariners expand,
And what the plains to those who traverse land.

H 2

Of spreading ocean the remotest horn,
Ample and deep a mighty stream is borne.
From springs remote his sounding waters glide,
And loaded ships may on his bosom ride,
Majestic Ister.   From Riphean hills,
Fill'd with the tribute of a thousand rills,   420
Swoln with the melting of perpetual snow,
Beyond the seats where Boreas 'gins to blow,
O'er many a region, from his mountain source,
He rolls at first with undivided force.   [gains,
When Scythian realms and Thracia's bound he
In sever'd streams he rushes o'er the plains.
One arm to meet the' Ionian wave he guides,
And one he sends, to swell Trinacria's tides
Through the deep bay that joins my native coast[6];
If I may knowledge of tradition boast.'   430
    He ceased.' The queen of heaven a sign dis-
Auspicious omen of celestial aid.   [play'd,
The heroes shout, exulting at the view,
And urge their chief his voyage to pursue;
To mark the course, where leading meteors fly,
And lambent lightnings flash along the sky.
Here Lycus' offspring[7] separates from the band,
And seeks his father's court, and native land.
They plough the waves, the wind their canvass fills,
They hold in view the Paphlagonian hills.   440
Not round Carambis do they wind their way,
But breathing gales and heavenly fires obey;
For still the breeze prevail'd, and splendour glow'd,
Until they came where swelling Ister flow'd.

[6] This is a very difficult passage in the original : the geography of the poet is rather unintelligible.
[7] Dascylus.

Their frustrate hours meantime the Colchians
        waste,
Through the Cyanean rocks a squadron pass'd.
Led by their youthful prince, a different train
Explored the seats where Ister seeks the main.
To cut off all retreat his course he sped
Across a branch where parted Ister spread; 450
Thence onward, round the narrow point of land,
His ships anticipate the Grecian band;
And while they [s] sail the jutting headland round,
By route compendious gain the' Ionian bound,
Indented bay.   By Ister's arms embraced,
In form triangular an isle is placed;
Peucé its name; that, dark with stately pines,
The spreading outlet of the stream confines.
The vertex meets the current and divides,
The' extended base resists the roaring tides; 460
The flood becomes another and the same;
Each parted branch assumes a different name.
Above, the turbid Arax seeks the waves;
That isle below the smoother Calon laves.
Through this the prince his Colchian followers
        drew;
The branch superior while the Greeks pursue.
There wide the verdant pastures were display'd;
And flocks, deserted by their keepers, stray'd.
The rude and timorous natives of the plain
Seem'd to behold, emergent from the main, 470
Devouring monsters, vast in bulk, arise;
For ships were strangers to their simple eyes;
And never yet the neighbouring tribes of Thrace
Had mix'd in commerce with the Scythian race,
The wild Sigynian, the Graucenian bands,
The Sindians, who possess the Laurian lands,

        [s] i. e. The Argonauts.

Wide-stretch'd and waste.　At such stupendous
　　　sight,
The savage tribes their safety placed in flight.
　　Near tall Angurus now the Minyæ steer'd,
And distant now the Cauliac rocks appear'd; 480
Where bellowing Ister breaks his ample horn,
To meet the waves in parted channels borne.
Now had they coasted the Talaurian land,
By shorter progress, while the Colchian band
Had reach'd already to the Chronian deep,
And all the outlets of the river keep;
Where, as they deem'd, the Greeks their course
　　　must shape,
That none the vengeance of their king might scape.
Not so the wary Minyæ.　Far behind
A safer passage up the stream they find;　　490
Two isles they reach, to virgin Dian dear,
To Dian whom the' Illyrian tribes revere.
One sacred structure boasts her awful fane,
One from their ship receives the' adventurous train,
Safe from the myriads, that, athirst for war,
With young Absyrtus guard the coast afar.
Those isles they shunn'd; for reverence of the place
Restrain'd the fury of that savage race.
But, these except, beset with arms they found
Each isle and shore that closed the channel round.
In every station adverse myriads stood,　　501
To Nestis' plain and to Salanco's flood.
　　Now crowds prevailing o'er undaunted might,
Had crush'd the Minyæ in unequal fight:
But treaty interrupts the rude alarms,
And sober compact stays the clang of arms.
The Minyæ by concession bear the fleece,
Hope of their voyage, to the shores of Greece;

The prize their chief by bold exertion gain'd,
In dreadful trials by the king ordain'd.   510
Though force or stratagem possession gave,
Let them retain, and waft it o'er the wave.
But for the maid, chief subject of debate,
In Dian's fane let her the future wait,
Till sceptred wisdom shall her fate decide;
Or, home returning, with her sire to bide,
Or with the sons of Phryxus, to explore
Unknown Orchomenus and Phthia's shore;
Or yet, more welcome to the' enamour'd fair,
To Hellas with the Grecian chiefs repair.   520
  In such alternatives for peace they sought;
But various passions on the virgin wrought.
She mark'd their views with agonizing mind;
For who the wakeful eyes of love may blind?
Apart their leader from the chiefs she drew,
Alike remote from hearing and from view.
Then streaming tears and mournful sounds ex-
          press'd
The painful thoughts that labour'd in her breast.
  ' Oh say, what blow thy secret counsel aims
Against the wretch who thy protection claims.
I know thy purpose; cruel and unjust,   531
To love injurious, faithless to thy trust.
Think of the splendours I have left for thee;
Think of the dangers whence I set thee free.
Oh, think what vows, what promises were made,
In hours of peril, when I lent my aid;
Oh, fatal promises! of shame bereft,
Through them, ingrate, my natal soil I left.
Through them, with frantic hand I cast away
Imperial pomp, beneath my parent's sway;   540
The dearest pledges have I left to weep
With plaintive halcyon, while I roam the deep.

And why? Alas! this dreadful price I give,
That thou mayst triumph; nay, that thou mayst live.
In fatal labours hence hast thou prevail'd,
And bulls infuriate fire in vain exhaled;
And hence, ungrateful! did that earthborn band,
Like feeble infants, sink beneath thine hand.
Hope of thy voyage o'er the distant wave,
The precious fleece, my happy rashness gave;
Happy to thee, but fatal to my fame;   551
To female honesty an endless shame.
What bond with thee a modest maid should send?
Am I thy bride, thy sister, or thy friend?
A time there was, the flatterer would bestow
Each tender name that may from passion flow.
Afflicting change! I feel thy love decline
With cold neglect; the wanton's name is mine.
On different terms I left my regal home,
On different terms with thee I deign'd to roam;
Yet, be it so; the' eternal lot is cast;   561
The dire irrevocable doom is pass'd.
Alone and friendless in thy train I go,
Heiress of shame, a monument of woe,
Encumbrance now, no partner of thy flight;
Yet drive me not dishonour'd from thy sight.
Leave me not now to sate my father's rage;
My blood alone his fury can assuage.
If any pity in thy breast remains;
If justice in thy soul her sway retains;   570
If yet remembrance can attention draw
To the soft compact, and the mutual law,
Pass'd in the moment when I thought we loved,
Vow'd by the tongue, and by the heart approved,
Is this too great a boon—my worthless breath?
Then draw thy sword, and end my woes in death.

Strike here, transfix this heart, 'tis meet I prove
From thee the punishment of foolish love.
Say, should that king, to whom on deep debate,
Inhuman, thou wilt trust a wretch's fate,   580
Sad office, to pronounce my fatal doom,
To hurl a mourner to the' untimely tomb,
A miserable thrall in that sad hour,
Should he consign me to my brother's power;
Say with what glory should I then appear?
Or how sustain my father's brow severe?
My frantic love what punishments await?
In what dire form must I encounter fate?
Yet hope not thou thy feelings to control,
To lull to rest the self-accusing soul.   590
For thee no breezes shall propitious blow;
Nor glad return thy guilty sails shall know.
Hope not a blessing from the powers above,
Not e'en from her the' imperial wife of Jove,
Nor aid nor joy from Juno be supplied,
Friend of thy labours, motive of thy pride.
Avenging furies shall my grief attend,
And late remorse thy perjured bosom rend:
And may that precious prize, the fleece of gold,
Fade like a vision from thy vacant hold;   600
Driven from thy native soil to shame and woe,
Medea's anguish thou shalt learn to know.
Thou who shalt cause this doting heart to bleed,
Learn thou what demons haunt the faithless deed;
In what deep character the gods record
Each violated oath and impious word.'
  She ceased, at once with grief and rage oppress'd,
And horrors roll'd tumultuous in her breast;
And now she thought with mad vindictive aims
To hurl the brand, and wrap the ship in flames. 610

The son of Æson trembles at her rage,
And soothing words her stormy grief assuage.
   ' My fairest, my espoused, thy terrors cease;
To that afflicted bosom whisper peace.
Think not so meanly of thy lover's heart,
Where no deceit or treachery has part;
Deem not so lightly of these heavenly charms;
Think, could I thus resign thee from my arms?
Those terms, so justly hateful in thy sight,
Were proffer'd to suspend the dangerous fight. 620
For fierce and numerous is the hostile band
Assembled round thy beauties to demand;
With vengeful fury young Absyrtus leads
The crowding natives from the shores and meads.
They think to bear thee a defenceless prey,
And yield thee captive to thy father's sway.
What hopes from combat with that hostile train?
Their numbers render skill and valour vain.
What doom is thine, in battle should we fall,
Exposed to vengeance, a deserted thrall?   630
Hence, 'tis the power of artifice we try,
Counsel may give what prowess would deny.
This treaty shall confound the mighty host,
And all their schemes of vengeance shall be lost.
The natives, that around by myriads arm,
No more shall strike our bosoms with alarm;
But home dispersing, cease their aid to lend,
While e'en Absyrtus shall appear our friend.
Abandon'd thus the Colchians shall remain;
Nor fear I then to meet the' embattled train, 640
Should they presume to thwart my homeward way,
Or think by force to bear thee for their prey.'
   Soothing he spake, and her suspicions heal'd;
Her fatal thoughts Medea thus reveal'd—

' Bethink thee, Jason, what the time demands,
Guilt is no stranger to these dangerous hands.
Such dire connexion links unhallow'd aims,
Crime builds on crime, and shame engenders
    shames.   [mind,
Since Heaven in errors plunged my wandering
From guilt to guilt my desperate path I find. 650
Meet not the Colchian bands in open field;
My arts their leader to thy power shall yield.
But thou with splendid gifts the way prepare,
That draws the'incautious victim to my snare.
If won by me, in conference apart,
The heralds lend assistance to my art;
What then remains? Absyrtus is our thrall;
He comes defenceless, by thine hand to fall;
'Reft of their leader, should the Colchian band
Provoke the fight, no longer stay thine hand.' 660
   Thus they their thoughts in direful aims employ,
Of mortal mischief to the princely boy;
Dissembled fondness, and perfidious smiles,
And hospitable pledges, mask'd their wiles.
Among the gifts was first and fairest seen
A veil, that graced that beauteous Lemnian queen[9],
A radiant purple web with hands of love,
Which heavenly Charities for Bacchus wove.
Where sounding ocean beats on Dia's shore,
Thoas, his son, received the gift of yore.   670
Among the treasures that her father own'd,
Hypsipyle the beauteous texture found;
That gift at parting, ere he plough'd the wave,
With toys and gems, her love to Jason gave.
A work more form'd the senses to delight,
Ne'er sooth'd the touch, or glitter'd on the sight.

       [9] Hypsipyle.

From all the web ambrosial odours flow'd;
That perfume the Nysæan god[10] bestow'd
In hours of bliss, when, with his ivory arms,
He held entranced his Ariadne's charms.   680
From Gnossus her the perjured Theseus bore,
And weeping left on Dia's lonely shore.
　　In converse with the heralds had the maid
In order due her fraudful counsels laid;   [gain
Well were they school'd with soothing speech to
The youth, and lead him to Diana's fane.
She mark'd the time. When night her veil extends,
And stealth inspires, and fallacy befriends.
Fictitious aims her artful words unfold,
From Jason to withdraw the fleece of gold,   690
And with the treasure to her father haste,
Peaceful oblation for misconduct pass'd,
No willing exile, so she feign'd, from home,
But forced by Phryxus' guilty sons to roam.
The' instructions ended, the delusive fair
Hurl'd spells and philtres through the spungy air,
Of power to stay the wildest mountain flock,
And draw the savage from his cavern'd rock.
　　Pernicious love, thou scourge of humankind,
Thou bane envenom'd of the reasoning mind, 700
What fell contentions, what distress and woe,
What pangs unnumber'd from thine influence flow!
Sovereign of torments, for our foes alone
Reserve the furies by that virgin known.
O Muse, relate what snares Medea spread
To join her brother with the silent dead.
　　The maiden, as by compact was ordain'd,
Within the fane of Artemis remain'd.
The Colchian vessels part. The Greeks display
Their sails, and homeward seem to shape their way.

                    [10] Bacchus.

Deceitful seeming! Jason and his band,   711
With mortal purpose, took their ambush'd stand;
In arms relentless, working to destroy,
With all his train that unsuspecting boy.
The fatal promises the boy misled,
In evil hour the' incautious sail he spread.
His vessel skimm'd the waves with rapid flight,
And reach'd the sacred isle in shades of night.
Medea waits alone, with mischief fraught,
Balm on her tongue, but murder in her thought. 720
Poor simple youth! he thinks, with childish art,
To wield her dark impracticable heart!
Vain thought! as soon, with feeble hand, the swain
The raging wintry torrent might restrain.
It scorns its banks, it deluges the ground;
It roars, it foams, and spreads destruction round.
Her airy fabric fancy joy'd to build,
And idle hope his witless bosom fill'd.
He dreams of aid his sister may afford,
And sees the Minyæ fall beneath his sword. 730
The wily sister these delusions fed;
In fraudful speech the stealthy moments fled;
While bland compliance smooth'd her oily tongue,
And present kindness pander'd future wrong.
    Now Jason from his ambuscade advanced;
Rear'd o'er his head the shining falchion glanced.
Terrific form! abhorrent turn'd the maid,
And o'er her eyes her ample veil display'd,
With heart presageful of the' impending deed,
Nor fully steel'd to see a brother bleed.   740
As, in the precincts of some awful fane,
The victim ox by sudden stroke is slain,
The' insidious Grecian aim'd a rapid blow,
And, gazing round him, fell'd the' unguarded foe.

E'en at the threshold of the sacred door
He falls expiring on the marble floor,
E'en at the fane the natives of his land
Had raised for Artemis, with pious hand,
Sunk on his knees. As forth the life-blood gush'd,
O'er both his hands the purple torrent rush'd, 750
As in the mortal agonies he press'd
The ghastly wound that gaped upon his breast.
E'en as his sister turn'd her head away,
Her head attire was dash'd with purple spray.
The darted rills that smoked along the ground,
Bedew'd her snowy veil that floated round.
Power all-subduing, ever unsubdued,
With piercing glance oblique the fury view'd.
Of terrors queen, of ills and crimes the cause,
E'en she with horror mingled her applause. 760
  The slayer took the first-fruits of the slain,
For mystic rites, that conscious fears ordain,
Atonements, that, in ancient days decreed,
Absolved the man of blood's atrocious deed.
Then from the wound the reeking skin he tore,
And suck'd with quivering lips the streaming gore.
Thrice from the panting breast he draws the blood;
Thrice from his teeth ejects the horrid flood.
Then, bathed in streams yet welling from the wound,
He gave the lifeless body to the ground.   770
There, still entomb'd, his bones for ever sleep;
And still the stripling's name the natives keep.
  Soon as the Greeks the glaring torch survey'd,
Appointed signal of the treacherous maid,
The reins to joy and martial thoughts they give,
And full against the Colchian vessel drive.
Then fall impetuous on the' astonish'd crew,
As pouncing hawks the timid doves subdue;

Or ravening lions, that in midnight hour,
To thin the fold with savage fury pour.   780
Fierce and destructive, the relentless train
Nor art eludes, nor courage can sustain.
Now here, now there they dart, with lightning's
    force,
And all existence withers in their course.
Now Jason flies to share the warlike deed,
And yield that aid his comrades scarcely need.
One care alone the social band possess'd;
Doubts of his safety fill'd each thoughtful breast.
    And now the' assembled chiefs in council sate,
The future voyage wakes the deep debate,   790
The princess on their consultations broke,
As Peleus thus among the leaders spoke—
' My counsel is, ere morn resumes the sky,
To man the vessel, and our oars to ply;
Mark where the foes attend in dread array,
And opposite direct your cautious way.
When morn shall come the past events to show,
Doubt and confusion will possess the foe;
'Reft of their leader mid the shades of night,
Nor scheme nor head combines them in the fight;
Dissension through their myriads shall prevail, 801
And unmolested leave our flying sail.'
    His counsel pleased. The warriors spring from
    land,
The benches line, and row with vigorous hand.
Their toil with nerves unfailing they sustain'd,
And now Electris' hallow'd seat they gain'd,
Last in their progress of that island train,
Where Po descends to meet the briny main.
    Emotions mingled of dismay and grief,
Possess'd the Colchians for their ravish'd chief. 810

Yet o'er the Chronian deep, with vengeful thought,
The Grecian vessel and her crew they sought.
In vain. The Argonauts were Juno's care;
To thwart their foes, terrific lightnings glare.
Final discomfiture, dispersed they roam,
Impress'd with horror, from their native home.
Æëtes' cruelty such terror bred,
That wandering far to distant climes they fled.
Absyrtus' name some bid those isles retain,
That yielded refuge to the Grecian train;   820
Some raise the distant towers, with exiled hand,
Where Panyasis bathes the' Illyrian land;
And where a monument of ancient fame
With Cadmus[11] joins his loved Harmonia's name,
As denizens augment the' Enchelian race,
And lose the memory of their native place.
Scared by the thunders of almighty Jove,
Some to the high Ceraunian summits rove;
And still the name records the dread event, 829
Derived from glancing fires through ether sent.
  When now the voyage seem'd from perils freed,
The heroes through the watery vast proceed.
Hyllean seats the' adventurous band explore,
And bind their cables from the rocky shore.
Along the coast, where clustering islets rise,
Dangerous and difficult the channel lies.
No more the Minyæ from the natives find
Repulsive welcome, and unfriendly mind;
Bland they receive them, in their counsels share,
And means to prosecute their course prepare. 840
A fair donation their affections won,
A hallow'd tripod of Latona's son.

[11] For the story of Cadmus and Harmonia, see notes at the
end.

Erewhile, to Jason had the god of light
Two polish'd tripods given, of fabric bright;
When Pythos' shrine oracular he sought,
And the long voyage fill'd his anxious thought.
A mighty privilege the gifts endow'd,
By fate, in that auspicious hour, bestow'd,
To guard the land, where treasured they remain,
From wasting inroad of the hostile train.   850
Deep in the bosom of the peaceful ground,
Where fair Hylleis lifts her towers renown'd,
The treasure lies conceal'd within the soil,
A depth inscrutable to human toil.
  No longer flourishing in youthful bloom
The king they found; he slept within the tomb,
Young Hyllus.   Him, on the Phæacian shore,
Fair Melita to strong Alcides bore.
For there a refuge in his youth he found,
When good Nausithoüs the sceptre own'd :   860
Press'd with a weight of guiltless blood he ranged,
And soon for Macris this asylum changed.
Some expiation there he hoped to find,
For conscious guilt lay heavy on his mind,
Since by their father's hand his infants bléd,
In frantic mood, of melancholy fed.
Thee, nursing mother of the roseate god,
Thy viny plains the' illustrious wanderer trod.
There, beauteous daughter of the Ægean main,
Fair Melita renew'd his amorous pain ;   870
She crown'd his love, and to the hero bore
The gallant Hyllus on that lonely shore.
High-minded youth, when manhood he attain'd,
The state subordinate his soul disdain'd.
He scorn'd the region where Nausithoüs sway'd,
And all his nod implicitly obey'd.

The native train he led, and wander'd wide,
O'er Chronian waves with freedom for his guide.
Phæacia's king his aid and counsel gave;
And here he ceased his wanderings o'er the wave.
Not long he rested in the seats he chose;   881
With fierce Mentorians deadly war arose,
To guard the numerous herds and rustic band,
And Hyllus sunk beneath the spoiler's hand.

But sing, ye Muses, how the' adventurous train
Pass'd from that sea to reach the' Ausonian plain.
Say, how to those Ligustic isles they came,
The Stœchades, so call their modern name.
Still do these regions true memorials hold
Of wanderings wide, and navigation bold.   890
What ruling winds the destination gave,
On shores unknown to bid their ensigns wave?
Say, goddess, why that devious course they held;
What good allured, or what distress compell'd?

Father of justice, sire of gods and men,
Who marks our actions with all-seeing ken,
Jove, from on high, beheld Absyrtus bleed,
And doom'd to punishment that impious deed.
Peace or remission none for them remain'd;
Eternal wisdom this decree ordain'd,   900
That guiltless blood should agitate the band,
And vengeful furies hunt from land to land,
Till rites, which Circé might perform alone,
Should chase those horrors, and for guilt atone.

The doom mysterious not a chief could read,
For darkness veil'd what righteous Heaven de-
    creed.
And now they pass from that Hyllæan plain,
Where countless isles lay clustering in the main,
And those Liburnian seats in order trace,
Of old the mansions of a Colchian race,   910

Resounding Issa, with her rocky steep,
Fair Pityæa, smiling on the deep.
Still forward borne, they to Corcyra came, [dame,
Where amorous Neptune placed the beauteous
Sprung from Asopus, nymph with golden hair;
From Phlius far he led Corcyra fair.
With forests clad the gloomy hills arise,
At distance blackening on the sailor's eyes.
And hence that isle is black Corcyra named,
An epithet to mark the' appearance framed. 920
The winds propitious'to their course prevail,
And Melita they pass with swelling sail,
The tall Cerossus, and with head more high
Nymphæa proudly towering to the sky.
Daughter of Atlas, here amid the deeps
Her magic court the fair Calypso keeps.
Distant, half veil'd in clouds and vapours blue,
Ceraunia's doubtful hills they seem to view.
    Then Juno read her consort's secret mind,
And schemes of vengeance 'gainst the Greeks
            design'd.   930
Hence, that the train lustrations might perform,
To thwart their course she sent the friendly storm;
They hurried retrograde with rapid flight;
Electris, rocky island, rose in sight.
Here, as the vessel plough'd the salt profound,
Sudden they heard a deep and awful sound.
With human speech endow'd, the groaning oak
In hollow tones amid the timbers spoke,
Where placed by Pallas from Dodona's wood,
With vocal powers, oracular it stood.   940
Amaze and horror fill'd the Greeks to hear
So strange a voice announcing words of fear.
' What dreadful tempests on your course await!
What endless wanderings by the doom of fate!

How long through pains and perils must ye rove!
Such the decree, and such the wrath of Jove!
Unless fair Circé shall remove the stain
Of blood, contracted from Absyrtus slain.
Yet more, the twins of Leda must repair
To win the favour of the gods by prayer;   950
With gales propitious, that the ship may keep
Her steady course along the' Ausonian deep,
Till Circé's island cheer the longing sight,
Daughter of Perseus and the god of light.'
   Thus Argo spake, as day began to close.
The sons of Tyndarus obedient rose.
The wishes of the Greeks their voice express'd,
Their lifted hands the heavenly powers address'd.
With downcast eyes the Minyæ stood around;
Their humbled spirits sunk in awe profound. 960
Their flying bark with swelling sails convey'd,
Within Eridanus was deep embay'd.
Where, blasted by the lightning's darted ray,
And rushing headlong from the car of day,
Young Phaëton, unfortunate as fair,
Expiring fell, and quench'd his flaming hair
Deep in the channel of the spreading stream;
The waters still emit a fiery steam,   968
As boiling from their lowest depth they swell,
Where pierced with fiery wounds the stripling fell.
There birds in vain their sounding pinions urge,
O'erpower'd they sink in that sulphureous surge.
The daughters of the sun, a mournful band,
Along the bank, enclosed in poplars stand.
Still from their leaves resounds the voice of woe,
And still for Phaëton their sorrows flow;
Still, sensible of grief, their loss recall,
While drops of amber from their eyelids fall,

That bright and liquid, scatter'd o'er the land,
Consistence from the chymic sun demand.   980
When loud and shrill the wintry storms arise,
And bid the swelling stream his bank despise;
Gloomy and deep the Po inundates round,
His waters sweep the treasure from the ground,
In giddy whirlpools.   But the Celtic race
To nobler origin that substance trace;
E'en to the tears by weeping Phœbus shed,
In fond remembrance of his offspring dead.
For much he wept, with grief and anger fraught,
What time the Hyperborean race he sought; 990
Stung by reproaches from the sire of gods,
For earth he left the starry-paved abodes.
Sorrowing for him, in Lacerea fair,
Whom to the god divine Coronis [12] bare.
Where to the main bright Amyrus descends,
The power that health to wretched mortals sends.
Such the tradition of the Celtic throng,
Preserved in fable, and rehearsed in song.   998
   No gleam of pleasure cheer'd the conscious crew,
No sense of thirst, no care of food, they knew.
All day they mourn'd and languish'd; where
       prevail'd
Mephitic vapours, from the stream exhaled,
That o'er the Po incessant baneful rise,
Since Phaëton fell flaming from the skies.
While gloom prevail'd, in accents sad and clear,
The mourning daughters of the sun they hear.
They wept their brother lost. The tears at morn,
Like drops of oil, were on the current borne.
   Then the deep courses of the Rhone they gain,
Who, mix'd with Po, fraternal seeks the main. 1010

        [12] Æsculapius.

Where steepy banks the narrow channel bound,
With bellowing voice the confluent waters sound,
From central depths, within the hollow ground,
The gates and resting place of night profound.
The Rhone, impetuous bursting, fiercely roars,
And hurls his raging stream on ocean's shores.
While here he hurries to the' Ionian main,
And there descends, Sardinian waves to gain.
Diffusive there seven ample mouths convey   1019
His parted waters through the spacious bay.
Onward they pass, where spreading lakes [13] ex-
Their squally shoals along the Celtic land. [pand
Here dangers unforeseen the' adventurous wait,
A sunken rock lies fraught with sudden fate [14].
The Greeks unconscious near perdition drew,
And never had return'd that gallant crew;
Here Argo, though by hands divine composed,
Her course disastrous had for ever closed,
But Juno provident, from fields of air,
Survey'd their peril with parental care.   1030
Descending on the' Hercynian mount she stood;
And loud recall'd them from the fatal flood.
Aghast they stood, with fear and wonder fill'd;
Through air around the warning accents thrill'd.
Obedient then a backward course they trace,
Through the known channels of that dangerous
                place.
Before the voice precursive lightnings broke,
The sacred presence pealing thunders spoke.
Yet still those straits the labouring bark detain'd;
And ocean's seabeat shore full late they gain'd.
While, by imperial Juno's counsel sway'd, 1041
Mid various nations of the Celts they stray'd.

[13] *Aliter*, marshes wide.   [14] See note on this passage.

Thus many a tribe of the Ligurian shore
Unheeding and unheeded they explore.
Still, as they pass, the guardian goddess shrouds
Their daring progress in a night of clouds.
The bark secure the midway channel keeps,
Incumbent on the noon while darkness sleeps:
And gains the Stœchades, while from above
Divine protection guards the twins of Jove. 1050
And altars still preserve their ancient praise,
Where sacred rites are paid in these our days.
And, first in that eventful voyage, shown
Their saving aid to mariners is known.
To Heaven exalted, by the will divine,
Propitious still to mariners they shine.
　　The Minyæ reach'd Æthalia's seagirt soil,
And bathed their limbs subdued with ceaseless
With pebbles on the shore that ready lay　[toil.
They chafed the skin, and cleansed the sweat away.
And still the spotted stones along the shore
Confess the labours that the heroes bore.　1062
And many a famous monument remains;
For still that isle their disks and arms retains;
And still a port, preserving Argus' name,
Records the memory of their ancient fame.
Borne on the swelling of the' Ausonian deep,
Full in their view the Tuscan shore they keep.
With rapid flight they reach the famous port,
Where skill'd in magic Circé held her court. 1070
　　Beside the waves they found the heavenly fair,
The braids adjusting of her radiant hair.
Appalling forms, in visions of the night,
Had fill'd her soul with wonder and affright.
Through all her chambers, and the courts below,
Redounding streams of blood appeared to flow.

The treasures of her art, the mystic arms,
The hoarded armoury of drugs and charms,
That stranger guests subdued beneath her sway,
On these the flames devouring seem'd to prey.
Then o'er the fire she cast the' impurpled stream,
With hurried hands, and quench'd the trembling
      gleam: **1082**
Then seem'd her fears to cease. With early dawn,
Her steps were to the seabeat margin drawn,
With pious rites, averting ill, to lave
Her hair and garments in the briny wave.
A train of beasts, not fierce like those of chase,
Nor yet in form of godlike human race,
But something mingled between brute and man,
With action mild, beside the' enchantress ran;
As gentle sheep, in myriads, where he leads, **1091**
Attend the shepherd through the flowery meads.
Their forms were doubtful, as when teeming earth
On living things bestow'd primeval birth;
While she, great parent, moist and pliant lay,
As yet unharden'd by the stroke of day;
From vital principles of every kind,
Her first rude work, she various limbs combined;
Ere nature's hand from time experience gain'd,
Decided figures genders ascertain'd.   **1100**
In mute attention thus around their queen,
Discordant shapes, ambiguous kinds were seen.
Stupendous scene! the heroes stood amazed;
And speechless wonder on the' enchantress gazed.
Soon as her port and features struck their view,
The sister of the Colchian king they knew.
   The nightly terror of her dream dispell'd,
Home from the beach her course the' enchantress
      held.

With soothing action and demeanour bland,
The train she beckon'd with deceitful hand. 1110
But Jason at the shore his comrades stay'd,
Alone proceeding with the Colchian maid.
They follow'd Circé; and together trod
The path that tended to her proud abode.
On splendid seats the' enchantress bade them rest;
But doubt and anxious thoughts her soul possess'd.
Their steps unsounding through the palace pass'd,
The vestal hearth they sought with silent haste;
Then, motionless, with downcast eyes they sate,
As suits the humble suppliant's piteous state. 1120
Stung with reproaches of the conscious mind,
Between her hands the maid her face inclined;
While leaning on the hilt with grief profound,
The youth infix'd his falchion on the ground;
Nor lifts to vengeful Heaven his drooping eyes,
While gloomy thoughts for slain Absyrtus rise.
Fair Circé mark'd their deep desponding mood;
She recognised the fugitives from blood;
Revered the suppliant's right with pious awe;
And bow'd submiss to Jove's imperial law, 1130
Who makes the suppliant his peculiar care,
And, e'en in punishment, inclines to spare.
The' atoning sacrifices she began,
That stains of blood remove from wretched man;
For refuge when he flies to Vesta's shrine,
And seeks remission from the powers divine.
High o'er their heads the little swine she held,
New from the dam, and paps with nurture swell'd.
She pierced his throat, and, cleansing blood with
          blood,
Her suppliants tinctured in the purple flood.
Then ceremonies fill'd the solemn hour,   1141
To calm the wrath of every vengeful power;

And lustral Jove was call'd, at whose command
Oblations pure absolve the slayer's hand.
This done, her train, full many a Naiad maid,
The' ablutions from the splendid dome convey'd.
Within, to sober vows and whisper'd prayer,
That bid the furies drop the scourge, and spare,
The flame with salted cakes the' enchantress fed;
And sweet libations o'er that offering shed   1150
Of mighty power, to sooth the gliding dead;
Whether a stranger's death their hands embrued,
Or the dire stain from kindred blood accrued.
    The solemn expiations were complete.
She call'd each suppliant to the polish'd seat,
Full in her view, and near.   The speech began,
' What climes they visited, what seas o'erran.
Say, graceful strangers, from what part of earth,
Ye claim protection at the sacred hearth?'
Still, with the memory of her dream possess'd,
Doubt and disquiet fill'd her anxious breast.
Fondly she listen'd, with attentive ear,   1162
The native accents of that maid to hear.
Soon as Medea lifted from the ground
Those eyes that beam'd celestial glory round,
That liquid golden fire, effulgence bright,
Which marks the beauteous progeny of light;
The daughter of that tyrant stern and bold,
In Colchian speech a tale of sorrow told.   1169
In tuneful sounds, her soothing words explain'd
The toils, the travels by the band sustain'd;
And how she fled her cruel father's wrath,
With Phryxus' offspring through the watery path;
But some events her cautious tongue forbore;
Nor spoke Absyrtus weltering in his gore.
    In vain.   Her inmost bosom Circé read;
Yet tears of pity for her sufferings shed,

And thus she spake—' Ah wretch, in evil hour,
Thy steps adventurous left the princely bower!
What saving hand thine anguish shall delay? 1180
What force protect thee from a father's sway?
His rage untired will hunt thee o'er the flood;
And e'en in Greece avenge thy brother's blood.
Great is thy guilt. Yet, since the suppliant's name,
And ties of kindred, my compassion claim;
From me, though merited, no mischief prove.
But hence I warn thee. From these walls remove.
Hence, with that stranger, 'mong whose followers
A father's curse and duty are thy scorn. [borne,
Hence with the partner of thy guilty choice; 1190
No more assail me with that plaintive voice.
Thy presence here the sacred hearth profanes;
I shrink abhorrent from thy guilty stains.
I shun thy counsels, nor assist thy flight
From fame and every form of fair and right.'
    She ceased. And, fill'd with grief, the royal maid
Before her eyes the shining veil display'd,
To hide her tears. Her frame with terror shook.
Her hand with gentle action Jason took,
And led her through the portal. Mighty woes,
In briny torrents, found a brief repose.   1201
Trembling she went. Thus from the doors they
            move;
Nor heedless was the imperial wife of Jove.
    Already by her faithful envoy shown,
Each circumstance was to the goddess known.
Erewhile, observant of the Grecian train,
Fair Iris left the starry-paved domain.
For Juno sought to learn, with anxious care,
When to their bark the Minyæ should repair.
This trusty instrument of her desires   1210
 Again she calls; again her aid requires;
                    K 2

' Haste, nymph beloved, my wishes to fulfil;
Toil is thy pleasure, when it works my will.
With rapid course on varied pinions sweep,
And summon Thetis from the briny deep.
Say, Juno seeks her aid.   From thence repair,
Where Vulcan's forges cast a ruddy glare
Along the strand, and deafening hammers sound
On massive anvils to the vast profound.
From labour let him cease, and still the blast, 1220
Parent of fire, till Argo shall have pass'd.
Thence to the caves of Æolus repair,
Supreme o'er winds the progeny of air.
My wishes to the stormy power explain.
Let peace and stillness through his empire reign;
No truant tempest issue from his caves
Nor angry surges curl the sounding waves.
Let gentlest zephyrs o'er the billows smile, 1228
And waft the heroes to Phæacia's isle.'   [tends,
     She ceased; the nymph her pinions light ex-
And swiftly through the fields of air descends.
Deep, deep she plunged, beneath the' Ægean tides,
In regal state, where hoary Nereus bides.
To Thetis first was Juno's mandate given;
And, urged by Iris, she repair'd to heaven.
Next the fair messenger to Vulcan came;
The bellows ceased to swell the roaring flame;
Attentive to his parent's high behest,
Through all his caves he bade the hammers rest.
Last the famed son of Hippotas [15] she finds, 1240
Immortal ruler of the stormy winds.
To him her message, while the nymph address'd,
And, pausing, bade her weary pinions rest;
Fair Thetis left her sisters of the waves,
And ancient sire, within the coral caves;

[15] Æolus.

And hasting to the blissful seats above,
Obedient sought the' imperial wife of Jove.
Her sovereign Juno at her right hand placed,
And thus address'd, with fair reception graced—
  ' Now, lovely Thetis, with attention hear 1250
The words I destine for thy private ear.
Thou know'st how much my cares for Jason wake,
And those brave spirits who his toils partake.
Their vessel through the wandering isles I bore,
Where, charged with fire, tremendous tempests
          roar;
Where pointed rocks the savage shore defend,
And thundering waves the mortal barriers rend.
But, if aright I read the page of fate,
The' adventurous train yet greater dangers wait.
Full in their path the rocks of Scylla lie,   1260
With dire Charybdis whirling to the sky.
Thee, from a child, I nursed with partial hand,
More prized, more loved, than all the seaborn band,
Since thy proud virtue scorn'd the vows of Jove,
That wanderer, ever prone to lawless love.
Mortals, immortals, in promiscuous throngs;
With all alike the nuptial couch he wrongs.
Thy pious mind revered the wedded law,
And Juno's rights inspired a virtuous awe.
Hence, as thou know'st, his wrathful doom he
          bound,   1270
By that dire oath the Stygian waves profound,
That never god, of all the' immortal train,
Should beauteous Thetis for his bride obtain.
Yet still resistance seem'd to fan the fire,
And still his glance betray'd unchaste desire.
Till Themis, venerable power, reveal'd
The high decree, from eldest time conceal'd.

Perdition seek, let Thetis crown thy love,
Produce a son, the conqueror of Jove.
His passion then he curb'd with prudent fear,
Lest in his son he should a rival bear.   1281
While I, to recompense thy prudent mind,
The first of mortals for thy spouse assign'd.
To meet thy chaste desires with mutual flame,
And glad thee with a mother's tender name.
The gods I summon'd to the nuptial rite,
And I myself sustain'd the nuptial light,
Rejoiced to give, in that auspicious hour,
Each mark of honour that my love could shower.
Yet more, without disguise, I shall unfold   1290
The destinies, by mystic fate enroll'd.
When thy loved son shall seek the' Elysian plains,
Whom Chiron now within his cave detains,
With gentle Naiads, who indulgent share
The wakeful duties of parental care,
There is he doom'd to wed the Colchian maid;
Thy future child demands thy present aid.
And Peleus too, I see thine anger flame;
But what existence is exempt from blame?
He may have err'd, but powerful Até flies,   1300
E'en through the blissful mansions of the skies.
Vulcan, I trust, will yield to my desires,
And hush through all his caves the raging fires.
While Æolus forbids the storm to sweep,
And only zephyrs wander o'er the deep.
Each element shall with propitious smile
Conspiring waft them to Phæacia's isle.
Thence I confide them to thy guardian care;
Their safe return thy counsels shall prepare.
Tremendous rocks the boding fears excite,   1310
And mountain billows teem with wild affright.

Yet from these perils, with benignant hand,
Thou and thy sisters may protect the band.
Let them not drive incautious through the waves,
In greedy whirls, where dire Charybdis raves,
Wheel'd by devouring eddies round and round,
Absorb'd to perish in the salt profound.
Nor let them Scylla's dire recess attain,
The monstrous terror of the' Ausonian main.
Appalling offspring, she from Phorcys came,
And Hecaté, whom men Crataïs name,   1321
Night-wandering power. Around her dogs of hell
The billows vex, with never ceasing yell.
The choice of heroes be it thine to save
From ravening jaws that gape amid the wave.
Safe let their bark the course of peril run;
However near, destruction let them shun.'
Then Thetis answer'd—' Let the tempests sleep,
And raging fires within their caverns keep;
No danger from devouring billows fear,   1330
Through them the vessel I profess to bear.
Let gentle zephyrs o'er the deeps prevail,
And safe to Greece I speed their flying sail.
But distant seats the' occasion bids me trace;
To meet my sisters of the Nereid race,
And gain concurrence of their friendly power,
No mean support in that laborious hour.
From thence with rapid flight I seek the land,
Where Jason's bark is anchor'd near the strand;
And urge the crew, when morn shall glad the sky,
To spread their sails, and o'er the billows fly.' 1341
     These accents ended, downward she repairs,
Through curling vapours and through eddying airs.
Her native realm, through azure waves profound,
She sought, and call'd the sister Nereids round,

When, crowding at the well known voice, they
     came,
She spake the will of heaven's imperial dame.
Prompt, at her bidding, from their parent caves,
They throng'd obedient through the' Ausonian
     waves.   1349
But Thetis, swifter than the lightning's gleam,
Or rapid progress of the solar beam,
That, parting from the morning's orient birth,
To western limits traverses the earth,
Full soon appear'd upon Æëa's strand,
Near the wide limits of the' Etrurian land.
   The Grecian youths beside their bark she finds,
With disk and javelin they relax'd their minds.
Peleus, her spouse, was with the gallant crew;
She seized his hand, and from the crowd withdrew.
To him alone his consort shone reveal'd;   1360
A mist her beauties from the rest conceal'd.
' No more inactive on the shore remain;
With dawn returning plough the watery plain:
So Juno wills, whose kind protecting power
Wakes for your safety in the dangerous hour.
She bids the' assembled Nereids of the tide
Your vessel through the wandering islets guide,
There lies the future voyage.   But beware,
Lest thou my presence to thy friends declare;
When to thine aid, emergent from the main, 1370
I join my sisters of the Nereid train.
Deep in thy bosom let this caution stay;
Nor wake my wrath, as on a former day;
Lest unextinguish'd hate my spirit keep,
And woes inflict, thy latest hours shall weep.'
   She ceased; and, vanishing with rapid flight,
The caves of ocean snatch'd her from his sight.

The hero gazed with anguish and surprise,
Long had her charms been strangers to his eyes;
Enraged, for young Achilles, since she fled, 1380
Forsook his mansion, and disclaim'd his bed.
O'er flaming lamps, amid the nightly gloom,
Her infant's mortal flesh she would consume,
Immortal being to the babe to give,
And bid him free from age and sickness live.
She pour'd upon his little limbs by day
Ambrosial streams, preventive of decay.
As starting from his couch, the' indignant sire
Beheld his darling panting in the fire;
Untaught to read the dictates of the sky,   1390
Forward he rush'd with a tremendous cry.
The goddess heard, with rage and grief profound,
And cast her infant screaming to the ground.
Like fading airy visions, forth she pass'd,
With motion swifter than the northern blast;
And wrathful plunged beneath the briny foam,
Divorced from Peleus, and estranged from home.
His soul with anguish fond remembrance fill'd,
Yet to the train he told what Thetis will'd.
Their sportive combats instant they forsook, 1400
And o'er the grass a hasty banquet took;
Along the turf they rested through the night,
To heaven's high vault till morning shot her light.
 Now rush the zephyrs forth with influence bland;
They man their bark, and hasten from the strand.
Their anchors from the briny deep they heave,
And fit their ship the watery path to cleave.
They strain the rigging from the mast on high,
And spreading yards, to bid the canvass fly.
As gales propitious bade the vessel glide,   1410
They soon a fair and florid isle descried.

There tuneful Syrens, with mellifluous strain,
Allure the' unwary sailors to their bane.
Them the bright muse Terpsichoré of yore,
Seducers sweet, to Acheloüs bore.
Their charming songs thy daughter Ceres loved,
Ere Pluto from Ennæan fields removed;
When, wreathing chaplets with the virgin throng,
She join'd the dance, and shared the choral song.
   Mix'd was their form, part shone with female
      grace,   1420
And part bespoke them of the plumy race.
Their station on the lofty rock they keep,
Where cliffs projecting shade the glassy deep.
Far distant heard their songs insidious flow,
And bid the mariner his home forego.
Deceived, enchanted, day succeeding day,
He pines, and wastes his idle life away.
And now, with soft and never ceasing sound,
The sweet deluders pour'd their notes around.
Delighted and entranced, the Grecian band 1430
Had cast their anchors on the fatal strand;
But soon the poet of celestial race [16],
Son of Æagrus, tuneful pride of Thrace,
Preventive melody, with heavenly fire,
And flying fingers, touch'd the native lyre.
He swept, with mastery, the hurried sound,
And notes of manly music floated round.
Loud o'er the soft voluptuous strain it thrill'd,
And every ear the martial descant fill'd.
Before the zephyrs, as they shoot along,   1440
Through gurgling waves they lose the siren throng;
Less heard and less, their voices melt away,
And, lost in undulating air, decay.

           [16] Orpheus.

Yet, Butes, son of Teleon, heard the strain,
With sweet seduction, wafted o'er the main;
He only, leaning from the polish'd stern,
The words of smooth enchantment could discern.
Instant he plunged amid the watery roar,
Possess'd with hopes to gain the fatal shore.
There had he perish'd; but the queen of love 1450
Beheld the youth, with pity, from above;
And safe to land restored him from the deep,
Where Lilybæum rears the' aerial steep.
Sorrowing the Grecian band their course pursue,
While in their path yet greater perils grew.
Here Scylla rose with dark and fearful head;
Loud bellowing there, Charybdis terror spread.
And while the Planctæ wander through the waves,
Against their sides the gushing billow raves.
There, from the burning rocks the flames arise,
With smoke in columns towering to the skies;
And, raging from the subterranean cells,   1462
The boiling deep the flame of Vulcan swells.
His anvils rested, but the furnace glow'd,
And, mix'd with sparks, redounding vapour flow'd.
The struggling sun diffused a feeble ray,
And pitchy clouds prevail'd upon the day.
    Around the vessel now the Nereids throng,
And Thetis following urged the bark along.
The dangerous course through floating rocks to
        guide,   1470
She grasp'd the rudder, and her force applied,
While winds propitious lent their airy wing.
Thus from the deep exulting dolphins spring;
Now in the van their beauteous forms appear;
And now they bend resplendent in the rear;

Now, parallel on either hand, they dart;
A prospect grateful to the sailor's heart;
Thus crowded round the ship the graceful band,
While Thetis steer'd her with unerring hand.
When to those wandering isles the vessel came,
Above her snowy knees each seaborn dame 1481
With eager haste her floating garments drew,
Then, wide dispersed, to share the labour flew.
On the sharp rocks, at intervals, they stood,
Where billows broke incessant from the flood;
And as they rush'd infuriate on the shore,
The foamy swell aloft the vessel bore.
Now airy light the nymphs to heaven ascend;
Now with the wave to blackest depths descend.
As when, upon the hard and yellow sands,   1490
With garb succinct, the sportive virgin bands
From hand to hand the gay contention ply,
And urge the ball quick circling through the sky,
Alternate caught amid the sportive crowd,
Alternate lost amid the fleeting cloud,
Earth still it shuns; the Nereids thus sustain
The flying ship alternate through the main,
High on the billow's back; while dashing round,
Through pointed breakers roar'd the salt profound.
Their labours Vulcan, sovereign of the fires, 1500
From the smooth promontory's top admires,
His hammer propp'd his shoulder as he stood,
And wondering gazed that animated flood.
    From starry seats the' imperial bride of Jove
Mark'd how the vessel with the billows strove.
Possess'd and palpitating with alarms,
She clasp'd Minerva in her trembling arms.
Around that vessel such was the delay,
As fill'd the compass of a summer's day;   1509

Ere freed from rocks the nymphs a passage gave,
To feel the favouring breeze, and skim the wave.
With gladden'd hearts the sailors forward run,
And pass Trinacria [17], favour'd by the sun.
Her flowery meads that happy land displays;
Untroubled there the flocks of Phœbus graze.
    The task of Juno done, the flitting train,
Like birds aquatic, dived beneath the main.
The Greeks the bleat of sheep unnumber'd hear,
And low of oxen vibrates on their ear.
The sheep, on grass with spangled dew bespread,
Sol's youngest daughter Phaethusa fed.   1521
With mildest rule her subject flock she sway'd;
A silver crook her lovely hand display'd.
A staff of shining brass Lampetia held,
And o'er the meads the lowing herd impell'd.
The flocks and herds were white as drifted snow,
And fed where springs the pastures moist o'erflow.
No dusky stain was through the number found,
And horns of gold their heads resplendent crown'd.
These meads they coasted with diurnal light, 1530
Then pass'd a deep and spacious bay by night.
Through shades rejoicing they pursued their way,
Till morning hail'd them with returning day.
    Beyond the' Ionian bay an island lies,
In wealth abounding, and of ample size;
With spacious harbours bless'd, Ceraunia named,
From elder time in storied legend famed.
And here 'tis fabled (heavenly Muse forgive;
I bid the tale with voice reluctant live),
Beneath the sickle lies, with horrid deed   1540
Distain'd, when Saturn doom'd his sire to bleed.
As others sing, this implement, of yore,
The bounteous Ceres to the harvest bore.

[17] Sicily.

For well the goddess loved the' exuberant soil,
And taught the Titans there the reaper's toil.
Such love she bore to Macris, after styled
Fair Drepané, nurse of Phæacians mild.
    Hither, through perils of the wave and land,
The Minyæ pass'd, from fair Trinacria's strand.
With fair reception, and a bounteous heart, 1550
The king and people social rites impart.
With joy Alcinoüs and the city came,
That seem'd a tribute to the kindred claim.
The jocund train while festive rites employ,
The brave adventurers share the common joy.
An inborn transport fill'd the' exulting train,
As though e'en now they trod Thessalia's plain.
Delusive joy! ordain'd by hostile fate,
Them fierce alarms from Colchian myriads wait.
With thirst of vengeance from the Pontus fraught,
Along the shores the Grecian band they sought.
Through the Cyanean rocks their squadrons came,
And every bosom raged with hostile flame. 1563
They claim to bear away the Colchian maid,
And no pretence may this demand evade.
These terms rejected, to maintain their right
They menace fierce interminable fight;
Both there, on land, and after on the main,
With proud Æëtes and his naval train.
But king Alcinoüs stay'd the rising war,   1570
Pleased to remove the flames of strife afar.
    With apprehensions dire the virgin fraught,
By turns the valiant friends of Jason sought.
Then near Phæacia's queen Areté stands,
And humbly clasps her knees with suppliant
       hands.
' With pity, queen, behold a wretched maid;
With generous hand extend thy timely aid.

Shall yon barbarians sate their fell desire,
To bear a victim to her vengeful sire.
By womanhood I urge thee, royal fair;   1580
Nor let her failings mar the suppliant's prayer.
Let not my faults that gentle bosom steel;
Mortal thyself, for human errors feel.
Most prone to faults is woman's wandering sense:
True, I have err'd; but venial my offence.
This orb of day, with courage, I attest,
No fires unchaste pollute my youthful breast.
Be witness, Hecaté, tremendous power,
Adored in orgies of the midnight hour.
No wish unhallow'd, no licentious thought 1590
My desperate steps to follow strangers brought;
But urgent fear, and conscience of a crime,
Drove me, a wanderer, from my native clime.
'Tis with reluctance being we resign,
And flight to save it, sole resource, was mine.
Yet still untouch'd, as in my native bower,
Still unpolluted to the present hour,
Such heavenly powers o'erawed the loose and
The dearest treasure of our sex I hold.   [bold,
O queen revered, thy royal husband bend, 1600
With generous hand, a maiden to defend.
So may the' immortals grant thee length of days,
A numerous offspring, and unenvied praise!
So may thy states possess renown and health,
Peace unmolested, and increasing wealth!'
   The virgin thus Phæacia's queen address'd;
And thus essay'd to melt each leader's breast—
' O noble chiefs, your labours cost me dear,
Since all these sorrows for your sake I bear.
O think, whose aid the fiery bulls subdued, 1610
And taught by whom, you quell'd that earthborn
       brood!

L 2

Think, who restores you to your native skies,
To glad Hæmonia, with the golden prize.
A wretched outcast, for your sakes I roam,
Deprived of parents, friends, and native home.
For you, relinquish all that life endears,
The mark of obloquy, the slave of fears.
I suffer, that to you I may restore
Friends, parents, homesteads, the paternal shore.
Oh, with what mingled pleasure and surprise 1620
Your welcome forms will glad the kindred eyes!
While Heaven has snatch'd away my crown of
    fame,
On strangers cast a burden and a shame.
And shall not, then, the solemn compact bind?
Shall awful oaths be scatter'd to the wind?
Think on the furies to the suppliant given,
And dread the future punishment from Heaven.
With pity think, how dire shall be my fate,
Return'd the victim of parental hate.   1629
What scorns, what tortures must the wretch sus-
    tain,
Whose only crime was kindness to your train!
To scape the doom for me remains no path;
No tower, no temple guards me from his wrath.
To you alone, sole tower of hope, I fly;
And cruel you the promised aid deny.
No soft compunctions a reception find;
No sense of shame can touch the harden'd mind.
A princess, trusting to your vows, is seen
An abject suppliant of a foreign queen.
When first the golden fleece appear'd in sight, 1640
Proud were your spirits, dauntless was your might.
You were not slow the battle then to wage:
Nor fear'd Æëtes dreadful in his rage;

But terrors now subdue the manly heart,
When of those Colchians you but find a part.'
  Each valiant chief as plaintive she essay'd,
He turn'd to comfort the desponding maid;
The brandish'd javelin lighten'd in her view,
And each the falchion from the scabbard drew.
'O virgin! with their lives, this faithful throng 1650
Shall ever guard thee from disgrace and wrong.'
  Amidst the troubles of the weary crew
The peaceful night diffused her balmy dew;
Night, that her mantle spreads on every soil,
And rest to mortals brings, and mortal toil.
But far her blessings from that virgin's breast,
And anxious sorrow robb'd her soul of rest.
As when, by night, the widow'd mother plies
The' unceasing distaff, mid her children's cries,
Oft for their sire they call, and oft for bread, 1660
Her grief redoubling for a husband dead.
As gloomy prospects agonize her soul,
Down her pale cheek the silent sorrows roll;
Thus flow'd Medea's tears, like drops of rain,
Thus was her heart transfix'd with amorous pain.
  Meantime, Alcinoüs and his consort fair
Revolved the virgin's fate, with anxious care.
The nightly couch together as they press'd,
The gentle queen her husband thus address'd—
'O spouse beloved, wilt thou not lend thine aid, 1670
And from the Colchians guard this wretched maid?
That with the Minyæ favour we may find,
And fill our neighbours with a grateful mind.
For near is Argos to Phæacia's strand,
And near the natives of Hæmonia's land.
No neighbourhood with us the Colchians claim;
Known but by rumour is their monarch's name.

A weight of sufferings has that virgin proved;
And much her fears my yielding soul have moved.
Let not these strangers thy kind heart engage, 1680
To give the mourner to her father's rage.
True, she offended.   Her unfilial hand
Imparted drugs, and charms, of influence bland.
She led the bulls, exhaling fire and smoke,
With passive necks, obedient to the yoke.
But one false step must from another spring;
And error in his train will error bring.
From cruel outrage of a father's hand,
She fled incautious with the stranger band.
But Jason, I am told, with solemn vows   1690
Is bound to make the maid his youthful spouse.
And would my love his virtuous aim control?
Or seek with perjury to load his soul?
Say, would thy gentle heart a maid return
To furious parents, who for vengeance burn?
The fair Antiopé recorded lives,
And warnings dire of rage paternal gives.
'Tis well remember'd, in the times of yore,
What sufferings Danaë through the billows bore.
From an injurious sire, in this our time,   1700
What deeds of horror stain a neighbouring clime!
How Echetus, the scourge of humankind,
Pursued his daughter with infuriate mind.
He doom'd the maid to pine in cheerless night,
And pierced with pointed brass the balls of sight.
Deep in a cell, to servile labour doom'd,
She pines, in darkness and despair consumed.'
   Thus she.   Her husband felt the soft control;
And kind expressions spake the melting soul.
' To glad my guests, and guard the virgin's charms,
Areté, I would meet the Colchian arms;   1711

But Jove, all-seeing Jove, my spirit awes,
And much I fear to violate his laws.
Nor hold Æëtes object of disdain;
His power is great, and wide extends his reign.
Enraged, no monarch were a fiercer foe,
And Greece, though distant, might his vengeance
I will not veil my purpose from thy love, [know.
And men, I trust, the sentence will approve.
If virgin yet remains the Colchian fair,   1720
To yield her to her father I prepare;
But, if already she is Jason's bride,
The wife I tear not from her husband's side;
Nor yield to foes, to cruelty, and scorn,
The tender progeny, as yet unborn.'
      He ceased; and sunk to calm repose consign'd.
His sayings deeply touch'd Areté's mind.
Her couch she leaves, and through the palace goes;
Attendant on the queen her women rose.
The herald, at her secret call, appears,   1730
And crafty counsel to the Minyæ bears.
' The maid let Jason wed with urgent haste;
No more entreaties on Alcinoüs waste;
For vain and idle are your tears and prayers,
To change the purpose that his voice declares.
If virgin yet the Colchian fair remains,
Home he returns her to her native plains.
The nuptial yoke if now the princess bears,
His soul the laws of wedded love reveres.'
      The' attentive herald pass'd without delay, 1740
To Jason's ear the mandate to convey.
Both what his queen suggests with warning kind,
And what the purpose of Alcinoüs' mind.
The bay of Hyllus the fair city crown'd;
Wakeful in arms the warriors there he found.

Beside their vessel, as he greets the band,
In words succinct he speaks the queen's command.
The heroes all received, with pleasure fraught,
Words thus according with each inward thought.
All to the' immortal gods their goblets crown'd,
And pour'd the pure libation on the ground. 1751
They led the victims for the hallow'd rite,
And spread the genial couch that very night.
     Sacred recess, a fair and spacious cave
Commodious chamber for the nuptials gave.
Exulting, they prepare the bridal bed,
Her days, of old, where beauteous Macris led.
From gentle Aristæus sprang the fair,
Who made the' industrious bee his favourite care,
And first from olives, with laborious hand, 1760
In balmy rills express'd the sweetness bland.
She, in Abantis first, Euboic soil,
For that fair child essay'd the nurse's toil,
Nyseian Bacchus, son of Jove; and press'd
The florid infant to her snowy breast.
From flames when Hermes bore him to the maid,
O'er his parch'd little lips she honey laid.
Her tender cares the queen of Jove beheld;
And, fill'd with anger, from that isle expell'd.
She sought far distant the Phæacian cave, 1770
And wealth exuberant to the natives gave.
     'Twas here the nuptial bed, capacious, placed,
Shone, with the fleece, resplendent covering graced,
Illustrious trophy, that renown supplied
To youthful Jason and his royal bride.
In their white bosoms, from the fragrant bowers,
The village maidens bore the fairest flowers;
With bounteous hands they strew'd them o'er the
          ground,
While beamy splendours darted all around.

So shone the precious fleece, like radiant fire, 1780
To light the lover to his fond desire:
The lovely rustics gazed with glad surprise,
And secret wishes lighten'd in their eyes;
Yet fear and modesty forbade the band
To touch the treasure with inquiring hand.
From various seats they came, of various line;
Some daughters of Ægeus, stream divine;
In uplands some of Meleteius bide;
Some cultivate the plains and meadows wide.
Impell'd by Juno, from each native bower, 1790
They throng'd to honour Jason's nuptial hour.
Still, in memorial of that night, the cave
Retains the name Medea's nuptials gave.
'Twas here entranced the youthful pair were laid,
And fragrant veils around them were display'd.
Without, the heroes shook the warlike spear,
Lest foes, with sudden onset, should appear.
With green and leafy boughs their heads were
        crown'd,
While Orpheus bade the tuneful lyre resound.
Before the bridal bower, the festive throng 1800
In cadence chanted hymeneal song.
    Yet different far did this event proceed,
From what the son of Æson had decreed.
His thoughts had destined, not Phæacia's reign,
Scene of his nuptials, but the native plain;
When, anchor'd in Iolcos' welcome port,
His gladden'd eyes should hail his father's court.
There too in fancy was Medea led,
To rest her hopes, and deck the bridal bed.
In vain the feeble race of hapless man   1810
Their airy schemes of perfect bliss may plan,
Unknown, alas! is happiness sincere;
When joy we taste, some anguish still is near.

Thus love's delights were poison'd by dismay,
And doubts what purpose might Alcinoüs sway.
The morn returning with immortal light,
Through ether chased the gloomy shades of night.
Her radiance gilt the smiling shores around,
And gems of dawning twinkled o'er the ground.
A busy hum in every street was heard;　　1820
The face of labour through the town appear'd:
Meantime, the Colchian armament from far
Around the point of Macris moved to war.
The just Alcinoüs, by his compact sway'd,
Came forth to judgment on the royal maid.
Of purest gold the sceptre he sustain'd,
Symbol that many a righteous doom ordain'd.
Behind, in armour formidably gay,
Phæacian cohorts pass'd in deep array.
The crowding consorts of the gallant band, 1830
Without the gates to view the pageant stand.
A train of rustics from their labour came;
For Juno round diffused the' unerring fame.
A lamb, the fairest of the flock, they brought,
And heifer, yet to bear the yoke untaught;
For due libations at the sacred shrine,
While others vases bore of sparkling wine.
The smoke arose in wreaths from sacred flames,
And bridal gifts were given by fairest dames;
Such female works as women wont to give, 1840
And fond of splendour gladly will receive;
Embroider'd veils, and gems, and golden toys,
That friendship pours on recent nuptial joys.
　The' assembled throng, with fond amazement,
　　view
The forms and features of the godlike crew:
And oft the Thracian bard, to charm the crowd,
Swept from his lyre a descant sweetly loud;

And soft and light, with evanescent sound,
His studded sandal nimbly beat the ground.
Nor heedless were the jocund virgin train, 1850
Of love and love's delights.   They added strain
Symphonious—hymeneal sweet—and sang—
That all the plain with charming carols rang.
Now sole they sang; now circling they advance,
And voice melodious join with choral dance,
As Juno taught.   She too the queen inclined,
To publish what her virtuous lord design'd,
Most upright doom.   Complete to her desire
All rites were done that nuptial laws require.
Firm is the king to guard the wedded pair; 1860
No selfish motives his resolves impair.
Threats of Æëtes and the Colchian band
Nor move his spirits nor unnerve his hand;
Determined firm remains the pious mind;
For sacred oaths and solemn compacts bind.
   When now the leaders of the Colchian host
Perceived the purpose of their mission lost,
And found him bent his honour to maintain,
And chase their navy from his ports and reign,
They fear'd the disappointed tyrant's wrath, 1870
And shrunk abhorrent from the homeward path.
Humbly they seek protection in that isle
Where equal laws prevail, and peaceful blessings
The happiness of quiet rule they felt,   [smile.
And long the settlers in Phæacia dwelt:
A race, that origin from Bacchus claim,
From Ephyræ, their native isthmus, came;
In aftertimes the peaceful mansions held,
And from their seats the colonists expell'd.
A neighbouring isle the banish'd Colchians gain'd,
Ere on the continent they seats obtain'd.   1881

Their place of rest Ceraunian hills they chose,
Where ancient dwellings of the' Abantes rose.
There, taking root and spreading o'er the ground,
Nestæan seats and Oricos they found.
Time, in his progress, these events survey'd,
And yearly still the solemn rites are paid;
Still are the fates, and still the nymphs revered,
Around an altar by Medea rear'd.
Where Nomian Phœbus fills his awful shrine, 1890
Author of just decrees, and source of light divine.
  And now, Alcinoüs to the parting band
The gifts of friendship gave with liberal hand :
And equal bounty mark'd the royal fair,
Her husband's feelings ever wont to share.
With soul compassionate, and thoughtful heed,
Of what a female's tenderness may need,
Twelve maids of her domestic train she gave,
To wait Medea o'er the distant wave :
Six days elapsed, the morn succeeding bore 1900
The godlike heroes from Corcyra's shore ;
The wind propitious through their canvass sings,
And speeds the vessel with his airy wings.
Nor yet did fates allow that toil-worn train
Thrice welcome Greece and native strands to gain;
That first of blessings ere the wanderers boast,
Much must be suffer'd on the Libyan coast.
With swelling sails Ambracia's gulf they fled,
And hallow'd seats where infant Jove was fed ;
Then, through the' Echinades their course they
      found,   1910
The dangerous strait where rocky islets bound.
Full in their view the land of Pelops lay,
When northern blasts arose with furious sway.
Nine dreadful nights the storm incessant roars ;
As many days it rends the Libyan shores.

The driving winds the helm, the pilot scorn,
Near the fell Syrtes was the vessel borne;
There shifting sands the labouring bark embay;
Thence never crew pursued the homeward way.
An hideous tract the slimy marshes spread; 1920
The putrid waves are motionless and dead.
A treacherous depth of seeming land is seen,
Devouring water clothed in fraudful green;
Along the brine a spume corrupted lies,
And pestilential vapours load the skies.
Inhospitable rise the sandy heaps,
No bird has dwelling there, no thing that creeps.
The winds conspiring with the refluent surge,
On these unhappy shoals the vessel urge;
Where tides resistless, with alternate roar, 1930
Now to the main return, now break upon the shore.
Part of the keel within the wave remain'd,
The greater portion now the land sustain'd;
The heroes sprang to shore, and grief profound
Possess'd each heart, to view the prospect round.
The' expansive skies, a cheerless blank and drear,
And tracts of sand to meet the skies appear,
Unvaried barrenness; no springs arise,
No path, no haunt of shepherds glads their eyes.
Nor tree nor herb was scatter'd o'er the plain, 1940
And mournful silence spoke it famine's reign.
Each turn'd with sad surprise and heartfelt groans,
And ask'd his comrade in desponding tones—
    ' What land is this? oh, whither has the storm
Driven us to perish, in some horrid form?
Better the dangers known again to brave,
Through clashing rocks, that float amid the wave;
To thwart the' Almighty's will, to brave his hate,
Heroic daring would adorn our fate;

But now what hope, or what resource remains? 1950
Confined by storms on these deserted plains,
Soon shall our little span of life be pass'd,
Despair unmingled reigns along the waste;
No means of life the burning sand supplies,
All nature sickens, vegetation flies.'
   Such sounds the phrensy of despair confess'd,
The sad Ancæus thus the train address'd,
Skilful to guide the helm—' 'Tis true, my friends,
A dreadful doom o'er every head impends.
In solitudes accursed we must endure   1960
Unutterable ills, without a cure:
If from the land the changing winds should blow,
And bear the waters back with refluent flow.
Far as these eyes the dismal view command,
Where turbid waves are mix'd with treacherous
        sand,
With dashing foam the' extended beach is hoar,
And billows break continuous on the shore.
The sacred ship our hope, our chiefest pride,
To fragments torn e'en now were scatter'd wide;
Did not the swellings of the salt profound   1970
Forbid her keel to strike the fatal ground.
But now, with rapid ebb returns the tide,
The sinking shoals the bottom scarcely hide;
Then pools innavigable round us spread,
And hopes of safety all are cold and dead.
Assume the helm some more experienced hand,
Give if thou canst salvation to this band.
Ah no! the day of our return is gone,
For ever fled. Our hopes and fears are done.
Soon shall we reap the fruit of perils pass'd; 1980
By Jove decreed to perish in this waste.'   [fill'd
   With tears he ceased. A like despondence
All who were best in guiding vessels skill'd.

Then every heart a mortal terror froze;
On every cheek a deathlike pale arose.
As when some tidings strange and dire prevail,
Men crowd the streets like sheeted spectres pale;
When tales of war and pestilence they hear,
Or future famine wakes presageful fear,
As inundation deluging the plain   1990
Devours the labours of the' industrious swain;
When from the statue bloody dews distil,
Or sacred shrines tremendous bellowings fill;
When dim eclipse o'erpowers the noontide glare,
And glancing meteors fill the troubled air;
With pensive steps, a wan desponding train,
The heroes stalk'd beside the' extended main.

   And now came on the sombrous evening's close,
Clad in a colour suited to their woes.   1999
With bursting tears they clasp'd each other's hand,
Tears sole indulgence of the wretched band;
Then parting, each pursues the sad relief,
And broods insatiate o'er the lonely grief.
Each far from other took his gloomy way, .
And stretch'd unsocial on the sands they lay,
As chance or choice the couch of sorrow found,
And mantles wrapp'd their drooping heads around.
They mourn'd, of food regardless, through the night,
No care of food return'd with morning light;
Such forms of horrid death were round display'd,
Such dire forebodings every heart dismay'd. 2011

   Apart the maids, that from Phæacia came,
With cries assembled round the Colchian dame.
As when the parent bird in quest of food,
Compell'd by hunger, leaves the callow brood,
Unfit to tempt the sky, an hapless flock
Within the cleft of some aspiring rock;

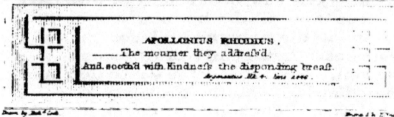

APOLLONIUS RHODIUS.

—— The mourner they addrefs'd,
And sooth'd with kindnefs the difponding breaft.

Argonautics Bk 4. line 1046.

Drawn by Rich.ᵈ Cook.   Engraved by E.ᵈ Scriven.

Published by Lackington Hughes & Co. London.
Jan.ʸ 1. 1814.

Abandon'd thus, if from the nest they fall,
In vain for help the piteous nurslings call;   2019
As where the swelling bank with verdant brow
Sees the rich streams of bright Pactolus flow,
The plaintive cygnets raise the doleful strain,
The borders far resound, the dewy plain,
The silver currents, mourn'd these virgins fair,
And mingled with the dust their golden hair.
All night their wailings rose most sadly sweet,
And lonely echo loved their voices to repeat.
    Unknown, unhonour'd by the race of man,
Their names extinguish'd with their glorious plan,
The first, the noblest of the Grecian host   2030
In deserts wild their gallant lives had lost;
But thoughts of pity to the suffering band
The heroines felt who sway'd the Libyan land.
When from her father's head in shining arms,
Severely bright, mature in virgin charms,
Minerva rose; their early cares they gave,
Her beauteous frame in Triton's lake to lave.
Thus had the nymph the love of Pallas gain'd,
And sacred honours o'er that realm obtain'd.
    'Twas noon.   The sun his keenest arrows cast,
Reflected fierce from all the burning waste. 2041
Their steps divine the nymphs to Jason guide,
From his fair head they gently drew aside
The shading veil.   Awe-struck the youth declined,
From glories that bespake the heavenly kind,
His reverent eyes.   The mourner they address'd,
And sooth'd with kindness the desponding breast.
    ' Why sink, sad youth, abandon'd to despair?
Know, that immortals make thy fate their care;
Thy fortunes past are not to us untold,   2050
Thy toils, thy wanderings, for the fleece of gold.

APOLLONIUS RHODIUS.

—— The mourner they addres'd,
And sooth'd with kindness the desponding breast.

Drawn by Head & Cook.

Engraved by C. Wanhrant.

Published by Mattaby Thomas & Dee London.
Jan'y 1 1811

We know thy sufferings o'er the wave and land;
We know the' achievements of thy daring band.
Nymphs of the fleecy care and rustic train,
We hold an humble and a local reign,
Pleased with the worship of our native soil,
The simple guardians of the shepherd's toil.
Rouse like a man from this despair profound,
And raise thy friends, that languish on the ground,
When Amphitrité shall unyoke the car   2060
That whirls her Neptune o'er the deeps afar,
Their tender parent let the train repay,
With due returns, for many an anxious day;
For painful throes and agonizing care,   [bare;
Since first their manly forms her womb parental
Then safely to the loved Achæan shore
Bear the rich fleece that shines with golden ore.'
   The nymphs evanish'd like an airy dream;
Yet still their accents sound, and near they seem.
As on that barren plain he sat half raised, 2070
Around in wonderment the hero gazed.
' Nymphs, honour'd nymphs, ye guardians of
            this wild,
Oh, hear your suppliant with indulgence mild!
Sustain his spirit in this hour of fear,
And safe through perils of these regions bear.
But dark the words that speak of our return;
Perplex'd with doubts my veering thoughts are
            borne;
United minds the' abyss of fate may sound,
Wherefore delay to call my friends around?'
   He rose impetuous from the sandy bed, 2080
Parch'd with the sun, with squalid dust o'erspread.
Forward he rush'd, and loudly call'd the train.
His voice resounded to the distant plain.

Thus in the wilds, that long have nursed his race,
The tawny lion, dusty from the chase,
Stalks through the forest with a fiery glare,
And roaring seeks the partner of his lair,
Tremendous call! among the mountains shake,
At his dire voice, the glens and tangled brake.
His roar the startling herds with terror fills, **2090**
His roar the guardian swains with horror thrills;
So loud were Jason's shouts.   But, to the heart
Congenial, no dismay the sounds impart.
The heroes all assembled at his cries;   [eyes.
With sadden'd minds they came, and downcast
Where, station'd mid the shoals and dangerous
Their vessel lay, they stood a gloomy band; [sand,
At Jason's mandate with the female train
Promiscuous join'd, they sat beside the main.

  ' Hear, loved companions, while my words un-
The tidings heavenly messengers have told; [fold
Late as I lay, the victim of despair,   **2102**
Three nymphs beside me stood, divinely fair.
No mortals they in skins of goats array'd,
With rustic cinctures of the shepherd maid,
Their simple vests from necks of ivory hung,
And graceful round their slender middles clung.
A while they stood above my drooping head,
And drew the veil that o'er my face lay spread.
With cheering words they roused me from the
                ground.   **2110**
They bade me summon you, my comrades, round;
And to your mother gratefully restore
Due recompense for all the pangs she bore;
For wakeful cares, and many an anxious day,
While yet unconscious in her womb we lay;
When Amphitrité shall unyoke the car,
That whirls her Neptune o'er the deeps afar.

With thoughts perplex'd, in vain my troubled mind
The purport of their accents toils to find.   2119
Celestial heroines so they spake their strain,
Daughters of Libya, guardians of the plain,
Our wanderings past, our various toils they knew,
By means superior open'd to their view.
They ended; and, in mist or cloud conceal'd,
No more the heavenly vision shone reveal'd.'
His words the crowd with silent wonder hear,
While motives mix'd of joy and grief appear.
What tongue can paint the' amazement of the band!
A mighty courser sprang from sea to land! 2129
He sought the plain. The locks redoubled deck,
On either side, his proud and arching neck.
Golden his mane, he toss'd his head on high,
And flakes of splendour lighten'd to the sky.
From his sleek sides he dash'd the briny foam,
Then stretch'd with zephyrs in his limbs to roam.
  This Peleus marking with elated breast,
And words of hope, the' assembled train ad-
        dress'd—   [bride
' Now, now, my friends, has Neptune's lovely
Unyoked the car that whirls him o'er the tide.
Now is the time.   Nor can my thoughtful mind
In those dark sayings other parent find   2141
Than the fair vessel in whose womb we pass'd,
With safety borne through many a watery waste;
For toils and perils she for us endured,
Our lives and safety have her groans procured.
Let pious shoulders then sustain the weight,
With nerves untired, of this maternal freight:
And with the burden o'er the sands proceed,
Where the swift courser shall direct his speed;
Observe his track along this arid ground;   2150
For sure he will not plunge in earth profound.

If hope mislead not, we shall thus explore
Some welcome harbour, some propitious shore.'
   He ceased.   The comment pleased the general
So has the Muse recorded in her song ; [throng,
And I but follow, with submissive tread,
An humble votary, where the Muses lead.
Their breath alone awakes poetic fire ;
Their words alone are suited to my lyre.
And thus they sang—
                          ' O first of regal line, 2160
Endow'd with virtues and with strength divine,
Whose vast exertions could the ship sustain,
With all her loading, o'er the desert plain.
Twelve times did Phœbus measure day and night,
While thus ye bare her with unwearied might.
What pangs, what miseries those heroes wrung ;
The tale of sufferance mocks the power of tongue.
O truly glorious was that godlike breed !
Their acts declare them of immortal seed.'
Thus, by the dire necessity compell'd,   2170
Their painful march the band of heroes held.
Onward they moved, till, source of glad surprise,
The lake of Pallas open'd to their eyes. [press'd,
Here first they paused, with toil and heat op-
Here first they bade their burden'd shoulders rest ;
Like famish'd dogs that prowl abroad for food,
Dispersed they flew to seek some spring or flood.
For burning thirst the fainting train assail'd,
And pain and misery o'er the mind prevail'd ;
Nor vainly sought.   They found in flowery prime
A sacred plain ; where to that instant time,
The serpent Ladon, with unwearied care,   2182
Was wont to guard the golden apples fair.
The parent stem, where fruits immortal crown'd,
The soil, the garden mighty Atlas own'd ;

And there Hesperian maids, with sweetest song,
The gentle monster fed, the fruits and flowers
    among.
Beside that tree, the region's boast and pride,
Slain by Alcides, late the guardian died.
The tail yet seem'd some feeling to betray, 2190
The trunk above all cold and lifeless lay;
The shafts unerring by the hero sent,
In many a wound the gaping skin had rent,
With active venom tinged of Lerna's brood;
The bane return'd, commix'd with putrid blood.
In swarms the greedy flies assembled round;
And drain'd the bile and gore from every wound.
Near him those tuneful nymphs, with streaming
    eyes,   [cries,
Their servant mourn'd with loud and piercing
High o'er their heads they raise the taper hand,
And o'er their faces snowy veils expand,   2201
And o'er their golden locks. The youths drew near,
Precipitate.   Possess'd with sudden fear,
The bashful nymphs dissolving from the view,
In dust and earth from mortal sense withdrew.
The bard of Thrace that prodigy explored,
And thus with prayer the deities adored—
' Nymphs, gentle nymphs, benevolent as fair,
With influence high, who make these fields your
    care;   2209
Whether you join the radiant throngs above,
Or powers terrestrial here delight to rove,
Or guardian maids of lawn and meadow wide,
O'er artless shepherds and their flocks preside,
With forms benignant glad our longing eyes;
Nymphs, sacred nymphs, old Ocean's daughters,
    rise.

Some rock disclose, where gushing springs have
  birth,
Some sacred fountain bubbling cool from earth,
That, temper'd with the sun's translucent ray,
May feverish pangs of ardent thirst allay!
And, if our bark may gain Achaia's coast, 2220
The richest gifts that deities can boast,
The sweetest perfumes that to heaven ascend,
To crown your rites, and glad your shrine, attend.'
 Fervent he prayed; and unperceived, though
  near,
His fervent prayer the' Hesperian virgins hear.
The suffering band they view'd, and felt their grief;
And soon compassion sent the wish'd relief.
They bade the teeming soil its wealth disclose,
And first a spring of tender grass arose; 2229
Then the long shoots of various herbs appear'd,
And quickly trees their taper forms uprear'd;
A shady elm fair Erytheis spread,
And Hespera sustain'd a poplar's head;
A sacred osier beauteous Æglé stood,
With branches ever bent to taste the flood.
Emergent then from trees, a portent strange,
The nymphs their forms assumed with sudden
 The fairest Æglé then, in gentlest words, [change.
Replied, and with their prayer her speech accords.
' Great is the' advantage that your weary band
Derives from him who first with impious hand,
Presumptuous daring, and irreverent toil, 2242
Deprived of life the guardian of this soil;
Then from the boughs the golden apples tore;
From weeping goddesses their treasure bore.
Scarce day preceding his career began,
Ere he appear'd, this rude oppressive man.

Well fitted he to wreak the mental storm,
Vast in his strength, and dreadful in his form.
His eyes dart fierce intolerable flame;   2250
A lion's spoils enwrap his giant frame.
His hand a ponderous trunk of olive bore, [gore;
Free from the workman's art, and stain'd with
And mighty bow from whence those arrows fled,
Too fatal shafts, that laid yon serpent dead!
His steps had traced a weary length of way;
And, thirsty from the parching glare of day,
He search'd for water through the plains around;
But none to cheer his eager eyes he found.
As rageful and despairing thus he stray'd,   2260
Or he discover'd, or some god display'd
Yon rock; near Pallas'[18] lake it stands alone,
And with his heel he smote the solid stone.
Freed by the stroke abundant waters sprung;
With eager transport to the ground he clung,
With ample chest outspread, and nervous hands;
Incessant draughts his furious thirst demands;
The fountain from its rocky bed he drains,
Prone like an ox that grazes on the plains.'
    She ceased. And to the fount that Æglé told,
Most sought, most wish'd, their joyful course
        they hold,   2271
Full soon discover'd; with contention loud,
And frantic eagerness, around they crowd;
As swarming ants, an active busy band,
Throng round a fissure in the thirsty land,
The granary where prudent toil has stored
The plunder of the barn, their winter's hoard;
Heap'd on each other, as the clustering flies
A formless mass compose, where honey lies,   2279

        [18] The lake Tritonis.

With restless murmur urge their greedy flight,
Pursue the sweets, and on each other light.
When the first draught some thirsty wretch had
How was Alcides to his heart endear'd! [cheer'd,
With moisten'd lips, and with expanding breast,
The soften'd soul these grateful words confess'd—
' E'en absent, godlike chief, the social band
Feel the protection of that peerless hand!
E'en absent thou hast saved the toil-worn train
From burning death upon a thirsty plain!
Oh might our search along the distant soil   2290
Regain the partner of our glorious toil!'
   Nor vain the word, the crowd to council went;
The general voice selected heroes sent,
By various paths, if tidings might be gain'd,
Where yet Alcides in those wilds remain'd.
Perplexing task! for on that sandy ground,
No lasting prints of human step were found;
The nightly breezes with incessant sway
Erased the vagrant traces of the day.
The sons of Boreas that hard task desired   2300
(Their airy pinions confidence inspired),
Euphemus, trusting in his footsteps light,
And Lynceus boasting of unequal'd sight;
A fifth to friendship true, bold Canthus came,
By ruling fates impell'd, and virtue's flame.
Still, still his heart recall'd the parted friend,
And social feelings bade him thus attend;
That, finding Hercules, he might demand
His Polyphemus at the hero's hand.
No fear of rousing that impatient ire,   2310
No face of toil abates the strong desire,
Resolved to learn what chances they had proved,
And where Alcides left the man he loved.

E'en then his friend had rear'd, in Mysia's soil,
A town that spake the founder's patriot toil;
Then ranged enamour'd of his native plain,
To seek the vessel and the social train,
Till in his course, o'er many a region wide,
He reach'd the Chalybes and ocean's side.
But there the fates ordain'd his resting place;
He fell in combat with that hardy race.   2321
Where the tall poplar waves, and billow flows,
Sacred to him the monument arose.
   But now the chosen missionaries pass'd
With eager footsteps o'er the trackless waste.
Their painful search the godlike man pursues;
Him Lynceus far remote and lonely views,
Or seems to view, as o'er the spreading lawn,
Through gray beginnings of the doubtful dawn,
And floating mists, the gazer darts his eyes, 2330
And sees, or thinks he sees, the moon arise.
Return'd with speedy step he warn'd the train,
That search prolong'd and anxious cares were
' Hope not the subject of our wish to see, [vain.
Remote and evanescent e'en to me;
Hope not that others shall his wanderings trace,
When Lynceus turns despairing from the chase.'
The swift Euphemus, and the plumed pair,
Alike to find the godlike chief despair.
   But mortal destinies on Canthus call.   2340
Forward he press'd in Libyan wilds to fall.
Encountering there the huts, and fleecy fold,
The wants of his companions made him bold;
He strove to bear away the bleating prize,
The guardian of the flock indignant flies;
The' ill fated spoiler with a stone he fell'd;
No feeble arm the ponderous mass impell'd;

For bold Caphareus, such the shepherd's name,
From heaven possess'd a spark of daring flame,
And with the' opponent match'd in vigour strode,
Derived from him, the Lycorean god [19],   2351
His grandsire. When resplendent beauty's boast,
Fair Acacallis sought the Libyan coast,
Sent by her sire, stern Minos, to that shore,
Her womb the progeny of Phœbus bore;
And gave to him, that guides the car of day,
An infant lovely as the father's ray,
Amphithemis or Garamas, for styled
By various titles was the graceful child.
When rising youth bade amorous feelings wake,
He woo'd a nymph of the Tritonian lake.   2361
The beauteous nymph a mutual passion own'd,
Their loves with Nasamon Caphareus crown'd.
To guard his flocks the careful shepherd bent,
To shades below the gentle Canthus sent,
Not long to triumph; for the Grecian band
Avenged their comrade on the slayer's hand.
With patient steps they sought him o'er the plains,
And mourning bore away his cold remains. 2369
O'er Canthus the sepulchral earth they spread,
While pious tears embalm'd the virtuous dead;
And seized the flocks, unhappy cause of strife,
Lamented price of their companion's life.
  To thee too, Mopsus, fatal was that day,
A doom relentless summon'd thee away.
Not all his skill in augury could save
The son of prescience from the' untimely grave;
For who may death elude? Immense in length,
A serpent shunn'd the day's meridian strength.
Stretch'd in the sand, o'erpower'd with sultry heats,
Tardy to follow where the prey retreats,   2381

[19] Apollo so called.

He shunn'd the' attack, relax'd in every spire,
Languid to strike, nor active in his ire;
But, once provoked, his fangs such mischief fill'd,
Such deadly venom from his jaws distill'd,
Might never living thing its influence bear;
The bane received, the mortal hour was near;
Where his fell tooth the slightest print applied,
The rankling wound e'en aid from heaven defied;
Not Pæan (author of the healing art,   2390
As legends tell) could ease the mortal smart.
When godlike Perseus, whom his mother styled
Eurymedon, high o'er the Libyan wild
The sever'd head of direful Gorgon bore,
Warm from the falchion and distilling gore;
In sable drops, where'er the blood was shed,
The teeming soil a race of serpents bred.
Such lay the serpent.   With unboding breast,
As Mopsus pass'd, the monster's spine he press'd.
Roused by the pain, the monster wreath'd around
His ankle, and infix'd the burning wound. 2401
Deep, deep with vengeful tooth the flesh he tore,
And mix'd his poison with the spouting gore;
Medea shriek'd, and shriek'd her female train;
The generous hero, unsubdued by pain,
The gory wound with hand intrepid press'd;
The poison thence but slowly reach'd his breast.
Ah wretch! he feels the stroke of fate advance,
From vein to vein inducing mortal trance.
O'er every sense a dire oblivion steals,   2410
His swimming eyes a waving blackness seals;
On earth reclined, with powerless limbs he lay,
And cold and rigid breathed his soul away.
Collected round aghast his comrades gaze,
Aghast their leader stood, in dire amaze.

N 2

A spectacle so sudden and so dread!
Their friend so quickly number'd with the dead!
Smote every heart. Nor could the dead remain,
Exposed a moment weltering on the plain,   2419
Beneath the sun; for now through all the corse
The subtle poison spread putrescent force.
From limb to limb the dissolution flew;
From every pore exuded clammy dew.
The brazen mattocks his companions wield,
And soon a trench is open'd in the field;
Deep in its womb the putrid mass they lay,
And heap with needful haste the' incumbent clay.
The mourning warriors and the softer kind
The shining honours of their heads resign'd. 2429
With trembling hands o'er all the grave they spread
Their parted locks, in honour of the dead;
And thrice with pious hand they heap'd the ground;
And compass'd thrice in arms the rising mound.
   Now to the ship return'd, as o'er the deep
The southern winds with humid pinions sweep,
Long time they hover'd; and, with doubting mind,
Some passage sought from Triton's lake to find.
No fix'd resolves the veering purpose stay;
Now here, now there, they shape the' uncertain
         way.   2439
As, smote by noontide shafts, the writhing snake
The path oblique with sinuous toil may make,
From side to side the hissing head he turns,
His flaming eye with fire malignant burns,
Nor ceases till he spies with piercing ken
The secret passage to his murky den;
Thus Argo long her course uncertain winds,
Ere yet an outlet from the lake she finds.
Till Orpheus bade them, from the ship display
A tripod, hallow'd to the god of day,

And consecrate the gift with pious hand,   2450
To native deities, that guard the land.
  When disembarking on the shore they laid
The sacred offering, first for Phœbus made;
Then Triton, ruler of the lake, appear'd:
A seeming youth his graceful form he rear'd.
A verdant sod he lifted from the plain,
As pledge of friendship, and address'd the train.
' Hail, gallant youths, from Triton's hand receive
A friendly pledge, that never shall deceive,
Assurance of protection, ere ye go;   2460
No greater can a deity bestow.
If haply ye desire, with anxious mind,
To learn (what mariners would seek to find)
What outlets of this lake, as yet untried,
May lead embarrass'd barks to reach the tide;
All this with truth unerring I can speak.
Ordain'd by Neptune guardian of each creek,
Harbour, and station of the Libyan main,
O'er all the coast a wide extent I reign;   2469
From distant climes ye come, yet haply fame
Has made your ears familiar with my name,
Eurypylus; this monster-teeming earth,
Subject of fable, is my place of birth.'
  Euphemus answer'd, with expressions bland,
The pledge [20] receiving with a grateful hand—
' Where Apis lies and where the seas of Crete,
If such thy knowledge, noble chief, repeat.
No vain inquirers we from shore to shore,
That, idly curious, distant realms explore;
But dire necessity controls our course,   2480
These realms we visit through the whirlwind's
      force.

[20] The sod.

Long tempest-toss'd our labouring vessel found
This continent, on earth's remotest bound.
And long with force combined, and weary toil,
We bore the ponderous vessel o'er the soil;
To shun the terrors that the Syrtes wake,
And float her safely, in this ample lake;
In pity then to strangers led astray,
To Pelops' land reveal the nearest way.'
   The Libyan answers, as Euphemus ends, 2490
And while he speaks his level'd arm extends;
Remote the sea in prospect wide he shows,
Near a deep outlet from the lake that flows.
' This passage to the main a vessel bears,
Where in the blackness, central depth appears;
White on each side the sandy banks arise,
And shallow there pellucid water lies.
The dangerous banks a narrow strait unfold,
Most needful 'tis the middle course to hold;
Yon sea, which scarce the dazzled sight explores,
Leads you past Crete to Pelopeian shores. 2501
When steering from the lake the right ye keep,
And now the bark is wafted to the deep;
With steady hand your vessel then restrain,
Pursue the shore, nor rashly seek the main;
Till boldly swelling, as your course you shape,
The land throws forward a projecting cape.
Then spread your canvass, onward plough the way
Your youthful vigour let no toil dismay.' 2500
   He spake benevolent. The bark they fill;
And through the lake exert the rower's skill.
With cries of joy proceed the' exulting band,
Meanwhile, the tripod shone in Triton's hand;
Full soon he vanish'd with the sacred prize,
Beneath the lake conceal'd from mortal eyes.

Inly rejoiced the' heroic band, to find
Their late instructor of celestial kind.
Then, Jason bids for sacrifice prepare
The first and fairest of the fleecy care,
So lately won, and pious vows to raise,   2520
To call protection on their future ways.
    The chosen victim at the prow was slain,
And prayers accompanied from all the train :
' Oh, thou divine, that here, to mortals shown,
Thy form reveal'd, thy title yet unknown,
Whoe'er thou art, assign'd these bounds to keep,
Or Triton, wonder of the vasty deep,
Phorcys, or Nereus, ruler of the wave,
Offspring of nymphs that in the billows lave;
Indulgent hear. Thy favour may we boast; 2530
Propitious guide us to the native coast.'
    Thus pray'd the chief, the victim as he slew,
And bleeding warm amid the billows threw ;
Then Triton awful from the depths arose,
His genuine form in majesty he shows.
As when some youth, in active vigour bold,
The fiery courser by the mane will hold,
And nimbly wheel him round with active force,
Through the large space where rival chariots
        course ;
The steed pursues his leader's rapid pace,   2540
His graceful neck curved high with haughty grace;
With champing teeth he makes the curb resound,
And white as snow the foam is dash'd around;
With mighty hand thus Triton grasp'd the keel,
And bade the ship resistless impulse feel.
His form above such majesty and grace
Combined as proved him of celestial race,
Fair to the middle, but the parts below
A fishy form, with strange discordance show ;

A tail enormous lengthens out his spine;   2550
With forky fins he ploughs the foamy brine;
Turn'd in a shining curve, such shape they wear
As when fair Luna's crescent horns appear.
On to the sea the vessel he impell'd,
And more secure the forward course she held.
That service render'd from their sight he fled,
And plunging sought old ocean's cavern'd bed.
     The portent fill'd the heroes with surprise,
From all the deck the shouts of wonder rise.
There, Argo's name the harbour yet retains; 2560
Still of that ship some monument remains;
For altars yet are seen with grateful hand
To Neptune raised, and Triton, by the band.
There for a day their voyage they delay'd,
The morrow's sun their spreading sails survey'd;
And swiftly gliding as the zephyr swept,
A desert land upon their right they kept.
When the next morn renew'd her rosy light,
Projecting far a headland rose in sight,
Retired behind a deep indented bay,   2570
A safe recess, beneath its shelter lay.
Now Zephyr ceased, and southern blasts prevail'd,
With joyful shouts the favouring breeze they hail'd.
Then Phœbus sunk, and Hesper raised his head,
To summon labour to his homely bed,
Sweet star of love, that brings, with solace fair,
Rest and oblivion of the peasant's care.
As night's still empire lull'd the falling wind,
They furl'd their canvass, and the mast inclined.
Incumbent then the polish'd oars they plied, 2580
And smote with vigorous arms the foamy tide;
All night, all day, they combated the wave,
Nor rest from toil the night succeeding gave;

From far the rocks of Carpathus appear;
Thence, onward to the shores of Crete they steer.
For chief of islands, Crete attracts their course,
But there opposed they meet portentous force.
　　High on a cliff the brazen Talus stands,
With brandish'd rocks he interdicts the lands;
No stranger may the' unfriendly port explore,
No vessel moor along the guarded shore.   2591
Son of that brazen race in elder time,
Derived from trees, robust for every crime,
Him sole remaining branch, the thunderer graced,
And him with demigods his favour placed,
Ordain'd to guard his loved Europa's charms,
And keep her favourite isle from rude alarms :
For annual thrice he compass'd all around,
With brazen feet, the precincts of that ground.
His giant frame he rear'd, untaught to feel ·2600
The trenchant brass or sharply pointed steel,
Save where a vein, that from his head extends,
Pursues the chine, then in his ankle ends.
Red through this duct, where vital currents bound,
The magic form was pervious to the wound.
The skin alone confined the purple tide,
And slightest barriers life from death divide.
The form terrific awed the' adventurous band;
Though present wants some friendly port demand,
They push from those inhospitable shores,   2610
And urge the labouring bark with bending oars,
Now, far from Crete their course they had pursued,
Though thirst and anguish every soul subdued;
But fair Medea thus the crowd address'd,
And comfort cheer'd each agitated breast—
　‘ Hear, warriors—brazen though this monster
Let not a visage with despondence lour;   [tower,

If mortal he the breath of heaven inhale,
Beneath my hand his boasted strength shall fail,
Your vessel station, and avoid the shock,   2620
Secure in distance from the volley'd rock;
There patient wait, until with art profound
I lay this monster prostrate on the ground.'
They row'd obedient past the range of harms,
The direful volleys from those brazen arms;
And waited to behold Medea's skill
The promised wonders of her art fulfil.

Before her face the Colchian fair extends
Her purple robe, and thus the deck ascends;
The son of Æson by the hand she drew,   2630
From bank to bank, where sat the gallant crew.
With sweetest witchery she chanted strain
Of soothing melody, and lull'd the train
Of destinies that harrow up the mind,
And fill with terrors feeble humankind.
The messengers of hell that wing the air,
And mortals fill with anguish and despair;
These were invoked, and thrice her magic song,
And thrice her prayers address'd the direful
   throng.   2639
The potent charms the giant's soul subdued,
The' enchantress then her victory pursued;
Her flashing eyes she fill'd with noxious ire,
His glances sunk beneath the deadly fire;
In rage she grew, her grinding teeth she gnash'd,
Infernal vapours on the foe she dash'd;
Goblins she call'd, and hateful spectres round,
And bade the forms of hell his soul confound.
' Oh! father Jove (he cried), what gloom o'er-
   shades,
What torpid influence every sense invades?

Must we not fear alone disease and wound? 2650
Shall distant foes with magic art confound?'
Though firm in solid brass the giant towers,
He feels the weight of magic's fearful powers;
Yet still his hands the task of warfare ply,
Still rocky fragments fill the darken'd sky.
    While massive volley thus, and menace rude,
The labouring vessel from the port exclude;
His vulnerable part, with mighty shock,
His ankle dash'd against the pointed rock;
Then ichor gush'd from the metallic frame,   2660
Like boiling lead dissolved before the flame;
Nor long his station on that rock he fills,
Like some enormous pine on airy hills,
Which biting axes, urged by rustic might,
Half-fell'd, abandon at the' approach of night;
Full soon nocturnal blasts the foliage rend,
Shake the tall stem, and on the rocks extend;
The limbs a while the giant form sustain,
Then faint it sinks, and thundering loads the plain.
    The harbour now receives the joyful band,
That night they pass upon the Cretan land; 2671
A fane they raised, when early morn appear'd,
To Pallas, by the sons of Crete revered.
With store of water from the spring supplied,
Again they man the bark, and plough the tide;
Eager to pass Salmonium's point around,
With bending oars they vex the salt profound;
As o'er the swell of Cretan seas they flew,
Unwonted terrors night around them threw;
Shrouded they were in blackness of the tomb,
No beamy star dispersed the solid gloom; 2681
The struggling glimpses of the moonlight fail'd,
And shades infernal o'er the world prevail'd.

The sailors know not, darkling as they rove,
Whether in Orcus or the deep they move;
And to the wind and to the wave confide
The random course they can no longer guide.
Then Jason, fill'd with anguish and dismay,
Fervent and loud invoked the source of day;
He call'd on Phœbus to protect the train,   2690
While copious tears distill'd like briny rain;
He vow'd oblations to the Pythian shrine,
To crown with offerings Amyclæ divine;
He vow'd to Delos gifts immense to bear,
For aid imparted in that hour of fear.   [light,
Thou heardst, propitious power; from realms of
With succour prompt, Apollo wing'd his flight;
Melantian rocks amid the waves arise,
And one receives him bending from the skies;
His right hand bare aloft the golden bow,   2700
Thence wide in air the streaming splendours flow;
Where thick the deep is sown with many an isle,
The clustering Sporades in prospect smile;
An islet of the group arises near,
Though small in compass, to the wishes dear;
Full opposite the small Hippuris rose,
And anchor'd here, the train respire from woes.
    The rising morn was fled, with pious care
A goodly shrine for Phœbus they prepare;
And place his altar in the sacred shade,   2710
Where stately groves religious gloom display'd.
They call'd Ægletes [21], bounteous source of light,
With appellation new and solemn rite;
They gave that craggy island's small extent
A name, expressive of the glad event;

---

[21] Ægletes, an epithet or appellation of Apollo.

Propitious Anaphé[22], reveal'd to sight,
With cheering radiance by the god of light.

Such vows were paid as poverty could find,
For scanty means the liberal heart confined;
Where neither lowing herds nor flocks were found,
Nor vines nor olives clad the sterile ground. 2721
But when the maids that from Phæacia came
Beheld the warriors by the torches' flame,
Along the margin of the rocky bay
Unmix'd libations from the fountain pay;
Loud bursts of laughter from the heedless breast
Their foolish scorn of indigence express'd;
And much they turn'd to transitory sport,
A scene so different from Phæacia's court; 2729
For there the blood of countless victims stream'd,
And altars there with wine and incense steam'd.
With taunts their levity the youths assail'd,
While secret pleasure at their mirth prevail'd;
Nor end they thus, the maidens quick replied,
And gay contention rose from side to side.
From their glad warfare in alternate strain,
Still does that isle the war of wit retain;
Ægletes bright, in Anaphé revered,
By mirthful sallies are thy rites endear'd.   2739
Their placid mirror the calm waves expand,
The heroes loose their halsers from the land.
Mindful of visions, in the night survey'd,
His vows to Maia's son Euphemus paid;
What Heaven design'd as yet untaught to know,
But thus his words described the mystic show—
'That sod, methought, the pledge of heavenly
Given to my hand, upon my breast I laid; [aid,
There the small mass, with milky currents fed,
Extending, warm with life a female spread,

22 From a Greek verb, that signifies *to show*.

A beauteous maid. I gazed upon her face,   2750
And fondly strain'd her in a dear embrace;
For sovereign beauty fill'd me with desire,
And shot from every pore resistless fire.
My passion sated, calmer thoughts succeed,
And keen remorse pursues the' incautious deed.
I mourn'd with horror that I had possess'd
My child, that infant nurtured at my breast.
But she, to cheer me with soft soothing grace,
" No daughter I, but born of Triton's race.
I come from Libya, my paternal land,   2760
Nurse of thy progeny, a gracious band.
Oh! youth beloved.   My father bade me share
A portion in the deep with Nereids fair.
Near Anaphé, surrounded by the main,
That mansion for thy children I retain;
Soon shall I bid the dimpling waves display
The surface fair, to drink the solar ray".'

Euphemus thus recall'd to Jason's thought
The forms of wonder that his vision wrought.
The chief revolved the prophecies divine,   2770
In times preceding given from Phœbus' shrine;
And thus replies—' No doubt the gods intend,
That fame immortal shall adorn my friend.
Their power shall bid the pledge that Triton gave
Become an isle when trusted to the wave;
Thy children's children shall possess that land,
Since Triton gave possession to thine hand;
Triton, for he, of all the' immortal train,
Bestow'd this portion of the Libyan plain.'

His answer with Euphemus' thought accords,
He hastes completion of the' auspicious words;
The hallow'd sod into the deep he threw,   2782
And where it plunged Callisté rose to view;

An isle where nature wore her happiest face,
The sacred nurse, Euphemus, of thy race.
That race in after ages Lemnos held,
By Tuscan inroad from those seats expell'd;
The wandering exiles reach'd Laconia's soil,
Where generous Sparta own'd their thriving toil.
The gallant Theras, from Autesion sprung, 2790
From Sparta led the' adventurous and the young;
At sweet Callisté they their wanderings closed,
And fix'd content their leader's name imposed.

But these events succeeding time display'd,
When swift Euphemus was an airy shade;
From thence the'adventurers urged their rapid way,
Till fair Ægina claim'd a short delay;
Though bent on speed they seek the friendly shores,
And eager thirst the cooling fount explores;
Then rose a harmless strife among the train,
Who first with water should the vessel gain; 2801
While double cause of prompt dispatch they find
In pressing want, and in the' impetuous wind;
And hence derived, as ancient story runs,
A custom lives among Thessalia's sons;
And youthful racers urns of water bear,
As to the goal with active limbs they steer.

Hail, gallant youths! hail, bless'd immortal breed,
Propitious to your poet now proceed!
More sweet, more tuneable, from day to day, 2810
From year to year resound the votive lay;
Exulting labour sees the goal appear,
That aspiration of my soul is near.
Great heirs of glory, ever famous throng,
O may your names immortalize my song!
Now let the poet with his heroes rest,
From weary vigils spare the harass'd breast.

By land no perils wait the gallant train,
No future tempests menace o'er the main;
Cecropian hills behold the vessel glide,   2820
With prosperous gale and gently swelling tide.
Near Aulis then they trace the level brine,
And Locrian cities of Opuntian line;
The bay of Pagasæ receives them last,
With shouts exulting o er the labours past.

═════

LINE 1. *Erato*.] The poet being about to sing the loves of Medea and Jason, which had such a considerable influence on the success of the Argonautic expedition, with much propriety invokes Erato, the muse who was supposed to preside over amatory poetry. Virgil, in imitation of our author, invokes the same muse, when he comes to a part of his poem where a love intrigue has a considerable share in the action: 'The wrath of Turnus for Lavinia disespoused.'—See book vii. ver. 37, of the Æneid—*Nunc age, qui reges, Erato, &c.* The Muses are said to preside over the different departments of science and the fine arts. Clio is supposed to have invented history; Thalia (probably from Θαλλω, *germino*) agriculture, and the knowledge of plants; Euterpe, the knowledge of mathematics; Terpsichore, the arts of educating youth; Erato, dancing; Polymnia, playing on the lyre; Melpomene, singing; Urania, astrology, and the knowledge of the heavenly bodies; Calliope, poetry. Two queries have been suggested (says the Greek scholiast), first, why the poet did not invoke the Muses at the commencement of his poem; and next, why he singles out Erato, and invokes her in preference to the other Muses. In answer to the first, he says, that it was natural for the poet,

at the commencement of the work, to invoke
Phœbus, the leader and president of the Muses;
and besides, it was highly proper to reserve his
invocation of the Muses, who were held to pre-
side (in addition to the provinces already enu-
merated) over nuptials, and other festive so-
lemnities, until he came to speak of incidents of
that nature.   It is said, in some of the Orphic
hymns, ' Mortals never cease to cultivate the
Muses, for they are the leaders in the choral
dance and delightsome festivities.'   As to the
second point, Érato, being the Muse who pre-
sided over the dance, was properly invoked by
the poet, when he was about to celebrate the
nuptials of Medea and Jason, to which dancing
and other festivities were appropriate.   Milton,
with equal propriety, invokes Urania, to cele-
brate divine subjects:

> Descend from heaven, Urania! by that name
> If rightly thou art call'd, &c.

41. *My sire produced me.*] Jupiter.   Apollo-
dorus the Athenian has given us a legend of the
birth of Pallas, which he seems to have borrowed
from some very ancient poet.   ' Jupiter, with
some difficulty, enjoyed Metis, who changed
herself into various forms to avoid his embraces.
When she became pregnant, he swallowed her;
because, he said, she was fated to produce a son,
after the girl who was first to be born of her,
who was destined to become the ruler of heaven.
Thus Jupiter became pregnant.   When the time
of gestation was expired, Prometheus (or, as
others say, Vulcan) striking his head with a
hatchet, near the banks of the river Triton, Mi-
nerva sprung from it, clad in armour.'—(Apollod.
lib. i. c. iii. ver. 1. edit. Heyne, p. 11.)   This

fable seems to intimate, by an allegory, that
Jove being filled with innate wisdom, which is
signified by his having swallowed Metis, or
counsel, displayed his wisdom outwardly joined
with power, which is meant by Pallas. Heyne
supposes that the fables respecting Jove and
Thetis were afterwards borrowed from the an-
cient one respecting Metis.—(See note in Apol-
lod. 39, 40.) It is observed, by the Scholiast on
Apollon. ver. 1310, that it was first related by
Stesichorus, that Pallas sprung armed from her
father's head. If this be true, the Hymn to Mi-
nerva, commonly ascribed to Homer, must be
more recent than Stesichorus, since it mentions
this circumstance. It is observed by Heyne
(*ubi sup.*), that several different divinities were
confounded together under the name of Minerva;
as the tutelary goddess of Athens; and Pallas,
a Libyan and Egyptian deity.

43. *Unskill'd I am, &c.*] There is a consider-
able degree of affectation and prudery in this
speech of Minerva. She professes to doubt the
influence and power of love; and boasts her ex-
emption from his sway, in the perfect style and
manner of an old maid.

55. *Erratic isle.*] The word, in the original,
is Plancta, on which a doubt may arise, whether
the forge of Vulcan must be supposed to be
placed in an island, called Plancta, or in an
island that floated: as no island of the name of
Plancta is mentioned by geographers, the latter
meaning seems to be preferable. The forge of
the god, according to ancient fable, was situated
in one of the Lipari or Eolian islands—the names
of which were Strongyle, Euonymus, Lipara,
Hiera, Didyme, Ericodes, and Phenicodes.
Homer says πλαγκτῇ ἐνι νησω; ' A floating isle,

high raised by skill divine.'——See, in a note pre-
ceding, a quotation respecting floating islands.

65. *When her guests.*] Apollonius has evidently
taken the hint of this visit of the goddesses to
Venus, from the application of Juno to that god-
dess in Homer. Virgil has availed himself of the
assistance both of Homer and Apollonius, in the
part which he assigns to Venus and her son, in
the plot and machinery of the poem. A more
particular imitation of our poet will appear in
different passages of Virgil.——See the passages
in the first Æneid, where Juno influences Æolus,
and where Venus instigates her son Cupid to
inspire Dido with a passion for Æneas. Virgil
seems to have had this conversation, between
Juno and Minerva on the one part, and Venus
on the other, particularly in his recollection,
when, in the fourth book, he introduced a con-
versation between Juno and Venus. The pas-
sage in the text of Apollonius, which shows the
goddess as entering and finding Venus employed
in combing her locks, is imitated by Claudian;
who says, speaking of Venus:

> Cesariem tum forte Venus subnixa corusco
> Fingebat solio, dextrâ levâque sorores
> Stabant Idaliæ, &c.

87. *Even should he try.*] Juno endeavours to
give the strongest proof of her attachment to
Jason, by saying that she would befriend him
even in an attempt to loose Ixion, who had most
particularly offended and insulted her, and was
doomed to punishment for a gross outrage against
her.——(See Hyginus, fab. 62.) Ixion was father
to Pirithous.

89. *Pelias.*] Juno, as has been already men-
tioned, had particular reason for being displeased

with Pelias, who had neglected her worship:
and the deities, according to ancient mythology,
never forgave such slights.

98. *In shape deform'd and old.*] It was the
opinion of the ancients, that the gods used often,
for the purpose of proving the piety of men, to
assume the mortal shape. Thus Homer, Odyss.
xvii. ver. 485; and see Ovid, Met. lib. i. ver. 212.
See, too, the fable of Baucis and Philemon.

119. *Thy son.*] There are different genealogies
of love. Apollonius makes him the son of Venus;
Sappho styles him the son of Earth and Heaven;
Simonides the son of Mars and Venus : ' Cruel
and deceitful son of Venus, whom she bore to
treacherous Mars.' Ibycus and Hesiod make
love the offspring of Chaos. In the Theogony it
is said ; ' Chronus or Saturn produced love, and
all the winds.'

136. *Menaces returns.*] This passage puts one
in mind of the fable, which is the groundwork of
the Adone of Marino. Venus chastises her son
Cupid with a rod of roses; and he, in revenge,
pierces his mother's bosom with an arrow, and
makes her fall in love with Adonis.

> 'Con flagello di rose insieme attorte,
> C' havea grappi de spine cha il percosse,
> E de bei membri onde si dolce sorte
> Fe le vivaci porpore più rosse
> Tremaro i poli e la stellata corte
> A quel fiero vagir tutta si mosse
> Mosse si il ciel che più d'amor infante
> Teme il furor, che di Tifeo gigante.
> *Adone di Marino.*

156. *Power of love.*] The circumstances related
by Apollonius, of Cupid and Ganymede playing
at dice, and Venus bribing Cupid with a couple
of golden balls, though they might shine in an

epigram, or an Anacreontic ode, are too light
and trivial to be admitted into an epic poem.
Prior, who has made a most pleasing use of an-
cient mythology, alludes to this fable in his poem
of Cupid and Ganymede. It must be allowed;
however, that there is uncommon prettiness,
grace, and ingenuity, in the fiction of Apollonius;
it is like the gay and sportive paintings of Albano,
which are full of little naked laughing loves.

158. *The little*.] There is an ambiguity in the
phrase in the original, Ἀπανευϑε Διος. It may
either mean, ' remote or apart from Jove, in a
flowery enclosure,' or (others being understood)
it will mean, that ' she found him, apart from the
crowd, in a flowery enclosure of Jupiter, peculiarly
sacred to that deity.'—Gr. Scho.

159. *Ganymede*.] Homer says, that Gany-
mede was carried off, not by Jupiter alone, but
by all the gods ; and he ascribes this act, not to
any improper attachment, but merely to their
wish to employ him as cupbearer to the gods.

161. *Struck with his beauty*.] This was a Cre-
tan fable ; and, as such, Plato takes notice of it
in his first book on Laws ; and says, therefore,
Παντες αυτον καϑηγορϑμεν. We all explode and
reprobate it, for falsity and impudence, accord-
ing to the saying of the poet, Κρητες αιει ψευσται.—
' The Cretans always liars.'—Yet, the scholiast
on the fourth book of the Iliad explains this fable
in an allegorical sense.—Hælzlinus.

164. *Wanton*.] Or madding, Μαργος Ἐρως,
by metonymy, because he renders wanton. Thus
we have frantic Bacchus, and Homer has ' pale
fear.'—Gr. Scho.

184. *Beauteous toy*.] The poet has made the
toy or *bijou*, which Venus offers to her son, a
plaything truly worthy of a divinity, and fit to

have amused the sovereign of the gods in his infancy. It seems to have been a miniature of an armillary sphere. It was composed of a number of concentric circles.

185. *Idæan cave.*] It is doubtful whether this cave was in Crete or in Mount Ida, near Troy; both the Cretans and Trojans claiming the honour of giving birth and nurture to Jove in his infancy, as Demetrius Scepsius asserts.—(Gr. Scho.) The claims of the Phrygians, however, seem to be best founded; as they were the most ancient. The volumes of Greece and Rome abound with records of the Phrygians. Arrian tells us, that they were the oldest of mankind. Their religious madness, in the worship of Cybele, renders them very remarkable in classic story. They were also remarkable for effeminacy. We have their character beautifully drawn by Virgil, in the contrast which he gives in the ninth Æneid, between them and the ancient Tuscans; ver. 614, *et seq.*

186. *Adrasté.*] Adrasté or Adrastea, together with Ida, was the nurse of Jove when an infant in Crete. They fed him with milk of Amalthea. Callimachus, Hymn to Jove, ver. 47, says— ' Adrastia lulled thee to rest in a golden cradle.' This plaything was worthy of an infant Jupiter.

201. *The gather'd playthings, &c.*] All this, and what follows, is wonderfully pretty and ingenious, though not altogether in the taste and style of the higher poetry. The puerile manners of Cupid are well marked and justly preserved : his eagerness to gain possession of the toy, and the unwillingness of Venus to give it until he had actually earned it (as well knowing the malignity and duplicity of him she had to deal

with), are admirably characteristic, and finely described.

222. *From the abode of Jove*.] In this and the following verses, the poet imitates a passage of Ibycus, in his ode to Gorgias, in which he speaks of the rape of Ganymede, and gives a description of Tithonus being carried off by Aurora.—Gr. Scho.

224. *A sloping path*.] It is not improbable that Milton, from this sloping path, took his idea of the sloping sunbeam bearing the angel downward in his passage to earth: ' which (as the poet says) bore him slope downwards.' The passages of Milton are, Paradise Lost, book iv. l. 555; and again, 589.

240. *Jason thus*.] The following speech is highly in character, and marks the prudent and cautious character of Jason.

264. *And murderous rites*.] The means by which Ino endeavoured to destroy her stepchildren, the offspring of Athamas by Nephele, were as follows: She contrived by some means to burn up the harvest, and there being a great scarcity in the district in consequence, Athamas sent to consult the Pythian oracle. The priests, being corrupted by Ino, replied, that he must sacrifice his son Phryxus. Virgil seems to have formed, on this legend, some of the circumstances of his story of Sinon, in the second Æneid: *Adytis hæc tristia dicta reportat, sanguine placastis, &c.*—Gr. Scho. and Hællinuc.

276. *From Circè famed, &c.*] The Circean plain was a large open space of ground near the city of Æa. It took its name from Circè; who, according to some accounts, was the sister of Æëtes, being the daughter of the Sun; according to others, the daughter of Æëtes and Hecaté,

and sister of Medea. This Hecaté was the daughter of Perses. Dionysius, the Milesian, concurs in the latter account; and adds, that two sons were born to Apollo, or the sun, in those regions: the name of the one, Perses; of the other, Æëtes. Æëtes reigned over the Colchians and the Mæotis; Perses, over the Tauric Chersonesus. This prince married a certain woman of the country, and by her had a daughter named Hecaté. Hecaté is said to have shown an uncommon predilection for masculine sports, to have been very much addicted to hunting, and to have discovered the properties and uses of poisonous and deadly roots and herbs. Of this knowledge she availed herself, in poisoning her own father; a parent fit to produce Circè and Medea. Circè, the elder daughter, is fabled to have even surpassed her mother Hecaté, nor was Medea inferior to her. Hesiod makes Circè the daughter of the Sun, in the verses where he says, ' Circè, the daughter of the heavenly Sun, bore in love to the much enduring Ulysses, Agrius and Latinus, blameless and puissant.'— Gr. Scho.

284. *Crude hides.*] This is a remarkable passage, respecting the funeral rites of the ancient Colchians; the reader will find it quoted, in a very curious article, in the Monthly Magazine for July, 1802, p. 540; a translation of the *procès verbal* of the disinterment of the kings and queens of France at St. Denis. ' On the nineteenth was opened the tomb, which contained the body of Lewis VIII. father of St. Lewis, who died in November, 1226. The body had been wrapped in a mantle of gold tissue, and in this dress had been buried, sewed up in very thick leather, which still retained all its elasticity. At St.

Germain des Prés a body was discovered, which had been buried in a similar manner. But a remarkable difference must be observed between the practice of the ancient Colchians and the Parisian accounts; the Colchians suspended the dead bodies in the air, whereas, by the Parisian account, they were interred.

290. *Various customs.*] These extraordinary rites of the Colchians are mentioned by Ælian in his fourth book; the earth and air are said to be the principal objects of their worship.

291. *Juno shrouds.*] This is imitated from the fourth book of the Odyssey, where Pallas spreads a veil of thick air around Ulysses:

> Propitious Pallas, to secure her care,
> Around him threw a veil of thicken'd air.

Virgil avails himself of these passages, and makes Venus afford a similar protection to Æneas, on his way to Carthage.

> At Venus obscuro gradientes aëre sepsit,
> Et multo nebulæ circum dea fudit amictu.

There is a peculiar propriety in the appropriation of this fiction by Apollonius. Juno being made frequently to signify the air in ancient mythology, she is more aptly and philosophically employed in producing a cloud and mist than either Minerva or Venus. Besides, Jason, who was on a perilous enterprise, and exposed to the rage of a jealous and ferocious people, had more need of this protection than either Ulysses or Æneas.

305. *Four springs.*] Compare with this passage ver. 68, and the following, of the Odyssey, lib. v. The description of the grotto of Calypso:

> Four limpid fountains from the clefts distil,
> And every fountain is a separate rill.   POPE.

309. *Pleiades.*] The Greek Scholiast here

blames Apollonius for want of precision, inasmuch as there are two risings and two settings of the Pleiades, as of all the fixed stars; the true rising and setting, and the heliacal rising and setting: the latter of which is more strictly the emersion out of, or immersion into, the sun's rays. And the objection of the Scholiast is, that the poet has not specified to us which of them had the effect he mentions on the springs. But, as Hælzlinus truly observes, if we were to analyze all poetical descriptions thus scrupulously, scarcely any of the ancient writers would be free from blame. The strictly minute and technical description would betray too much exactness, and take off from the dignity and poetical spirit of the passage. It would, in fact, savour more of the historian, or the naturalist, than of the poet. Indeed, few modern poets could bear this sort of hypercritical observation. The Pleiades, from whom the stars in question take their name, are said to have been the daughters of Atlas and Plione, who was the daughter of Ocean. They are said by some to have taken their name from their mother; but the better opinion is, that it comes from a word which denotes fulness or pleonasm; because the appearance of the Pleiades, taken together, in their different vicissitudes, indicate the fulness of the year, as composed of summer and winter. They are always said to avoid Orion, and pursue a course contrary to his. The reason is given thus :—it is said in ancient fables, that Orion having met Plione, with her daughters, in Bœotia, fell in love with the mother. Their flight from his violence was incessant; until, at last, they were changed into stars, which still continue to fly from Orion.—(Gr. Scho.) The Pleiades were

called, in Latin, *Virgiliæ;* from the vernal season
when they rise. They rise about the vernal equi-
nox, and set in autumn.   Some derive the name
of Pleiades from ωλεω, ' to sail;' because these
stars were observed, with peculiar anxiety, by
those who were about to sail on voyages; as the
heliacal rising of the Pleiades was commonly
attended by storms.   These Pleiades are small
stars, in the neck of Taurus.   There were origi-
nally seven of them, as appears from various
ancient writers; but one of them must have dis-
appeared in the course of time, since at present
only six of them are observable.   The largest of
these stars is of the third magnitude, and is called
Lucida Pleiadum.   The evening rising of the
Pleiades—the rising is the appearance of a star,
after having been concealed by the sun; and the
evening rising is, when it appears in the evening
after the setting of the sun.

The names of the Pleiades, according to an-
cient mythology, were Maia, Electra, Taygeté,
Asterope, Merope, Halcyone, and Celano. They
were called Atlantides, from their father Atlas.
They were carried off, it is said, into captivity,
by Busiris, king of Egypt.   Hercules, having
conquered this prince, restored them to their
father.   It was after this that they were perse-
cuted by Orion.

316. *Brazen hoofs.*] Pherecydes agrees with
Apollonius, in saying that these bulls had hoofs
of brass, and breathed fire.—Gr. Scho.

317. *Plough.*] In the original Ἀυτογυον.—
There were, among the ancients, two kinds of
ploughs, Ἀυτογυον, which was all of one piece;
and Πηχλον, which had the sock or tail, the part
into which the coulter or ploughshare was in-
serted, fitted to the pole; that part of the plough

which, with the yoke, went on the necks of the
cattle. The cutting part of the plough was called
'υνις, from ὑς, a swine, because it turned up the
soil, like the swine's snout; and, perhaps, re-
sembled it in form. The ploughtail, in which
the share was inserted, was called ἰλυμα. The
piece of wood which stretched from the plough-
tail to the oxen, was called γυης. The part
which the ploughman held, and on which he
leaned, and turned the plough, was called 'ιστο-
βοευς. The part of the yoke which was put on
the necks of the oxen was called ζευγλαι, or
μισσαβα. Such was the composition of the
πηχϊον. The ἀυτογυον, as has been already ob-
served, had the pole and ploughtail all in one
piece.—(Gr. Scho.) The reader will find an
ample description of a plough in the Works and
Days of Hesiod, ver. 427.—And see the Georgics
of Virgil, lib. i. ver. 169 and 199 : and the learned
notes and disquisitions of Professor Heyne on
the passage; where the structure and component
parts of the ancient plough are critically and mi-
nutely considered, and various writers are enu-
merated who throw a light on this subject.

320. *Phlegræan.*] Phlegra was an extensive
plain near the city of Pallene, in the Chersonese
of Thrace; or, according to others, in Thessaly;
where the battle between the gods and the giants
is said to have been fought.—(See Gr. Scho.)
The same region seems to have been called, at
different times, both Phlegra and Pallene; the
region of Pallene bore evident marks of the ruin
occasioned by the intestine commotions of earth-
quakes and subterranean fires. Hence this place
was made the scene of the battles between the
gods and giants. The name of Phlegra was in
aftertimes transferred to other places which ex-

hibited the ravage of intestine fires; thus there were Phlegræan plains near Cumæ, in Italy, a country subject at all times to shocks of earth-quakes; where some also lay the scene of these famous battles of the giants.—See Strabo, book v. in different passages. Others place the Phlegræan plains, and the combats of the giants, at Tar-tessus, in the extreme western part of Europe.—Sée Heyne, not. in Apollod. p. 70.

330. *Asterodea.*] The author of the Naupactica calls her Eurylyte. Dionysius, the Milesian, says that Hecaté (as has been already menti-oned) was the mother of Medea and Circè. So-phocles assigns them, as their parent, Neera, one of the Nereids. Hesiod says, ' Æëtes, son of the resplendent god who enlightens mortals by the will of the gods, wedded the beautiful Idyia.' Epimenides says, that Æëtes was a Corinthian by descent, and that his mother was Ephyré. Diophanes, in his History of Pontus, book i. says, that Antiope was the mother of Æëtes; and that Absyrtus was own brother to Medea, and the eldest child of Æëtes, by Aste-rodea, the daughter of Oceanus and Tethys.

376. *Billets sere.*] Milton, ' Ivy never sere.' Shakspeare, ' The sere, the yellow leaf.'

382. *The breeze by rustics.*] Virgil describes this insect, Georgic. iii. ver. 147. His translator uses the word ' breeze.' It is also employed by Merrick; version of Tryphiodorus.

385. *Shaft untried.*] This passage is imitated from the fourth Iliad, where Pandarus is repre-sented as shooting an arrow, which had never been discharged before, at Menelaus.—See ver. 117.

404. *Smother'd brand.*] Apollonius seems here to have had in his recollection a passage of Ho-

mer, Odyss. v. 488. Virgil has obviously imitated our poet, in Æneid viii. ver. 408.

411. *Pernicious love.*] So Virgil, Æneid iv. ver. 67.

430. *Sister Circè.*] Our poet, following Hesiod, says that Phœbus conveyed his daughter Circè, in his chariot, to an island which lay on the Tuscan coast; where she settled in Italy, which took the name of Hesperia, from its western situation, in respect of Greece and Asia. The promontory of Circeum, now Circeii, took its name from Circè. See, with respect to this subject, a subsequent note.

436. *Speech of Æëtes.*] The haughty, ferocious, inhospitable, and suspicious character of the Colchian king, is well preserved in this passage. He does not seem to be inwardly well pleased, even with the return of his grandsons. He deigns to address them alone; and examines them very strictly respecting their companions. And Lydgate makes Æëtes give a much more courteous reception to Jason.—(See Warton, Hist. Poet. ii. p. 89.) When Jason arrives at Colchos, he is entertained by king Æëtes in a Gothic castle. Amadis or Lancelot were never conducted to their fairy chambers with more ceremony or solemnity. He is led through many a hall and many a tower, by many a star, to a sumptuous apartment, whose walls, richly painted with the histories of ancient heroes, glittered with gold and azure.

> Through many a halle, and many a riche towre,
> By many a tourne, and many divers waye,
> By many a gree ymade of marble gray,
> And in his chambré, englosed bright and cleare,
> That shone full shene with gold and with asure,
> Of many image that ther was in picture.

See Lydgate's Troy Book, a translation from

Colonna's prose history.   In Mr. Ellis's Speci-
mens of early English Poetry, more lines are
quoted, descriptive of the ceremonial used by
the Colchian monarch after Jason's first audi-
ence.

> But first of all, this mighty man Jason,
> Assigned was by the kinge anon.
> For to sitte at his owne borde ;
> And Hercules, that was so great a lord,
> Was sette also faste by his side.

437. *Before his brothers, &c.*] Argus was in
haste to speak before his brothers, from an ap-
prehension that they might be frank and un-
guarded, and make some answer that should dis-
close too much, and compromise the safety of
Jason and his companions, together with their
ship.   Orpheus, in his Argonautics (see ver. 775)
differs somewhat from Apollonius in his account
of the meeting of the Minyæ and the Colchian
king.   He represents him as terrified by inaus-
picious dreams, calling his children round him,
and, having ascended his chariot, hasting to the
banks of the Phasis, with his daughters, to meet
the Argonauts.

477. *Far have they wander'd.*] Virgil has imi-
tated this passage, Æneid i. ver. 2.

511. *My table.*] The rites of hospitality and
the table were held sacred among the ancients,
in the heroic ages particularly.   And this spirit
of hospitality prevails at this day all through the
east. Insomuch that among the wandering Arabs,
who subsist by robbery and violence, if a person
can contrive to eat and drink with them, he is
thenceforward respected as a guest, and exempt-
ed from all danger of outrage.

516. *Lies—blasphemies.*] Because Argus had
said that Telamon was descended from Jove, and
that all the followers of Jason could trace their

pedigree to some divine origin. Telamon, in consequence, shows peculiar resentment.

526. *No hostile purpose.*] Virgil has imitated this passage. Æneid i. ver. 527.

568. *Thy king.*] Æëtes lays an emphasis on the words ' thy king,' to taunt and insult Jason, as being his inferior. He reminds him, that he is a vassal and a dependant, acting, not from himself or for his own benefit, but in subjection to the commands of another.

570. *Silent the hero.*] The picture of the feelings and conduct of Jason is natural and beautiful; and highly characteristic of the prudence and good sense which the poet uniformly ascribes to his hero. Jason sees all the difficulties of his situation. His mind is not free from fear; but, by an effort of resolution and prudence, he conquers or conceals his emotion. His answer is discreet and short. An inferior poet would have thought this a fine opportunity of shining; and might have put into the mouth of Jason a speech full of rant and bravado, and made him accept the proffered trial without any hesitation. But would this have been equally true to nature?

594. *Æëtes thus.*] The ferocity and pride of the Colchian king are finely represented here, and are happily contrasted with the steady mildness of Jason.

603. *Held her veil.*] The description of Medea holding her veil aside, and taking a sidelong and stealthy glance at the graceful stranger, is very natural, and beautifully described.

607. *Dream.*] With eager, yet unavailing and painful endeavour—

———— Nequicquam avidos extendere cursus
Velle videmur, et in mediis conatibus egri
Succidimus.   LUCRETIUS.

614. *Absent Jason.*] Virgil has followed this passage of our author closely, in the fourth book of the Æneid, ver 3.

The following picture of Medea's growing passion is not inelegant:

> For as she sat at meat, though in that tide,
> Her father next, and Jason by her side,
> All suddenly her fresh and rosen hue
> Full oftetime gan changen and renew,
> An hundred sithes in a little space.
> For now the bloode from her goodly face
> Unto her heart unwarely gan avale ;
> And therewithal she waxeth dead and pale :
> And eft anon (who thereto gan take heed)
> Her hue returneth into goodly red.

It is given by Lydgate, in his Troy Book, and quoted by Ellis, in his Specimens of early English Poetry, vol. i.

639. *Daughter of Perses.*] Hecaté. Her mother was Asteria.—Apoll. Some make her the daughter of Jove. In the Orphic Hymns her genealogy is deduced from Ceres :—' Then Ceres bore Hecaté the divine.' Bacchylides makes her the daughter of Night. ' Hecaté, daughter of the torch-bearing and vast bosom'd Night !' Musæus makes her the daughter of Asteria and Jove : Pherecydes makes her the daughter of Aristeus, the son of Pæon. Some books call the father of Hecaté, Perses; others, Perseus.

655. *Hast thou not heard, &c.*] The poet has not given us this conversation, in which Argus is supposed to have had in view, and represented to Jason, the magical acquirements of Medea.

693. *Peleus at length.*] The poet seems to have had in view that part of the seventh Iliad, ver. 161 and 199, where Hector challenges some Grecian champion to single combat. The host is at first dismayed ; but, at the reproach of

Nestor, a number of heroes afterwards arise and offer themselves.

723. *From every drug.*] Virgil's description of the magical powers of the Massylian priestess (Æneid iv. ver. 487) is manifestly borrowed from the passage in the text.

757. *Idas alone.*] Here again the poet shows his attention to the preservation of character, and his skill in discriminating its shades from each other. Peleus and Idas are both brave; but their bravery has different features. There is a gallantry and generosity about Peleus, while Idas is ferocious, envious, and contemptuous. The behaviour of many of the Minyæ, who are represented as secretly approving the speech of Idas, is very natural. The populace are usually disposed to applaud violent counsels.

768. *Deep resentment.*] It appears that Jason was moved with an extraordinary degree of shame and indignation, at the scornful and insulting manner in which Idas spoke.

798. *Son of Maia.*] Virgil has imitated this passage in the first Æneid, ver. 303. The son of Maia is dispatched by Jupiter to render Dido favourable to the Trojans.

—— Regina quietum
Accipit in Teucros animum, mentemque benignam.

821. *Sole cause of fear.*] The confidence of Æetes, that no danger could possibly arise to him from his daughters, the very source of his danger, is uncommonly artful and happy, and truly in the spirit of tragedy. The passage before us reminds us of that in Shakspeare, where he says, after having experienced the unkindness of Gonerill : ' Yet have I left a daughter—I can be happy—I can stay with Regan—I and my hundred knights.'

843. *Visions.*] The dream of Medea is beautifully imagined, and highly natural. It is made up of circumstances which might be supposed to have occurred to the mind of Medea while she was waking: at the same time, it is well calculated for disposing her to pursue the conduct which, in fact, she afterwards adopts. The dream of Eve, in Paradise Lost, has the same apposite felicity.

873. *But why.*] The solicitude of Medea, to impose on herself, and blind her eyes, even to her own motives and feelings, by ascribing to sisterly affection what she does, under the influence of her passion for Jason, is very natural; and shows that Apollonius had a profound knowledge of the human heart. It is also very ingenious, and well imagined in the poet, to make the love of Chalciope for her children subservient to the plot of the fable. She is thus induced to meet the wishes of her sister half way. And this concurrence of Chalciope, in the secret views of Medea, and even anticipation of her unsettled designs, emboldens the latter to give way to her passion without control; and to reveal to Jason the secret of her heart, at which she herself at first started with abhorrence.

889. *Trembling steps.*] Orpheus, in his Argonautics, gives a very different account of the feelings and behaviour of Medea; and, certainly, by much a less natural and interesting one. Orpheus, indeed, represents the Colchian princess as a bold and forward wanton, without any sense of decorum. (See Orph. Argon. ver. 874.) He exhibits her there as possessed with amorous fury; going unsolicited and boldly to the ship, and offering herself to the wishes of Jason; as disregarding alike the anger of her father, and

the ties of shame; as throwing herself on the neck of Jason, and kissing his face and bosom. How much has the poet improved on this, by introducing the conflicts of Medea with her fatal passion! How much more beautiful and interesting, and, at the same time, more consonant to the decorum of the female character, and to the dignity of a princess, as well as more agreeable to probability, is the conduct of the enamoured virgin, as delineated by Apollonius!

935. *That I and mine might flee.*] This speech of Chalciope is very artfully introduced, to encourage Medea in her passion. The idea of flying away to some distant region, where she might never more expect to see her father's roof, or hear the name of Colchos, is calculated to render Medea more communicative, and serves to prepare the way, and dispose her to the thoughts of flying with the Argonauts. The share which Apollonius here ascribes to Chalciope, in leading her sister to disregard the voice of prudence, and concur in the wishes of Jason, seems to have suggested to Virgil the part which he ascribes to Anna, the sister of Dido, in making her the chief instrument by which the queen is brought to abandon herself blindly to her fatal passion.

947. *The answer of Medea.*] There is much artifice and ingenuity shown by the poet in the speeches of the two sisters; each doubtful of the other, and not fully acquainted with her secret feelings and disposition. Thus there is a sort of trial of skill between them: the one, actuated by maternal tenderness and anxiety for the safety of her children; the other, by love. The superior artifice of Medea, however, prevails; and she has the address to make the proposal, for their assisting Jason, come from Chalciope; and

to make her sister offer what she feared to demand.

974. *To vex thy rest*.] Virgil has imitated these lines in the fourth Æneid, ver. 385 :

> Et cum frigida mors animâ seduxerit artus,
> Omnibus umbra locis adero, dabis improbe pœnas.

The ancients had the same popular superstition which yet prevails so generally, that the spirits of departed persons return to earth, to haunt and plague those who injure and oppress them. Such, according to Horace, was the power of the Manes. Apuleius, in his book on the god of Socrates, explains at large the power of the soul, in its state of separation from the body.

989. *Earth*.] Here the word is taken to signify 'earth,' as a divinity.

1014. *Thy sons*.] How beautiful and natural are the sentiments and conduct of Medea! With what art and delicacy does she endeavour to impose on her sister and herself, and to set down the part which she acts to the account of natural affection! This is a delineation worthy of Shakspeare.

1016. *Daughter*.] Chalciope being so much older than Medea, that she had assisted in her education; the latter naturally says, that she considers her in the light of sister and parent at once.

1033. *Now night*.] Compare with this Virgil's famous description of night, in the fourth book of the Æneid, ver. 522. It is not easy to decide between them. The description of Virgil is in a higher tone, more grand and majestic; that of our poet is more amiable, more tender, and affecting. The circumstance of the fond mother even ceasing to mourn her lost children is very sweet and natural. In fine, Virgil has imitated Apollonius so happily as to leave it doubtful whether most praise is due to the original or the copy. There is a very beautiful description of night in Theocritus, Idyll. ii. ver. 38. Milton also has a similar description in Paradise Lost;.

Silence accompanied, for bird and beast, &c.

The sweetness and softness of the foregoing line are observable.

1054. *Trembling lymph.*] Virgil was struck with the beauty of this simile, and has imitated it; Æn. viii. ver. 22.

But the similes are employed for very different purposes. Apollonius means only to illustrate the quick palpitation of Medea's heart, within her bosom: Virgil proceeds further, and applies the comparison to illustrate the movements of the mind; to show the uncertainty and quickness of thoughts glancing from one subject to another.

1086. *For Greece.*] Literally the Achaian land.

1112. *Pendulous.*] Hanging seems to have been the favourite death with the female suicides of antiquity. Jocasta dies in that manner in Sophocles; so does the wife of Cizycus, in the first book of our poet. It was natural, however, that the alternative of taking poison should occur to Medea, who was so skilful in the preparation and power of noxious drugs.

1127. *She ceased.*] The uncertainty and conflicts in the mind of Medea are admirably described. How natural too is it, that, at the very moment when she is about to destroy herself, all the terrors of death, and all the charms of existence, should rush upon her mind!

1158. *To mark the' approach.*] So Virgil, Æn. iv. ver. 586.

Q 2

1178. *Vanish'd every care.*] Either from feminine vanity, because she was delighted to see herself look so well in her fine clothes, or because the thoughts of love, and the prospect of an interview with Jason, banished all other considerations from her mind.

1180. *Evils of the future.*] When she should be despised and rejected by the ingratitude of Jason. Poets are fond of these prophetic anticipations.

1189. *Prometheus' name.*] *Herba Promethea.* It was supposed to spring from the blood of Prometheus, which flowed to the ground as the vulture preyed upon his liver. This plant was supposed to possess many extraordinary properties, and was much used in magical rites and incantations. Its juice was black, its flower something like that of the crocus, and of the same colour; and by the description given of the root, which was forked, it much resembled the circa or mandragora. In an allegorical sense, this herb may signify reason, which subdues the fiery emotions of the soul. A similar sense may be ascribed to the Moly of Homer; the golden bough of Virgil; the Κρηδεμνον, or fillet of Ulysses; the Porphyris of Agamemnon; Valerius Flaccus (book vii. ver. 355) has introduced Medea as employing this herb in incantations. Propertius talks of a potent herb, which he calls Promethean, the effect of which was to produce antipathy and hatred.

> Invidiæ sumus; num me deus obruit? an quæ
> Secta Prometheis dividit herba jugis.

The mention of these opinions of the ancients, respecting the power of herbs, in charms and incantations, shows that they are not unlike the popular opinions which prevail very generally at this day. The reader can hardly avoid recollecting, on this occasion, the beautiful fiction in the Midsummer Night's Dream of Shakspeare, respecting the use of the two flowers; one of which had the power of producing love, the other hatred.

1193. *Persephone.*] It is, in the original, 'Sole begotten' Daira, *quasi* Daiera, from the Greek verb δαιειν, 'to burn,' from the light of torches, which were used in the solemn rites of Hecaté. 'To whom the secret flames of midnight torches burns, mysterious dame.'

1201. *Caucasian.*] Caucasus is called, by Propertius, the Promethean mountain, because Prometheus was there chained : and the magic herbs, for which it was famous, were said to have sprung from his blood. See a preceding note.

1212. *Corycium.*] A mountain and district of Cilicia, where the best saffron was anciently produced. Strabo mentions it in his fourth book. The juice of this root was preserved, in shells, from the Caspian strand, because that shore was supposed to produce cockle-shells of an uncommon size. The poet, to excite the attention of the reader and create a greater interest, makes every thing respecting the charms and medicaments of Medea extraordinary and marvellous, —See Gr. Scho.

1214. *Brimo.*] Hecaté was called Brimo, which means something tremendous and appalling, from the spectres and phantasms which were supposed to be attendant on her.

1221. *Plant of Titan.*] So called, because it sprang from the blood of Prometheus, who was of the race of Titans.—Gr. Scho.

1224. *Screams.*] Hence seems to have arisen the vulgar tradition, that screams and lamentable

cries are heard, when the roots of mandrakes are
plucked out of the ground.   Shakspeare alludes
to this notion when he says,

> Shrieks like mandrakes torn out of the earth.

1235. *Parthenius.*] A river of Paphlagonia;
so called from Diana, the goddess of chastity.

1236. *Amnisus.* A river and city of Crete, sa-
cred to Dian.—See Callimachus (Hymn to Ar-
temis, ver. 15.)

1237. *Virgin Dian.*] Apollonius has imitated
this simile, from the sixth book of the Odyssey.
Homer there applies it to Nausicaä, with her
fair attendants.   Virgil has endeavoured to im-
prove both on Homer and Apollonius; when,
speaking of Dido and her train passing through
Carthage, he says,

> Qualis in Eurotæ ripis aut per juga Cynthi
> Exercet Diana choros, quam mille secutæ
> Hinc atque glomerantur Oreades.

The simile of Apollonius is more original and
ingenious, and at the same time more apposite
and descriptive, than that of Virgil.   The Latin
poet merely describes a beautiful woman, with a
numerous train of attendants.   In our poet all
the circumstances concur most exactly.   Diana
is a virgin, so is Medea; the princess is borne
rapidly along, so is the goddess; and, in both
cases, the attendant nymphs run after their mis-
tresses.   The circumstance of the beasts sporting
and gamboling, at sight of the goddess, is very
noble and beautiful.   Milton, it appears, was
peculiarly struck with it; and has imitated it in
his Paradise Lost, where he represents the beasts
fawning round our first parents in Paradise.

1291. *Endowments rare.*] This passage is imi-
tated by Ovid, Met. lib. vii. ver. 84.   Apollonius

himself has imitated a passage in the Odyssey; where Homer represents Minerva improving the appearance of Ulysses, and adding grace and majesty to his form. Virgil, in imitation of Homer and Apollonius, makes Venus adorn her son. Æneid i. ver. 589.

1303. *Claps her sable wing.*] This passage is exquisitely fanciful and elegant. In what a truly poetical manner does our author contrive to tell us, that it occurred to Mopsus, that it would be proper to leave his friend alone, to meet the lady!

1350. *Bright as Sirius.*] Nothing can be more happy or illustrative than this simile! The beauty and splendour of Sirius, joined with his supposed pernicious influence on health and life, are finely compared with the appearance of Jason, resplendent in youth and beauty, which was to be attended with such fatal consequences to the peace and happiness of Medea; the smoothness and sweetness of versification, in the original, are beyond all praise.

1362. *Her feet beneath.*] The description of the emotion and confusion of Medea is highly beautiful and natural; and shows our author's knowledge of the human heart. I am, perhaps, to blame in repeating the same remark so often; but I am anxious to do justice to a poet who has been too much neglected.

1369. *Whose peaceful heads.*] Valerius Flaccus has imitated this passage, book vii. ver. 403. It is a very fanciful and original simile.

1406. *Climes remote.*] In the original, ' When they shall return to Hellas;' which properly means that part of Thessaly called Phthiotis: for it is to be recollected that most of the Argonauts were, like their leader, Thessalians.

1417. *Ariadne.*] Daughter of Minos, king of Crete and Pasiphaë. Jason artfully introduces the mention of Ariadne, who saved Theseus from perishing in his enterprise at Crete, and after sailed away with him; as an example and encouragement, to lead Medea to assist the Argonauts, and accompany them afterwards in flight. He conceals, however, the subsequent part of the story.

1425. *Garland.*] The crown of Ariadne is a constellation, supposed to be formed by the garland of that princess, which was placed in heaven. The lines of Catullus, on the meeting of Theseus and Ariadne, deserve a place here.

—— (Nuptiæ Pel.)

Magnanimum ad Minoa venit sedesque superbas,
Hunc simul ac cupido conspexit lumine virgo
Regia, quam suavis expirans castus odores
Lectulus, in molli complexu matris alebat.
Qualis Eurotæ progignunt flumina myrtos,
Aurave distinctos educit verna colores
Non prius ex illo flagrantia declinavit
Lumina, quam cuncto concepit pectore flammam
Funditus, atque imis exarsit tota medullis,
Hei misere exagitans immiti cordi furores,
Sancte puer, curis hominum qui gaudia misces, &c.

1439. *Tried in vain.*] Valerius Flaccus has imitated this passage, book vii. ver. 433.

1474. *Daughter of Perses.*] Hecaté, or the goddess who presided over the moon, was called 'sole-begotten,' because, says the annotator on Hesiod, the moon was thought by the ancients (though in this they were mistaken) to be the only celestial body of the kind.

1481. *Turn thy head.*] It was held to be highly irreverent and indecorous, and to be attended with fatal consequences, to interrupt the rites of sacrifice, when once they were com-

menced, on any pretence whatsoever.   We have
a remarkable instance of the firmness and pre-
sence of mind of a Roman, who was told that
his son was dead just as he was engaged in
sacrificing.

1496. *Its force is bounded by a single day.*] It
is very surprising, that the learned and accurate
Heyne, in his notes on Apollodorus, p. 203,
should have overlooked this passage of our author;
and asserted, that it is not to be found in Apol-
lonius, that the efficacy of the medicament was
confined to one day.—*Sed quod medicamenti per
unum tantum diem efficax vis fuit in Apollonio
non legitur.*

1520. *Remember me.*] This passage is very
affecting.   Valerius Flaccus has imitated it, lib.
iv. ver. 475.

1527. *Who is that virgin.*] It is very artful in
the poet to make Medea inquire particularly
about Ariadne.   It shows that her conduct had
made an impression on her mind; and furnishes
a pretty broad hint to Jason, to lead him to pro-
pose the example of the flight of Ariadne, as a
pattern for the imitation of Medea.

1545. *Hæmonia.*] Thessaly so called. Hella-
nicus (says the Scholiast) relates that Prometheus
reigned in Thessaly, and erected there an altar
to twelve gods.   This region is watered by a
variety of rivers, of which the four most remark-
able are the Peneus, the Apidanus, the Panisus,
and the Enipeus.—Gr. Scho.

1546. *Deucalion.*] Here Apollonius, according
to the generally received opinion, supposes Deu-
calion to have been a native of Greece.   He was
the son of Prometheus, the son of Iapetus, and
of Pandora (as Hesiod asserts in the first of his
catalogue, says the Greek Scholiast); by his

wife Pyrrha, Deucalion had a son named Hellen, who gave an appellation to the country where he lived. The poet represents Deucalion as the first of men through whom religious rites were renewed and cities founded. Philo is of opinion, that Deucalion was the same person with Noah. The scholiast makes it doubtful who was the mother of Deucalion by Prometheus. He enumerates four persons of the name; a second, who is mentioned by Hellanicus; a third, the son of Minos, who is mentioned by Pherecydes; a fourth, the son of Abas, of whom Aristippus speaks in his Arcadics.—See the Gr. Scholiast.

1549. *Hæmonia.*] Thessaly was at first called by this name. It had also other appellations. It was called Pyrrodia, from Pyrrha, the wife of Deucalion. Rhianus says, 'Thessaly was called Pyrrha by the ancients, from Pyrrha, who in old times was the wife of Deucalion.' It was called Æmonia from Æmon, the eldest son of Pelasgus; and Thessalia, from Thessalus, the son of Æmon. Thessaly was divided into four regions—Pelagiotis, Thessaliotis, Iolcitis, and Phthiotis. It was a region abounding in poisons, and frequented by witches and enchanters.

1553. *Minyas.*] He is called Æolian, not as being the immediate offspring of Æolus, but as being descended from his stock. Sisiphus, the son of Æolus, had two sons, Almus and Porphyrion. Minyas, the builder of Orchomenus, was the son of Neptune, by Chrysogone, the daughter of Almus: thus he was a descendant of Æolus by the mother's side.—Gr. Scho.

1556. *Cadmus.*] On the report of the rape of Europa, her father, Agenor, sent every where in search of her; and particularly ordered his son Cadmus not to return until he had found her.

Cadmus, having traversed a great part of Greece, without gaining any intelligence of his sister, settled at last at Thebes.

1563. *Oh might!*] How artfully and delicately does Jason gradually prepare the mind of Medea, and lead her on insensibly to give her consent to elope with him and his companions, by dwelling on the example of Theseus and Ariadne, and wishing that the father of Medea might consent to their union! Jason artfully conceals the subsequent part of the story of Ariadne, and designedly passes over, in silence, the ingratitude and desertion of Theseus.

1593. *Wish not, my fairest.*] The reply of Jason here is truly tender and insinuating: and there is wonderful delicacy and decorum, at the same time, in the thoughts and expressions.

1647. *Limbs spontaneous.*] That is to say, without the concurrence of her will or impulse of volition; as if she were unconscious of what she did, and even by a sort of mere mechanical motion. It is very natural in Apollonius, to make Jason, who was not so completely enamoured as Medea, and had his mind filled with thoughts of obtaining the fleece, the first to take notice of their situation, and to propose their parting.

1659. *Down on a humble seat, &c.*] The conflict of passion, and the fluctuation of purposes, in the mind of Medea, are finely depicted. It is the same kind of representation which strikes us forcibly in the Macbeth of Shakspeare.

1667. *Attendants.*] Mopsus and Argus, who had remained, and waited for him during his conference with Medea.

1673. *Idas alone.*] The contentious, unmanageable, and envious character of the ferocious Idas is here well preserved.

VOL. II.   R

1686. *Aonian snake.*] Bœotian. Bœotia was anciently called Aonia; and Thebes, Ogygian; from Ogyges, who anciently reigned there. Corinna says, ' that Ogyges was the son of Bœotus, and that from him the gates of Thebes were called Ogygian.' Lysimachus, in the first book of his Thebaics, relates many wonderful stories, and much miscellaneous matter, respecting the arrival of Europa and Cadmus at Thebes.—Gr. Scho.

1687. *Cadmus.*] Hellanicus, in the first book of his Phoronis, relates, that Cadmus, by the direction of Mars, sowed the teeth of the dragon which he had slain: whence five armed men were produced; Oudeus, Cthonius, Pelor, Hyperenor, and Echion. But Apollonius supposes their number to have been very great, and that they mutually engaged and slew each other in war. In the third book of the Titanographia of Musæus, it is said, that Cadmus proceeded, in obedience to the Delphic oracle, to journey, with a heifer for his guide. Hippias the Delian, in his ' Derivations of the Names of Nations,' says, that a certain nation, to which he came, were called Sparti; and in like manner Atromelus speaks. Pherecydes, in his fifth book, says, ' When Cadmus built his settlement in Thebes, Mars and Minerva gave to him half of the teeth of the serpent, the other half to Æëtes. Cadmus sowed those which he received in the furrow, by the directions of Mars: and being struck with terror, when the armed men began to spring up, threw stones at them; at which they, supposing that they were struck and attacked by each other, engaged in fight, until they were all exterminated, except five, Oudeus, Cthonius, Echion, Pelor, and Hyperenor, whom Cadmus saved, and settled as colonists and denizens; assigning to them habitations in his newly founded city of Thebes.' Such is the account given by the Greek Scholiast. I have presented the reader with the passage thus at length, because he quotes different works of ancient writers, of which no fragment has reached us.

1687. *Ogygia.*] This was one of the ancient names of Bœotia. It was derived either from Ogyges, an ancient sovereign of that country, in whose time the famous deluge happened; or rather from Ogygis, who (see Apollod. edit. Heyne, 197), was one of the daughters of Amphion, by Niobé, the daughter of Tantalus. Ogygia was also the name of an island in the Tyrrhenian sea, which was the residence of the goddess Calypso.

1707. *Now behind earth.*] He means here that the sun sunk beneath the horizon. The poet seems to suppose that the confines of Ethiopia bounded the two hemispheres. The ignorance of the ancients in geography was very extraordinary. It appears, that Herodotus did not believe that the earth was of a globular form. In Melpomene, 36, he says, ' I cannot but think it exceedingly ridiculous to hear some men talk of the circumference of the earth; pretending, without the smallest foundation or probability, that the ocean encompasses the earth; and that the earth is round, as if mechanically formed.'

1689. *Cadmus.*] Some writers make Cadmus the son of Agenor, others of Phœnix. Pherecydes, in his fourth book, says, ' Agenor, the son of Neptune, married Damno, the daughter of Belus; from her sprung Phœnix and Isca, who was married to Egyptus and Melia, who was married to Danaus. Afterwards Agenor attached himself to Argiope, the daughter of the river Nilus by whom he had Cadmus.'—(Gr. Scho.) Apollodorus (lib. iii.) speaks thus of Cadmus: ' Agenor was the brother of Belus, and son of Neptune and Libyé. He married Telephessa, by whom he had a daughter named Europa, and three sons, Cadmus, Phœnix, and Cilix. Cadmus was accompanied, in his wanderings, by his mother Telephessa, Thasus, the son of Neptune or, as Pherecydes says, of Cilix, and Phœnix. The latter, finding his search fruitless, settled in the region which, from him, was called Phœnicia. Cilix settled also in the same neighbourhood, and gave his name to the country of Cilicia. Cadmus and Telephessa resided in Thrace, as did also Thasus, who built a city which bore his name. Here Telephessa died, and was buried by Cadmus. After this he proceeded to Delphi, to inquire concerning Europa. The god desired him not to trouble himself about Europa, but to follow a heifer as his guide, and build a city wherever she should fall down with weariness. Cadmus departed, and following the steps of a heifer, which belonged to the stalls of one Pelagon, was conducted by her into Bœotia, where she lay down in the place where Thebes now stands. Being desirous to sacrifice this heifer to Minerva, Cadmus sends some of those who accompanied him to procure water from the fountain of Mars. A serpent, who guarded this sacred spring, attacked and killed most of those who were sent. Cadmus, enraged at this, killed the snake. The armed men, who were produced by sowing the dragon's teeth, were called Sparti. After this, Jove gave him as a wife, Harmonia, the daughter of Mars and Venus; and all the gods, leaving heaven, came to partake of the nuptial festivity, at the citadel of Thebes.'—See Apollod. edit. Heyne, vol. i. p. 173, 174, 175; 184, 185, 186.

1712. *Fix'd on heaven.*] Jason kept his eyes fixed on the stars with anxious attention, to watch the progress of the night, that he might not let slip the hour appointed by Medea.

1719. *Solemn rite.*] The rites of Hecaté bore some resemblance to those which, in more modern times, have been practised by sorcerers, who have pretended to raise the dead, or to call up evil spirits from the infernal regions. The passage in the text, which is very sublime, seems to have struck the imagination of Virgil most forcibly. He alludes to it in various places. Hecaté (the same with the moon, or Diana) was so called, because she was appeased with hecatombs; or from the power she was supposed to possess, of obliging those who were unburied to wander a hundred years. There may be a third etymon of the name, from the Greek εκας, *procul* —from the awful and mysterious attributes of the goddess, and her repulsion of the profane : *Procul, O procul, este profani.* Virgil applies to this goddess the epithet of Tergemina; and Horace, that of Triformis; to denote her threefold character and functions. She was called in heaven, Luna, or the moon; on earth, Diana; in hell, Proserpina, Hecaté, and Brimo. It is under the latter character that she is made, by the poet, to show herself on the present occasion. It is not extraordinary that Diana, under her character of the moon, should be invoked by women in childbed, because the moon has a considerable influence over persons in that situation; but it is rather strange that Diana, the goddess of chastity, should be represented as promoting the success of illicit amours. However, mythologists inform us, that Diana and Venus were one and the same divinity. The scholiast on Theocritus says, it was customary with men to invoke the sun; with women, the moon, for success in amours.

1741. *Snakes with oaken.*] That Hecaté was crowned with snakes, entwined with oaken boughs, appears also from Sophocles; who, in his play called Rizotomi, has introduced the chorus, saying, ' O sun, thou lord of light, and thou, sacred fire of Hecaté, invoked beside the beaten paths, her radiant darts fly numerous through Olympus, she appears, on earth, in the sacred spaces, where three roads meet, having crowned her head with oak, and many spires of serpents are coiled upon her shoulders.'—(Gr. Scho.) Apollodorus, as quoted by Athenæus (lib. vii.), says that the Trigla, or mullet fish, which was so called from its breeding thrice a year, was sacrificed to Hecaté, on account of the similitude of name, Hecaté being called Trimorphus. The pedigree of Hecaté is variously deduced by various writers.—See Sch. Apoll. 867—1034. Sch. Theoc. 2.

1748. *Phasis.*] This river is called Amarantian, from the Amarantii, a race of barbarians beyond Colchis, in whose country, according to some, the river Phasis springs. There is also a mountain of Colchis called Amarantium, whence the Phasis descends.

1757. *Phlegrean Mimas.*] Mimas was one of the Titans, or earthborn brood, which engaged with the gods in combat at Phlegra, near Pallene, in Thrace; or rather in Thessaly.

1767. *The king excepted.*] In imitation of Homer's description of the weight and size of the spear of Achilles, and of the difficulty of bending the bow of Ulysses.

1769. *Fair Phaeton.*] Timonax, in his second book of Scythics, agrees with our poet in saying, that Absyrtus had also the name of Phaeton.— Gr. Scho.

1776. *The king, like.*] This description of Æëtes is very sublime. The comparison of the king to Neptune, like all those of Apollonius, excels in propriety, and quadrates in every circumstance. The vast strength of the god of ocean illustrates that of Æëtes; both the deity and the prince are awful in their appearance, and stern in their nature; they are borne in their chariots; and they proceed to view the spectacle of severe contests of strength exerted to win an important prize.

1777. *Isthmian games.*] These games were celebrated on the isthmus of Corinth, whence they took their name. They were celebrated every three years. They were held at first in honour of Neptune, and afterwards of Melicerta, by the orders of Sisyphus, the son of Eolus, who at that time was king of Corinth; when, seeing the body of Melicerta thrown ashore by the waves at Corinth, he perceived that it was the corse of his nephew, the son of Athamas, the son of Eolus, and associated him in a share of the honour of these games. Musæus, in his work on the Isthmian games, says, which is most probable, that there were two sets of games on the Isthmus; the first, in honour of Neptune; the latter, in honour of Melicerta. The crown, in the Isthmian games, was originally of pine. It was afterwards made of parsley.—Gr. Scho. It appears from Pindar, that Isthmian games, or rather games in imitation of Isthmian, were celebrated at Syracuse; the people of which city were a Corinthian colony. The isthmus of Corinth was a very narrow neck of land, which separated the Egean and Ionian seas, as those inlets of the Mediterranean were called. It is said, that the people of Corinth, being afflicted by the plague which ravaged the Isthmus, applied to the oracle for advice; in obedience to which, they performed solemn funeral rites in honour of Melicerta, and established games to his memory.—(See Pindar, second Nemean Ode, third Strophe.) There is a description of Neptune proceeding to the Isthmian games. It was supposed that the god was personally present on that occasion; and, therefore, the young men used to receive their divine guest with the joyful sound of fifes, flutes, and other musical instruments. Pindar, in his sixth Nemean Ode, alludes to the Isthmian games, by the expression Ταυροφονω τριετηριδι; by which he intimates, that a bull was offered to the god, and that these games took place every three years. But Pliny makes the interval greater. Perhaps, in process of time, the period of celebration had been changed before the days of Pliny. His words are: *Isthmus pars altera cum delubro Neptuni quinquennalibus inclyto ludis.*

1778. *Tænarus.*] This was a promontory of Laconia. Lerna was a fountain of Argos, sacred to Neptune.—Gr. Scho.

1779. *Onchestus.*] This was a city of Bœotia, sacred to Neptune. It seems there was a famous temple of Neptune and consecrated grove in this city. It had its name of Hyantian Onchestus, from the Hyantes, a Bœotian tribe, who were so very rude and barbarous that thence came the name of ' a Bœotian swine.'— Gr. Scho.

1780. *Calaureia.*] Was a place where there

was a temple of Neptune. This temple had formerly belonged to Apollo; and the Pythian shrine to Neptune; the deities interchanged by mutual consent. The Emonian rock was a place in Thessaly, where games were held in honour of Neptune. Gerestus was a promontory of Eubœa.—Gr. Scho.

1806. *As when the charger.*] One cannot read this simile without recollecting the fine description of the war horse in Job. The Old Testament was certainly accessible, nay perhaps familiar, to the poets of Alexandria, in the translation of the seventy interpreters. It is very probable, that the fine verses in the text may have been suggested by the animated description in the Hebrew writer: ' Hast thou given the horse strength? hast thou clothed his neck with thunder? canst thou make him afraid as a grasshopper? the glory of his nostrils is terrible. He paweth in the valley, and rejoiceth in his strength: he goeth on to meet the armed men : he mocketh at fear, and is not affrighted ; neither turneth he back from the sword : the quiver rattleth against him, the glittering spear and the shield. He swalloweth the ground with fierceness and rage. Neither believeth he that it is the sound of the trumpet. He saith among the trumpets, ha, ha. He smelleth the battle afar off—the thunder of the captains, and the shouting.' Homer also has a simile of a horse; but it is a horse under a different aspect, and introduced to illustrate far different qualities and circumstances. It is the stalled horse, pampered and luxurious, breaking forth from the stable to the pastures and the mares : it is employed to exemplify the wantonness of youth and pride of beauty; it shows the graceful and high spirited but luxurious Paris, breaking forth from the bosom of ease and soft indulgence, from the bower of love. Virgil had both Homer and our poet in view, in his noble description of the horse in the third Georgic; that part, particularly, of his noble and animated description:

> Stare loco nescit, micat auribus, et tremit artus—
> Collectumque premens volvit sub naribus ignem:

seems to have been suggested by our poet.

1856. *Sudden from their stalls.*] The talents of our poet for the sublime and terrible, appear fully in this description of the encounter of Jason with the fiery bulls; which, perhaps, is equal to any thing in Homer, or any other poet ancient or modern; and ought, singly, to vindicate our poet from the charge of insipid mediocrity, so unjustly brought against him by Quintilian and Longinus. I entreat the reader to pardon my solicitude on this subject.

1887. *Firmly striding.*] The picturesque genius of Apollonius is exhibited fully in this passage. The representation of the youthful hero having thrown aside his shield, incumbent over the fiery bulls, now subdued and pressing them down, while he applies and fixes on them the brazen yoke, would furnish an admirable subject for a painter.

1910. *Goad.*] In the original, Pelasgic goad: this was a staff of ten feet in measure, pointed at the end, and used both to drive on the team of oxen and to measure land, as is remarked by Callimachus : Ἀμφότερον κεντρον τε βοων και μετρον ἀρουρης.—(Gr. Scho.) With respect to the Pelasgi, who are so often mentioned by ancient authors, and the epithet Pelasgic, which frequently occurs, the reader is requested to consult the note on ver. 387 of the fourth book of this poem.

1929. *Dragon's teeth.*] The manner in which Cadmus happened to kill this serpent was as follows: Cadmus having sent his companions into a grove, sacred to Mars, to procure water from a spring which was there, they were devoured by a serpent which guarded it. After this, Cadmus slew the monster, and having sown part of his teeth (as has been already mentioned), replenished his new city with subjects. Plato, in his treatise on Laws (lib. ii.), has given an ingenious explication of this Sidonian fable (as he calls it) of the dragon's teeth. He says, ' It is meant to show the power which legislators and rulers have, by laws and institutions, of infusing a warlike temper of mind, and forming a race of soldiers from any materials.' Hence he is said to have sown these teeth under the direction of Minerva and Mars— wisdom and valour.

1930. *Oft he turn'd.*] This is a natural and well imagined circumstance. Jason, no doubt, expected that the armed men should spring up instantaneously; and therefore turned, with anxious solicitude, to wait for them. They did not, however, spring up instantly, as the hero supposed they would have done.

1956. *And shields, &c.*] This description is very sublime and fine, and shows great powers of imagination in Apollonius.

1976. *With mute and blank amaze.*] This and the following lines are all taken from Eumelus, who makes Medea give a description of this event to Idmon. Sophocles likewise, in his Colchides, agrees with our poet. He has introduced the messenger of Æëtes, inquiring about the foregoing circumstances, in the following terms, which our poet has also imitated:

Has not the crop, appropriate to the soil,
Compacted horrent in well crested phalanx,
Sprung up all bright, in brazen panoply?—*Gr. Scho.*

1984. *As shoots a star.*] The word in the original, is ἀναπαλλεται—very expressive of the sudden and vibratory motion of the falling star. Some copies, says the scholiast, have ἀπολαμπεται; but the former reading is more poetical and forcible. This simile is as happy and expressive as can possibly be imagined, and wholly different from the preceding simile, drawn from the dark clouds clearing away, and showing the stars by night. The suddenness, the brightness, the ominous appearance of the falling star, are all illustrative of Jason, with his shining falchion, falling rapidly on the earthborn race.

1994. *As when a land.*] This simile is new; and, as far as I can find, peculiar to our author. It is highly ingenious, and illustrative of the subject. The haste and anxiety of the youth to cut down the earthborn warriors, before they should have time to range themselves in battle array; the circumstance of their falling immature, before they had fully extricated themselves from the furrow, are happily designated by the anticipated harvests of the alarmed husbandman.

2018. *As youthful plants.*] This simile is imitated from Homer. Virgil has imitated our poet, Æneid, lib. ix. ver. 435; and Ovid appears to have paid particular attention to the narrative which our poet gives, of the loves of Medea, and the acquisition of the fleece; Metam. lib. vii. ver. 104. Indeed he, in some parts, literally translates Apollonius.

NOTES AND OBSERVATIONS

ON

BOOK IV.

LINE 13. *Juno struck with fear.*] This fear was inspired by Juno, that Medea, being apprehensive of her father's severity, might the more readily be disposed to accompany the Argonauts to Greece, where the designs of the goddess required her presence, as an instrument of vengeance on Pelias, who had offended her.

14. *Timid deer.*] A fawn in the most tender state. The word, in the original, is Κεμας, which, the Greek Scholiast says, differs from νεβρος, in denoting the animal in a more helpless and infantine state, while it yet lies in the covert or cave, as yet unable to go abroad for food. In the text Apollonius intimates that Æëtes lay in wait for the Argonauts by night. The author of the Naupactica, whoever he was, relates, that he was lulled to rest by Venus.

28. *In her breast she placed.*] She placed her hoard of magic drugs and charms in her bosom, both for safety and secrecy; considering it as her most precious treasure.

29. *Kiss'd her bed.*] It was customary among the ancients to kiss inanimate things in this manner, by way of taking leave of them at parting, or gratulation on their return to them. Thus, in the Philoctetes of Sophocles, we have,—' Let us depart, O youth; first having kissed that uninhabitable cheerless seat within.'—Again,—' Go;

VOL. II.   s

having kissed the earth.'   In Virgil, Æn. ii. ver.
490.

Amplexæque tenent postes, atque oscula figunt.

34. *A tress of hair.*] It was the custom, among
the ancients, to offer up locks of their hair to
different deities.   Medea consigns hers, as a re-
membrance, to her mother.

57. *The bolts and bars, &c.*] Milton might have
taken from hence the idea of the gates of heaven
opening spontaneously to the angel.   The open-
ing of bolts, locks, and doors, in this manner, is
a favourite circumstance in the stories of sorcery
and incantation. Thus, in Macbeth; ' Open locks,
whoever knocks.'—The conflict of passion in
Medea's mind, previous to her flight, is very na-
tural and beautiful.   The poet, all through the
poem, shows himself solicitous to account for her
conduct, in deviating from the line of piety and
strict propriety, by the pressure of external cir-
cumstances, not by internal disposition to ill.
Thus, instead of exhibiting Medea as a *monstrum
nullâ virtute redemptum*, and overstepping the
modesty of nature, he consults decorum and con-
sistency of character, and gives an instructive
and moral delineation of such a personage as fre-
quently occurs in real life; of a personage, with
good natural dispositions, borne away from the
paths of rectitude by strong passions and unfor-
tunate circumstances.—How differently would a
modern German writer have drawn Medea!

68. *By paths, &c.*] There is something very
sublime and awful in this picture of Medea flying
by night; making the city gates open by her spells
and charms; and tracing the paths that she had
so often trod in quest of poisonous herbs.

75. *Goddess of the silver, &c.*] Titanis, in the

original Diana, is so called, because, as Hesiod says, ' The sun and moon were the progeny of Titan and Thea.'—Gr. Scho.

78. *Latmian.*] This was a mountain of Caria, where was a cave, in which Endymion was laid asleep; and near it was a city called Heraclea.— Gr. Scho.

80. *Endymion.*] Hesiod makes Endymion the son of Aethlius, the son of Jupiter and Calice. He is said to have obtained from Jupiter the privilege of commanding the period of his dissolution, so as to die when he pleased. With Hesiod agree Pisander, and Acusilaus, Pherecydes, and Nicander in the second book of his Etolics; as also Theopompus, in his Epopæi. But in the work entitled Μεγαλαι ηοιαι it is related, that Endymion was taken up into heaven by Jupiter; and having been beloved by Juno, and being imposed upon by the false form of a cloud, with which he became enamoured, he was cast out from heaven and descended to Hades. Sappho, and Nicander in the second book of his Europa, give us accounts of the love of the Moon for Endymion. She is said to have descended into this cave of Mount Latmos, to visit him. Epimenides says, that Endymion, being admitted into the society of the gods, was beloved by Juno; and, finding that Jupiter was enraged on that account, he demanded and obtained the privilege of sleeping perpetually. Ibycus says, that he reigned over Elis; and that, having been immortalized for his signal justice, he obtained from Jupiter the privilege (if it may be so called) of sleeping without intermission. Some writers say that he was a Spartan; others make him an Elean. Some explode altogether the fable of Endymion's being wrapped in sleep; and say

that he, being fond of hunting to an excess, used to rise by night, and pursue his sports by the light of the moon; because, at that time, the wild beasts were accustomed to come out from their lairs to feed; and that by day he used to repose, after his toils, in a cave: whence the fable arose of his being always asleep. Others attempt to allegorize the fables respecting Endymion in a different manner; and say, that he was the first who applied himself to the philosophy of the air and meteors, and to the observation of the heavenly bodies; and that, having bestowed a great proportion of his time on the contemplation of the moon, and successfully explained the phenomena of her phases, it came from thence to be said, that the moon was enamoured of him. As he watched through night to attend to his studies, and slept by day, thence came the story of his being always asleep. Some again will have it, that there really existed a person of an uncommonly drowsy habit, of the name of Endymion, who either lay in a long trance, or was so negligent of his affairs, that he always seemed to be asleep. In allusion to whose situation was formed the proverb, ' The slumber of Endymion.'

88. *Glimpses pale, &c.*] It was related in ancient legend, and believed by popular superstition, that enchantresses used to draw down the moon by their sorceries. The witches of Thessaly, in particular, were said to have possessed extraordinary powers of this kind; and, among others, Aglonicé, the daughter of Hegemon. The true meaning of the story is, that she, being skilful in astrology, was enabled to foretell when the eclipses of the moon were to happen; on which account she was supposed, by the igno-

rant people among whom she lived, to bring to
pass the alarming phenomenon which, in fact,
she only predicted. This woman was involved
in misfortunes; for, killing one of her domestics,
and being prosecuted for her crime, she gave rise
to the saying, ' They draw down the moon:' to
denote unfortunate persons.—(Gr. Scho.) The
ancients believed implicitly in the extraordinary
powers of sorcery. We find in the classics in-
numerable passages that refer to the force of
magical incantation, to draw down the moon from
her sphere. This was done to favour those rites
which were supposed to require an hour of solemn
darkness, or the ascent of departed shades and
demons, who were thought to have strong ob-
jections to the glare of light. Virgil describes
the power of enchantment in strong terms, in
Æneid iv. ver. 487 :

> Hæc se carminibus promittit solvere mentes, &c.

Tibullus gives a similar description of an en-
chantress. The poetical superstitions of the mo-
derns seem to resemble those of the ancients,
respecting the power of magic to darken the
moon, and the dislike which spectres and evil
spirits have to clear light, either of sun or moon.
To these received opinions Milton alludes, in
Par. L. ii. 665 :

> —— To dance
> With Lapland witches, while the labouring moon
> Eclipses at their charms.

And Shakspeare, in Hamlet :

> —— Thou dead corse, again, in complete steel,
> Revisit'st thus the glimpses of the moon.

97. *In flight, &c.*] The author of the Naupac-
tica says that Medea did not go out to the Ar-
gonauts by her own choice; but that, being called

out on some pretence to the temple of Vesta,
while Æëtes, who had laid an ambuscade to cut
off the Argonauts, and burn their ship, was with-
drawn from the prosecution of this scheme by
the embraces of his wife Eurylyte, the adven-
turers, at the suggestion of Idmon, took advan-
tage of this conjuncture, and sailed away, bear-
ing Medea with them.—Gr. Scho.

125. *The golden fleece.*] Apollonius represents
Medea as flying from her father's palace to the
Argonauts, before they had obtained the fleece,
and promising to put it into their hands. But the
author of the Naupactica represents her as car-
rying the fleece with her from the palace of
Æëtes; where, according to him, it was depo-
sited. Herodotus relates, that, after the de-
barkation of the Argonauts, Jason was dispatched
by Æëtes to obtain the fleece; and that he, hav-
ing proceeded on his mission, killed the dragon,
and brought away the fleece to Æëtes; who, with
the treacherous intention of destroying the Argo-
nauts, invited them to a banquet.—Gr. Scho.

141. *My fairest, &c.*] There are great delicacy
and truth of nature, in this picture of the feelings
and remorse of Medea, at finding herself a stranger
among strangers. The gallantry, politeness, and
decorum of Jason, on the occasion, are exem-
plary, and would do honour to modern manners.
The solicitude of Medea to exact his oath—an
unavailing pledge in her circumstances, is happily
imagined.

159. *Now had she rush'd.*] All these conflicts
of passion in the mind of Medea are admirably
affecting. Perhaps there is nothing in classic
lore equal to them, except the picture of the sub-
sequent distress of Medea, or of the fatal passion
of Phedra in Euripides.

171. *Fabled ram.*] Dionysius, in his Argonautics, says, that Crius was the name of the preceptor of Phryxus, who being the first to perceive the treacherous designs of his stepmother, counseled his pupil to save himself by flight, and accompanied him. Whence arose the fable, that Phryxus was saved by a ram and conveyed to Colchis.—Gr. Scho.

177. *Jove.*] Jupiter Phyxius, who was supposed to protect the movements of fugitives.

179. *Hermes.*] See Hyginus, book ii. fable 3; and the commentators on him. He is said to have offered up that ram to Jove.

183. *Sacred grove.*] In the Argonautics ascribed to Orpheus (see ver. 909) is a more particular description of this grove, and the various plants which its environs produced; of which the supposed Orpheus gives a long catalogue.

186. *Expanded wide.*] Valerius Flaccus has imitated this passage in book viii. ver. 114.

193. *Baleful and shrill.*] Virgil has imitated the passage of the original, and particularly the circumstance of the mothers clasping the infants to their bosoms:

—— Protinus omne
Contremuit nemus, et sylvæ intonuere profundæ.
Audiit et triviæ longe lacus, audiit amnis
Sulfureâ Nar albus aquâ, fontesque Velini:
Et trepidæ matres pressere ad pectora natos.

The circumstance of the mothers clasping their infants to their breasts, which is mentioned in the preceding verses of the original, is in itself highly natural and beautiful, and very tender and affecting, and seems to have been a great favourite with poets. Thus, for instance, we find it introduced in the Troades of Euripides; and Camöens has employed it in a passage where he professedly imitates Apollonius and Virgil:

Such was the tempest of the dread alarms,
The babe, that prattled in his nurse's arms,
Shriek'd at the sound: with sudden cold impress'd,
The mothers strain'd the infants to the breast,
And shook with horror.——
Lusiad by Mickle, book iv.

195. *Titanian, &c.*] So called from the river
Titanus, which gives name to the region around,
and is mentioned by Eratosthenus in his geogra-
phy.—Gr. Scho.

197. *Lycus.*] The name of a river, which, part-
ing from the Araxes, hastes to mingle with the
Phasis; and then, losing its own name, is borne
onward to the sea. The same happens with
respect to the Onochonus, a river of Thessaly,
the Parmisus, and the Sperchius; for when they
all meet at one place, they are called the Sper-
chius. The Araxes is a river of Scythia. Me-
trodorus, in his first book, respecting Tigranes,
says, that the river Thermodon was also called
Araxes.—(Gr. Scho.) There seem to have been
some doubt and difficulties arising from there
being two rivers, one Armenian, the other Scy-
thian, which bore the name of Araxes. Hero-
dotus (Clio 201) speaks thus of the Araxes:—
' The nation of the Massagetæ lay beyond the
Araxes. Some reckon this river less, others
greater, than the Danube. There are many
islands scattered up and down in it; some of
them equal to Lesbos in extent. Like the Gyndes,
which Cyrus divides into a hundred and twenty
rills, this river rises among the Matienian hills.
It separates itself into forty mouths; all of which,
except one, lose themselves in the fens and
marshes. The largest stream of the Araxes
continues its even course to the Caspian sea.
Cyrus the Great, in his attack on the Massa-
getæ, advanced to the Araxes, and threw a bridge

of boats over it.' Herodotus proceeds to give some account of the people who inhabit the islands in the Araxes. He says that they subsist, during summer, on such roots as they dig out of the earth, preserving for their winter provision ripe fruits. They have among them a tree, the fruit of which has a singular quality ; according to his account, much like that of tobacco. Having assembled round a fire, made for the purpose, they used to throw the before-mentioned fruit into it, the fumes of which had an inebriating quality. For, as the smoke ascended, these people became exhilarated, as others are with wine ; and, continuing to throw on more and more of this fruit, they began at length to leap, and dance, and sing. The Cyrus, and the Araxes (now called the Cur and the Arash), anciently flowed to the sea by different channels. See Spenser's Fairy Queen, book iv. canto xi. stanza 21 :

Oraxes feared for great Cyrus' sake ;

where, instead of Oraxes, we should read Araxes. —See Jortin. Virgil alludes to the tempestuous violence of this river, Æneid, lib. viii. l. 728: *Pontem indignatus Araxes.*—See also Chardin, tom. i. p. 181.—*On a bâti diverses fois des ponts dessus l'Araxe, mais quelques forts et massifs qu'ils fussent comme il paroit à des arches qui sont encore entières, ils n'ont pu tenir contre l'effort du fleuve. Il est si furieux lorsque le dégel le grossit des neiges fondues des monts voisins, qu'il n'y a ni digue ni autre bâtiment qu'il n'emporte.* Larcher remarks, that what Herodotus says of the Araxes applies to the Volga, which empties itself into the Caspian sea, and that by a great number of channels, and has in it many islands ; but does not (nor, indeed, could possibly) come from the Martienian or Median mountains. Herodotus, in fact, seems to have confounded the Armenian with the Scythian Araxes.

198. *Caucasian sea.*] The Euxine sea, which washed the foot of Mount Caucasus, is thence called Caucasian. The region of Caucasus overlooked the Sarmatian plains; that is to say, the desert of Astracan and the country of the Don Cossacs.

220. *Entranced, dissolved.*] Virgil has imitated this passage in the sixth Æneid, where he has described the effect of the soporific medicament on Cerberus :

> ——— Immania terga resolvit
> Fusus humi, totoque ingens extenditur antro.

He has even borrowed the very expressions of Apollonius, which are less expressive and happy in him; being applied to the serpentine species in the original, and to the canine in the imitation : *Immania terga resolvit—fusus humi, totoque extenditur antro;* which was more applicable to the serpent uncoiling his spires.

231. *A branch of juniper.*] Medea, having dipped this bough in magical drugs, bore the charm to the dragon, and accompanied it with spells and mystic songs; and thus took away the fleece, and retreated with her companion to the ship, while the monster lay asleep. Antimachus agrees with our poet in this account : but Pherecydes, in his seventh book, says, that the dragon was killed by Jason. The Arceuthus was a certain prickly plant, consecrated to Apollo; it is mentioned in the third book of the works ascribed to Musæus.—Gr. Scho.

231. *In drugs bedew'd.*] Virgil has imitated

the passage in the text, Æneid v. ver. 854, and
vi. ver. 420. See also Ovid, Met. vii. ver. 149.

249. *As when exulting.*] This simile is truly
original, and shows great ingenuity and powers
of fancy in Apollonius.

262. *Achaia.*] Or rather Achænea, Achana, or
Achanæ, was a city or district of Crete, which
abounded in stags of an extraordinary size, with
very branching horns, like our red deer. This
region of Crete is not to be confounded with
Achaia, a state of Greece.—See Gr. Scho.

269. *Now in his hands, &c.*] The behaviour of
Jason is very natural.—His youthful exultation
in the possession of the fleece, and his anxiety
lest he should be disturbed in the possession of
the treasure, are happily imagined, and well ex-
pressed. Mr. Warton is of opinion, that Virgil
had this passage in view when he described the
delight of Æneas at receiving the shield, the gift
of Venus.—See Æneid viii. ver. 618:

Expleri nequit, atque oculos per singula volvit,—
Miraturque, interque manus, et brachia versat, &c.

So Spenser, in his Fairy Queen, book vi. canto ii.
The account which Orpheus, in his Argonautics,
gives of the manner in which the fleece was
obtained and carried away, is very curious and
circumstantial; and differs, in some respects,
from that of our author. The reader, perhaps,
will not be displeased to see it in a literal trans-
lation. It extends from ver. 885 to ver. 1025,
in the original: ‘But, when Medea came clan-
destinely from the house of Æëtes to our ship,
we debated in our minds, in what manner we
should take away the golden fleece from the
sacred beech. She very quickly made us sen-
sible of what was to be done; nor had one of

us divined the unexpected labour. A direful task was presented to all our heroes, an abyss of evils yawned before us: for in front of the mansion of Æëtes, and near the guarded river, at the interval of nine ells, a vast fortification encloses it, with embattled towers and polished bars of iron. This enclosure is environed with no less than seven walls; thence open triple brazen gates, of enormous size; and within those, a lofty wall overtops, round which are golden buttresses. At the threshold of the gates sits the queen sublime, diffusing a fiery glare around, whom the Colchians worship under the name of Artemis, the keeper of the gate, resounding in the chase. Dreadful she is in aspect and in voice, to those rash men who dare approach her with steps unhallowed, before due lustrations and solemn expiatory rites are performed. These rites, concealed in mystic and awful privacy, are only known to Medea (skilful as she is in fatal and pernicious arts), and to the Colchian virgins, her companions. Nor could any man, whether native of the soil or stranger, intrude by force to tread that path of fear. For the terrors of the goddess prohibit all approach; inspiring with frantic rage. In the most secret recesses of that sanctuary a grove extends itself, shady and dark, with trees of luxuriant growth, there are many laurels and cornel trees, and lofty planes, with shrubs and plants of a less aspiring kind beneath, flourishing in the shelter of the trees: the asphodel, the honeysuckle, the beautiful adiantus, the seagrass, and the reed; the galingal, the slender and delicate aristereon, clary, wild cresses, and cyclamen divine; the stæchas or cotton lavender, the peony, the organy with branches low, the mandrake, the polion (whose leaves appear white in the morning, purple at noon, and blue when the sun declines). With these, the subtle dittany (or garden ginger), the fragrant crocus, the nasturtium, the lion's foot, the creeping smilax, the chamomile, the sable poppy, marsh-mallows, wound-wort, or all-heal, and capasum and aconite, and many other plants of noxious power, sprung up on that soil. In the midst, aspiring to the clouds, and furnished all around with wide-spreading branches that shade a great part of the grove, rises the beech, from whence hangs the fleece of gold, fastened on either hand to a long extended bough. A tremendous dragon, stationed near (a more horrible monster, and object of greater terror to man, than tongue can explain), guarded this fleece. The monster, shining with golden scales, twined around the trunk of the tree his spires of immense magnitude (a portent belonging to the Stygian realm); and guarded the treasure committed to his care, for ever twisting from side to side the baleful pupils of his green eyes. On having this unquestionable narrative of the situation of things, and particularly how the dragon kept watch around nocturnal Hecaté (all which was related to us in the clearest manner by Medea), we began to inquire, whether we might expect any prosperous end to our labour; and whether, by any means, we might appease and propitiate Diana, so as to approach that Stygian monster unharmed, and, possessing ourselves of the fleece, to return to our native land in safety. Then Mopsus arose among the heroes (for he was skilful in augury and divination, and this was suggested by his art); and advised, that they should all entreat me [Orpheus speaks here, as he always does, in the first person] to join with them in the work of rendering Diana favourable, and lulling the dreadful monster to rest. In consequence of this they came round and entreated me; but I directed the son of Æson to send away two men of might; Castor, famous for managed steeds, and Pollux, renowned for the cestus, together with Mopsus, the son of Amycus, to the projected scene of our future labour. Medea alone followed me, at a distance from the crowd. When we arrived at the temple of the goddess, and the consecrated space, there, in the level plain, I dug a trench in three rows; and quickly bringing together billets of juniper, and dry cedar, and the sharp buckthorn, and black poplar, with its whispering leaves, I raised a pyre beside the trench. Medea, supremely skilled in all the arts of incantation, brought me many things; taking them from a coffer, which she had conveyed from the fragrant recesses of her apartment. Presently, covered with a veil, I mixed the drugs and magical ingredients, then cast them on the pyre, and mixed with the blood vitriol, and the plants called Struthion (or fuller's herb), bastard saffron torn in shreds, obscene psyllium or flax-wort, the ruddy bugloss of suffocating power, and chalcimus; with this composition I filled the cavities of the bellies of the victims, and placed them on the pyre. I mixed the crude and gory intestines with pure water, and poured them about the trench. Then, robed in a sable stole, and striking at intervals the martial cymbals, I poured forth prayers. Instantly, Tisiphone, Alecto, and the awful Megera, heard me bursting the barriers of the cheerless and dark profound; shaking their torches, that emitted a lurid and ensanguined light. In a moment the trench was in a blaze, and the consuming fire crackled; the ardent flame sparkled, and wreathed around great volumes of smoke. Immediately those powers, tremendous, astonishing, inexorable, unapproachable, emergent from hell, were seen breaking through the fire. And she, with frame of iron, whom earthly mortals call Pandora; she came; and with her the phantasm, endowed with various forms, reared her threefold head (a monster dreadful to behold, nor even to be conceived by human thought), Hecaté, daughter of Tartarus. Over her left shoulder was the head of a horse; over her right that of a dog; in the midst that of a wild stag: in both her hands she wielded a sword, with an immense hilt. Pandora and Hecaté circled round the trench, and passed from side to side; and the furies followed them.— Then, the guardian form of Artemis cast to the ground the torches from her hands, and raised her eyes to Heaven. The dogs that attended her crouched with fawning tails. The bolts of the silver locks were unclosed, the beautful gates of the broad wall flew open, and the guarded grove was unfolded to view. Then I was the first to pass the threshold. After me the maid, the daughter of Æëtes, and the illustrious son of Æson; and the sons of Tyndarus then pressed on together, and Mopsus followed them. As soon as the beautiful and spreading beech appeared in nearer prospect, and the seat of hospitable Jove, and the station of the altar where the dragon rolled in spires immense; turning round, he raised his head and menacing jaws, and hissed most dreadfully. The vast expanse of air resounded; the trees resounded, shaken to and fro from the very roots; the gloomy grove resounded. Then terror seized me and my companions. Medea alone preserved an undaunted spirit within her bosom. She grasped in her hands portions of magical plants of potent influence; and I added the divine tones of my lyre. It was then that joining my piercing voice in harmony with the highest notes of the shell, and running down to the lowest keys, I sung in numbers now high, now softly deep. The song was an invocation of sleep; of sleep, the tamer of gods and men; that he might come and sooth the fury of the dragon. The power of sleep obeyed; and visited the Colchian land. He lulled to rest, in his passage, the various tribes of men, the powerful blasts of wind, the billows of the deep, the gushing springs of perennial waters, the courses of the rivers, the beasts, the birds, and all that live and move, causing them to sink down in sleep. On golden pinions he was borne; he came, and hovered over the rough but flourishing realm of the Colchians. On the instant, a drowsy influence seized the eyes of the monstrous dragon; a sleep like that of death. He wreathed about from his long spine his powerless neck and head, that seemed oppressed with its own scales. Medea, skilled in sorceries, was agreeably astonished at the sight; and encouraged the illustrious son of Æson, that he should expeditiously snatch away the fleece of gold from the tree. He, bearing away the vast fleece, proceeded to the ship.' Such is the passage of Orpheus, which is well deserving of attention, both for its poetical merit, and for the singular display of magical rites and incantations which it contains. Apollonius tells us that Æëtes, being frustrated in his intention of setting fire to the ship of the Argonauts, returned in his chariot, which was driven by the young Absyrtus. But Dionysius the Milesian (as quoted by the ancient scholiast) says, that Æëtes, finding the Argonauts at their ship, actually attacked them, and slew Iphis, the brother of Eurystheus, and many others, in the combat which ensued, and in which the Colchians were finally routed.—Pherecydes, in his seventh book, says that Medea took away Absyrtus out of his bed, and carried him to the Argonauts, at the suggestions of Jason ; and, after they were pursued, killed him, and having cut his body into small pieces scattered them in the river. In his Scythians, Sophocles says, that Absyrtus was not the uterine brother of Medea : they were not the offspring of one bed ; the youth was newly sprung from a Nereid.—Eiduia, the daughter of Ocean, bore the virgin.

310. *The leader from the sheath.*] So Virgil, Æneid, iv. ver. 579.

314. *Beside the plighted maid.*] There is something very graceful and gallant in the whole conduct and deportment of Jason on the present occasion; so that one can scarcely wonder, every thing considered, at the sacrifices Medea makes for him. There is also something highly animating in the address of the young hero to his companions. The figure of Jason, standing near Medea, with hope, love, and exultation in his countenance; the mixture of contending passions, love, grief, shame, and terror, in the looks of Medea; and the various expressions in those of the Argonauts, according to their different characters, would furnish a fine subject for a painter.

330. *A branch of flaming, &c.*] For the purpose of setting fire to the ship of the Argonauts.

353. *Not ships but feather'd, &c.*] This comparison very well illustrates the noise of the sailors, the number of their vessels, their being closely

crowded together, the whiteness of the sails, and the hurried motion of the vessels.

371. *Phineus.*] This communication of Phineus appears in the second book.

374. *Argus, &c.*] Argus convinces them that Phineus had really told them truth: since there actually was to be found a homeward route, different from that by which they had reached Colchis, which was pointed out by the Egyptian priests. Herodotus, however, in his Argonauts, says that they returned through the same sea by which they had proceeded to Colchis. Hecateus the Milesian says, that the Argonauts passed from the river Phasis to the ocean; from thence afterwards to the Nile; and from thence again to the Egean sea. This is contradicted by Artemidorus the Ephesian, who says, that the river Phasis does not fall into the ocean; and with him Eratosthenus agrees, in the third book of his geography. Timagetus, in the first book of his work on ports and lakes, says, that the Ister descends from the Celtic lake; that, after this, its waters are divided into two branches; the one of which falls into the Euxine, the other into the Celtic sea; that the Argonauts sailed through this latter mouth, and arrived at Tyrrhenia, or Tuscany. Hesiod, Pindar in one of his Pythian Odes, and Antimachus in his Lydia, say, that the Argonauts passed through the ocean to Libya, and, having carried their vessel over land, arrived at the Egean sea. With this account Apollonius agrees.—(Gr. Scholiast.) Hælzlinus blames the Scholiast for saying, that Apollonius follows the account given by Timagetus, which is not the fact; for the Argonauts are conducted by our poet through the Eridanus, or Po, and the Rhone, to the Adriatic gulf; nor was that

gulf called, at any time, the Celtic sea.—See
note of Hælzlinus.

381. *Oldest of mortals.*] Our poet asserts that
the Egyptians were the most ancient inhabitants
of the earth; but Herodotus attributes that ho-
nour to the Phrygians. Cosmes, in the first
book of his Egyptiacs; Leon, in the first of his
books addressed to his mother; and Knossus, in
the first book of his geography of Asia; all con-
cur in saying, that the Egyptians were the most
ancient of men, and that Thebes was the first
city built in that country; and with them Ni-
canor, Archimachus, and Xenagoras agree: the
second of these writers in his Metonymiæ; the
third, in the first book of his Chronology. Hip-
pys also says, that the Egyptians were the most
ancient people in the world, and the first who
formed conjectures about the temperature of the
air, and the mixture of the aerial elements which
compose the atmosphere. He adds, that the
Nile was the most productive of streams; whence
he accounts for Egypt being the land first peo-
pled. Apollonius says, that ' they lived before
all the constellations appeared:' by which he
must mean, before their nature had been explored
and understood; and their names imposed on
them. He adds, that they called the twelve
signs of the Zodiac, Θεοι βελαιοι, or ' gods en-
dowed with volition.' The planets they called
Ραβδοφορoι, or ' bearers of wands.' Herodotus
asserts that the Phrygians were the first of men;
and, in support of this opinion, tells a story, how
Psammitichus, king of Egypt, ascertained the fact
by an experiment. ' He delivered (says the
historian) two infants to a shepherd, with strict
orders to suffer no person to speak to them; but
to have them suckled by a goat. When the chil-

dren began to' articulate, the first sound they uttered was *bek*, which, in the Phrygian language, signified "bread." Hence the king concluded, that the Phrygians were the real aboriginal people, and parent stock, whence other tribes proceeded, and overspread the face of the earth.' This was but a simple conjecture, however; since it is very obvious, that this noise which the children were first observed to make, was not an attempt to speak any language, but merely an effort to imitate the sounds which they had heard from the flocks.—(Gr. Scho.) 'Certain it is, that there are few nations in the world which can pretend to an equal antiquity with the Egyptians. Their country is the only one in the world which has borne the name of a son of Noah; though it is uncertain whether Ham himself made any settlement there. However, his son Mizraim certainly peopled Egypt with his own issue, under the names of Mizraim, Pathrusim, Casluhim, and Caphtorim. And yet the Egyptians themselves, by being ignorant of their true descent, pretended even to a greater antiquity than this, asserting themselves to have been the first men in the world; which (as well as animals) they imagined must have been originally produced in their country, rather than in any other part of the world, because of the benign temperature of the air, the natural fecundity of the Nile, and its spontaneous bringing forth several kinds of vegetables; a proper food for the newly produced men and animals. And, to support this opinion by fact, they instanced in the great numbers of mice, which were every year bred out of the mud left by the Nile on its retreat; some of them, as they say, appearing alive, and formed so far as the fore part of the body only, the other part being inanimate, and without motion, as having not yet quite put off the nature of earth.'—Ant. Univ. Hist. vol. i. 8vo. p. 431.

384. *Arcadians.*] The Arcadians were said to have been before the moon, as Eudoxus relates in his Periods. Theodorus, in his twenty-ninth book, says, that the moon appeared a little before the war of the giants. And Aristo the Chian in his Theses, and Dionysius of Chalcis in the first book of his Ctisis, say the same thing, and that the race of men who peopled Arcadia were called Selenites. Mnaseas says, that the Arcadians possessed a dominion before the appearance of the moon. Aristotle, in his Polity of the Tegeates, asserts, that the Barbarians (by which, it is to be supposed, he meant the Asiatics) dwelt in Arcadia, but were expelled by an attack which the native Arcadians made on them, before the appearance of the moon, *i. e.* before its rising; whence these Arcadians obtained the name of προσεληνοι, or men anterior to the moon. Duris, in his fifth and tenth books of Macedonics, says, that Arcas, from whom Arcadia took its name, was the son of Orchomenus, the founder of a city of Arcadia, which bore his name. Some say, that Endymion, who was an Arcadian, found out the different periods of the various phenomena of the moon, and the arithmetical calculations, by which they might be ascertained; and that, from him, the Arcadians were said to be older than the moon. Some, however, ascribe these discoveries to Typhon. Xenagoras gives them to Atlas.—Gr. Scho.

The foregoing note of the Scholiast is very curious; as it shows what extraordinary opinions were held by some of the ancients. Indeed the ignorance even of learned and intelligent men among them, on many subjects of astronomy and geography, was very surprising. It appears, for instance, that Herodotus, a very inquisitive and well informed writer, did not believe that the earth was of a globular form. He expresses himself to this effect; (Melp. 36): ' I cannot but think it exceedingly ridiculous, to hear some men talking of the circumference of the earth; pretending, without the smallest reason or probability, that the ocean encompasses the earth; that the earth is rounded, as if mechanically formed so; and that Asia is equal to Europe.'

In addition to the observations of the scholiast respecting the Arcadians, it is to be observed, that some writers endeavoured to explain their boast of being older than the moon, by saying that the Greeks generally ordered their affairs according to the appearance of the new and full moon. The Spartans considered it as criminal to begin any great design before they had considered the moon, as she appeared when new, and in the full. Thus, we find, that previous to the battle of Marathon, the Athenians applied to the Spartans for succours, who agreed to furnish them, and ordered their troops to be ready to march, but at the same time declared, that they would not depart in less than five days; one of their laws forbidding them to march but at the full of the moon, of which it was then but the ninth day. The Arcadians, who were but a savage, uncouth race, contrary to the general practice of the other Greeks, transacted their business of importance before the appearance of the new moon, or that of the full, and were therefore called, in derision, προσεληνοι; which term of reproach the Arcadians artfully turned to their commendation; and affirmed, that they were older than the moon.

387. *Deucalion's blood, &c.*] The descendants
of Deucalion reigned over Thessaly, as Hecateus
and Hesiod write. Thessaly was called Pelas-
gia, from Pelasgus, who reigned in the country.
—(Gr. Scho.) The Pelasgi have been an object
of attention and curiosity to different learned
writers. The reader will find a disquisition on
the subject in the transactions of the French
National Institute, by Dupuis: ' If we believe
Ephorus (says he) and some other writers, as
Strabo, in his fifth book, and the scholiast on
Dionysius Periegetes, ver. 348. the Pelasgi
were originally Arcadians, who embraced the
profession of arms, and pushed their conquests
and colonies to a great distance from thence.
Pausanias pretends that the first savages who
inhabited Arcadia took the name of Pelasgi, and
their country that of Pelasgia; and that the name
of their king, who civilized them, was Pelasgus.
Hesiod also supposes that Pelasgus was an an-
cient indigenous prince or hero, who gave his
name to the people who were, in aftertimes,
called Danai and Argivi. These made them-
selves out to be the indigenous inhabitants of the
region. Pelasgus, *is quasi* Pelargus, a saunterer
or wanderer. Others suppose the name Pelas-
gus to be derived, with some change, from Pe-
largus, which signifies a crane; from the preva-
lent habits of this people, and their disposition
to emigrate. Herodotus distinguishes many
branches of the Pelasgic nation; as the Athe-
nians (who were called Cranai), the people of
Lemnos, the Ægialensians. This people were
only known in Asia and Europe by their hostile
incursions. Far from being the aboriginal inha-
bitants of Greece, it appears, from the language
and religious rites of the Pelasgi, that they

seemed to derive their origin from the Scythians, that is, the Celts or Scandinavians.' The Pelasgi are mentioned by Thucydides, in the beginning of his works. Some writers suppose, that the descendants of Peleg (the fourth in descent from Shem; the son of Noah, whom they imagine to have been the father of the Scythians) were the first who peopled Greece; and that they only softened the name of their progenitor Peleg, and called themselves Pelasgi. Some learned critics support this opinion, by a supposed affinity between the Hebrew and ancient Greek; and by the various dialects and pronunciations of the latter, which, in the Doric, comes nearest to the Eastern tongues, and from the remainder of those tongues, especially in places where the Pelasgians have been. The first improvements which the savage people of Greece made in their manner of living (such as exchanging their old food for more wholesome. acorns, building themselves huts to sleep in, and covering their bodies with the skins of wild beasts) were ascribed to Pelasgus, whose memory was much honoured among them on that account.

391. *Triton*.] Different causes have been assigned, by the ancients, for the overflowing of the Nile. Anaxagoras says, that it owes its increase to the melting of snows. With him Euripides agrees, saying, 'The stream renowned for virgin beauties, rolling along, swelled by the melting of the snows, irrigates the soil.' Eschylus and Sophocles conjectured also, that great snows fell in the region of Egypt, the melting of which produced the overflowing of the Nile. Nicagoras says, that the Nile flows back from the Anteci. Democritus, the natural philosopher, was of opinion, that the Nile received the super-

fluous water from the sea on the south, which was confined and overflowed; and, as to the sweetness of the waters, he endeavoured to account for that, by the length of its course over a vast interval of country; and by the heat of the sun, which evaporated the salt, and changed its taste. The opinion of Aristo the Chian was, that the sun in winter being beneath the earth, draws in and contracts the water; but in summer, being above the earth, he no longer does so, by reason of the earth's being more heated; on which account, her veins are relaxed and expanded, and she throws out the more water from her hidden and inward springs. Ephorus says, that Egypt is full of subterraneous springs and streams that flow under ground, and that the hot sun in spring, causing the earth to crack and open, gives them a passage, and thus enables them to rise to light, and increase the waters of the Nile. Thales the Milesian was of opinion, that the clouds, driven together by the Etesian winds, and congregated at the mountains of Ethiopia, were there broken; and, descending in torrents of rain, caused the waters of the Nile to swell. In addition to this, he said, that the Etesian winds, blowing all the hot season over the Mediterranean sea in a contrary direction to the course of the river, obstructed the passage of the waters of the Nile, as they flowed to the sea; and, by causing them to accumulate and rise above their banks, produced an inundation of the country. The opinion of Democritus was, that the overflowing of the Nile was caused by the sun's attraction of snowy vapours from the frozen mountains of the north, which being carried by the wind southward, and thawed by warmer climates, fell down upon Ethiopia in

deluges of rain. And the same thing is advanced
by Agatharcides of Cnidus, in his Periplus of
the Red Sea. Diogenes of Apollonia was of
opinion, that the augmentation of the Nile was
caused by the action of the sun raising the
waters of the sea, so as to cause them to be
poured into the bed of the Nile. He also thinks
that the Nile is increased, in summer, by the
sun's turning into it the dews and exhalations
from the earth. Such are the opinions enume-
rated by the Greek Scholiast, on the 269th verse
of our poet. There were other opinions equally
chimerical; as, for instance, that of Herodotus.
' The Nile overflows in summer, because in win-
ter the sun, driven from his usual course by
storms, ascends into the higher regions of air
above Libya; and to whatever region this power
more nearly approaches, there the rivers and
streams are dried up: thus in winter the Nile is
diminished, by the near approach of the sun in
the regions near Egypt; while in summer the
greater distance of the sun diminishes the cause
of evaporation, and allows the waters to swell.'
This opinion, which is obviously very absurd, is
fully refuted by Diodorus Siculus. The reader
will find all the various opinions on this subject
recounted in the oration of Aristides on the
increase of the Nile.

The Nile, at different times, bore different ap-
pellations. It was at first called the Triton; it
afterwards obtained the name of Nile, from
Nilus the centaur, the son of Tantalus, who
reigned over the country, as Hermippus relates.
(See Gr. Scho.) The name given to the Nile, in
Homer, is Egyptus: it also had the name of
Cronides, in ancient times. Pliny says, that the
Nile was called Siris. With this denomination

the Scriptures agree, which speak of the waters of Seir.

396. *A valiant chieftain.*] Sesostris, or Sesonchosis, was king of all Egypt. He reigned next in succession after Orus, the son of Isis and Osiris. This monarch, having made an inroad into Asia, subdued it, and also a considerable part of Europe. The most accurate account of his actions is found in Herodotus. Theopompus, in his third book, calls him Sesostris, not Sesonchosis. Herodotus relates, that if he happened to overthrow any nations in war, he erected columns expressive of the manner of his conquest. If the people in question had made a feeble and pusillanimous defence, the columns bore certain attributes, or ensigns, of the softer sex. If, on the contrary, they had made a brave and vigorous defence, the columns bore the attributes of the male kind. As to the time when Sesonchosis lived, Apollonius says only, in general terms, that he was very ancient. But Dicearchus, in his second book, says, that Sesonchosis affected the Grecian manner of living; and was said to have established laws, by which it was ordained that the son should not forsake the trade of his father: the permitting of which, he apprehended, would tend to too great an irregularity of ranks and conditions. They say, too, that he was the first who taught men to ride on horseback; though some refer these institutions to Cyrus.—Gr. Scho.

This institution which the Scholiast mentions, confining the son to the profession of his father, is noticed by other writers. Not only the husbandman and shepherd were obliged to follow the vocation of their fathers; but this ordinance extended to all arts and trades: and each person was confined to that which his ancestors had exercised, without a power of meddling with any other. Thus, being cut off from all hopes of rising to the magistracy, and having no room for popular ambition, they stuck closely to what they professed. They were never permitted to concern themselves with civil affairs; and if they attempted it, or undertook any business which did not belong to their hereditary profession, they were severely punished. There is something like this in what prevails at this day in the East Indies, where the people are divided into casts or classes, and each class is confined to a certain hereditary art or employment, and prohibited, under the most formidable penalties, from intermeddling with that belonging to another.

Sesostris was called by various names, as Sesoosis, Sesonchis, Sesonchosis, Sesothis. Sir Isaac Newton is of opinion, that Sesostris is the Osiris of the Egyptians, the Bacchus of the Greeks, and the Sesac of the Scriptures; and, among other arguments, draws one from the passage quoted from Dicearchus by the Scholiast of Apollonius. He not only overran all the countries which Alexander afterwards invaded, but crossed both the Indus and Ganges; and thence penetrated to the Eastern ocean. He thence turned towards the north, and attacked the nations of Scythia, until at last he arrived at the Tanais, or Don, which divides Europe and Asia. Justin, however, tells us that Sesostris, dispatching ambassadors to summon the Scythians to surrender, they sent back his messengers with contempt and defiance, and immediately took up arms. Sesostris, being informed that they were marching towards him, faced about suddenly, and fled before them; leaving his baggage and warlike apparel to the pursuers, who followed him till they had reached the borders of Egypt. Pliny relates, that he was overthrown by the king of Colchis, lib. xxxiii. c. 3. And Valerius Flaccus intimates (Argonaut. lib. v. ver. 420), that he was repulsed with great slaughter, and put to flight in these parts. Whether he had good or bad success in these countries, it is a common opinion that he settled a colony in Colchis: though Herodotus, who is most worthy of credit, does not decide whether it was of his own planting, or whether part of his army, tired out, loitered in the rear, and voluntarily sat down on the banks of the river Phasis. He says, from his own experience, that the inhabitants were undoubtedly of Egyptian descent, as was visible from the personal similitude they bore to the Egyptians, who were swarthy and frizzle-haired; but more especially from the conformity of their customs, particularly circumcision, and from the affinity of their language with that of Egypt. And many ages afterwards at Eä, the capital of Colchis, they showed maps of their journeys, and the bounds of sea and land, for the use of travellers; and hence came geography.—(See Hesiod. Diod. Sic. lib. i. Univ. Hist. vol. ii.) It is rather extraordinary (as some of the commentators of our author, and Mr. Bryant observe), that Apollonius, who was himself an Egyptian, when he comes to mention the exploits of this prince, suppresses his name. Perhaps he was doubtful by what appellation most properly to distinguish him, as he was known under so many. The Scholiast quotes an ancient writer, named Scymnus, who composed a description of Asia, as corroborating what is said by Herodotus respecting the conquests and colonies of Sesostris.

It is said by some, that the repulses which Sesostris experienced, together with the revolt of his brother Danaus, put a stop to his victories; and that, in returning home, he left part of his men in Colchis and at Mount Caucasus, under Æëtes and Prometheus; and his women upon the river Thermodon, under their new queens, Marthesia and Lampeto: for Diodorus, speaking of the Amazons, says, that they dwelt originally in Libya, and there reigned over the Atlantides; and, invading their neighbours, conquered as far as Europe.　Mr. Whiston is of opinion, that Sesostris is the very Pharaoh who perished in the Red Sea, and the very Typhon of the mythologists.　Dicearchus (as quoted by the Scholiast, on this present passage of Apollonius) says, in his first book, that from the reign of Sesonchosis to Nilus was a period of two thousand five hundred years; from the reign of Nilus to the fourth Olympiad, four hundred and thirty-six years: so that the whole time made a period of two thousand nine hundred and thirty-six years.　The passage, in the original, is obscure and difficult; but is certainly curious, as being connected with the history and antiquities of Egypt.　It is one of those in which Apollonius indulges his passion for ancient history and tradition: and as he was a man of great reading, he must be considered as preserving many things from other ancient writers.

405. *Eä's walls.*] The poet makes Argus say, that Eä had remained unshaken and prosperous from the irruption of Sesostris to his time; and that the descendants of those who had been planted in Colchis by that conqueror still subsisted.—Gr. Scho.

411. *Tablets sculptured.*] The ancient Egyp-

tians were the inventors of many useful arts and sciences. Geometry is, on all hands, agreed to have been first found out in their country. It is generally supposed too, that astronomy was invented by them; as, by reason of the constant serenity of the air, and the flatness of the country, they could observe the heavenly motions earlier, and with more ease, than other people. The Egyptian learning was partly inscribed on columns, and partly committed to writing, in the sacred books. Not only the Egyptians, but several other ancient nations, used to preserve the memory of things by inscriptions on pillars; to say nothing of those which Seth (as it is pretended) set up, before the flood, for the same purpose. We are told, that the Babylonians kept their astronomical observations engraved on bricks; and Democritus is said to have transcribed his moral discourses from a Babylonish pillar. But the most famous of all were the columns of Hermes in Egypt, mentioned by many authors. On them, he is said to have inscribed his learning, which was afterwards explained more at large, by the second Hermes, in several books. It is certain, at least, that, from these pillars, the Greek philosophers and Egyptian historians took many things. Pythagoras and Plato both read them, and borrowed their philosophy from thence. Sanchoniatho and Manetho made use of the same monuments, which were still remaining in the time of Proclus, or not long before. They stood in certain subterraneous apartments near Thebes. To these inscriptions succeeded the sacred books, somewhat more recent, but not less famous; to which Sanchoniatho and Manetho are also said to have been beholden for the perfecting of their histories. These books not only contained what related to the worship of the gods, and the laws of the kingdom, but historical collections; nay, even all kinds of miscellaneous and philosophical matter of considerable moment; which accounts for their having those memorials touching the course of the Danube. For it was part of the business of the priests, or sacred scribes, to insert in those public registers whatever deserved to be recorded and transmitted to posterity, as well as carefully to preserve what had been delivered down to them from their ancestors.—See Ant. Univ. Hist. vol. i. p. 480.

411. *Tablets sculptured.*] Κυρβεις, in the original, which the Scholiast says, means the tables or columns of stone on which the laws used to be written in popular states, as is mentioned by Apollodorus. These tables were called Κυρβεις, *quasi* Κορυφεις: first, by a syncope or abbreviation of the word; and, after, by changing the letter φ into β. This account of the origin of the name in question is to be found in the ancient Scholiast on the ' Clouds of Aristophanes.' It is said, that in process of time, when the laws came to be written on tablets of wood painted white, they were also called *cyrbes*; although the word properly denotes the tables, or columns of stone only, which contained sacred writings; as we are assured by Eratosthenes. The tablets at Athens, on which the laws were written, were called Ἀξονες. Some, who pretend to superior accuracy, say, that the ἀξονες were four square stones; the Κυρβεις triangular; and that the laws were inscribed, indifferently, on both the one and the other.—(See the Greek Scholiast, l. 280.) In conformity with the foregoing account, it will be recollected, that the laws of Moses were written by God on tables of stone. But, as is justly ob-

served by Hælzlinus, it does seem that the poet, in the passage before us, meant not to speak of the tables on which laws were inscribed; but rather of such tables as are mentioned by Elian, in the third book of his Written History, and called by him *πιναχια*; which, in fact, were geographical monuments or delineations of different countries, executed on columns of stone, plastered over, and after that painted. We have had an instance of a work, in the present times, of a nature somewhat analogous; a map, or geographical delineation of France, according to its later boundaries, engraved or sculptured on marble, and coloured.

415. *Remotest horn.*] All rivers are said to be horns of the ocean. The Ister is said to be a remote horn, because it springs in Scythia, a distant region.—Gr. Scho.

419. *Majestic Ister.*] The poet says that the Danube is the same with Ister; whence Ovid calls the Ister Binomian: and that it descends from the country of the Hyperboreans and the Riphean hills—(in this he follows the authority of Eschylus, in his ' Prometheus freed'), and is divided between the Scythians and Thracians. And also, that one branch falls into the sea which bathes the shores of Greece, the other into the Adriatic gulf. The Riphean hills are situated to the eastward: a circumstance to which Callimachus alludes. Eratosthenes, in the third book of his geography, says that this river flows from desert regions, and surrounds the island of Peucé. But no one, except Timagetus, whom Apollonius followed, pretends to say that the Argonauts sailed through the Ister into the Grecian sea. Scymnus asserts, that they sailed through the Tanais into the great sea, and thence into the

Grecian sea: he conjectures that the Argonauts,
when they arrived at the continent between the
two seas, carried their vessel on poles or great
lances, until they reached the other sea. Hesiod
asserts, that they sailed through the Phasis:
Hecateus, consulting him, says that the Phasis
could not bring them from Colchis to the sea;
nor will he allow that they sailed through the
Tanais. He maintains that they held the same
route homewards which they had pursued in their
way to Colchis; as Sophocles, in his Scythians,
relates, and Callimachus: whence they say it
happened that the Scythians, who sailed into
the Adriatic sea, did not meet with the Argo-
nauts, while others, who passed through the
Cyanean rocks, overtook them at Corcyra. But
the Ister, as soon as it comes into the region be-
tween Scythia and Thrace, is divided into two
branches; and the one discharges itself into the
Euxine, the other into the Tyrrhenian sea.—
(Gr. Scho.) Such is the note of the ancient
annotator on our poet: it is not very clear or
intelligible. Probably the text may have been
corrupted: I have given it in his own words.
It is, however, curious, and deserving of notice,
as it shows the strange notions which the ancients
entertained; and their gross ignorance on geo-
graphical subjects.

It is not surprising that our author, and other
poets, either from real ignorance, or from their
desire of entertaining their readers by fabulous
and fanciful embellishments, and marvellous inci-
dents, should depart from physical and geogra-
phical truth, as they have done in many instan-
ces; and from authentic history; since we find
such material deviations, in this respect, in such
a sober and judicious writer as Herodotus, who

took considerable pains on the subject of geography. The Danube was the greatest river, excepting the Nile, known to Herodotus. He conceived, that it underwent two variations in size in Summer and Winter; (Melpom. 48—50.) —See, too, his errors as to the relative position of the Caspian, Euxine, and Persian seas, to each other, and to the Mediterranean. It is observable, too, that Apollonius does not here speak in his own person, or pledge himself for the truth of what is advanced respecting the course of the Danube, the face of the country, or the different routes by which the Argonauts might expect to reach Greece from Colchos. He cautiously puts all that is said on the subject into the mouth of Argus. who professes to derive his knowledge from the traditions of the ancient Egyptians; and in making him deviate from the truth, one might imagine that the poet thought he gave a more faithful picture of the rudeness and ignorance of the age he meant to describe; did we not find him, in the sequel, actually conducting his Argonauts home by a route which sets geography at defiance.

The poet must confound the Riphean of Scythian mountains, at the heads of the Tanais, with the Alps; or else must have been wholly ignorant of the true source of the Danube; which rises (see Cox's Travels into Swisserland, vol. i. p. 3), near the Alps; in that part of the circle of Suabia, on the west, which adjoins the Swiss bounds, at a place called Donauschingen. ' This place is the principal residence of the Prince of Furstenberg, and in the court-yard of the palace the Danube takes its rise.'—See too Pliny, lib. iv. cap. 12.

422. *Boreas 'gins to blow*.] The springs of the

Ister are not exactly to the north of Greece, but to the north-west.   Nor is what the poet says of the Riphean hills (which, with respect to the Danube, must be taken to be the same with the Alps), namely, that they are seated beneath the north pole, to be exactly scrutinized.   It is actually a part of poetic skill to seem to think, and really to speak, with the vulgar; and to mask the truth, by choice, in fables, that it may not shine out too palpably, and become less susceptible of ornament.   Stuckius says, that by Riphean mountains here, Apollonius means the Rhetian Alps.—Hælzlinus.

428. *Trinacria's tides.*] The sea that washed the shores of Sicily, called Trinacria; from its three promontories, Pachinus, Lilybæum, and Pelorus.   The poet means to say, that one branch of the Ister flows into the Adriatic, the other into the Tuscan sea; which, by catachresis, he calls the Trinacrian sea.—Gr. Scho.

429. *My native coast.*] Greece.   Argus here speaks of himself as a Grecian; and properly does so, being sprung from Athamas: and he confirms his assertion by adding, Greece is my native land, as sure as Achelous is a Grecian river.—See the Gr. Scho.

437. *Lycus' offspring.*] Dascylus, son of Lycus, king of the Mariandyni, who had been sent by his father as a guide to the Argonauts, and had hitherto accompanied them.—See book ii.

454. *Ionian bound.*] The Ionian sea was properly that which bathes the coast of Italy on the one hand, and part of Greece and Dalmatia on the other; and into which the Adriatic opens. It took its name from Ionius, a person of Illyrian race; as Theopompus mentions in his twenty-first book.—(Gr. Scho.)   Or rather, from the

tribe of Ionians, who peopled great part of Greece and Asia Minor, and are supposed to be the descendants of Javan. Thus Milton says: 'The Ionian gods, of Javan's issue held gods.' It was called by some, anciently, the Adriatic; indeed the two names of Ionian and Adriatic were used indifferently.

457. *Peucé*.] Eratosthenes, in his geography, writes, that in the Danube there is an island of a triangular form, equal in dimension to Rhodes; that this island abounds in pines, whence it takes its name; that the vertex of the triangle is turned towards the course of the river, dividing the stream; and that the base or broadest side is presented to the sea. Its two other sides are thus placed parallel to the banks of the river.—Gr. Scho.

465. *Through this*.] The two channels, by which the Danube is said here to discharge itself into the sea, were called Arax and Calon. The Argonauts passed through the former; Absyrtus, with the Colchians, through the latter.—Gr. Scho.

469. *The rude and timorous, &c.*] Dryden endeavours to describe an impression of this kind, in his play of the Indian Emperor (Act. i. Sc. 2); but exaggerates the thoughts to bombast; as is too frequently his manner.

474. *Scythian race*.] The country of the Scythians answered to that of the Ukraine, the Nogais Tartars, and the Don Cossacs. This is a flat country: the Laurian plain here spoken of was one of those extensive plains in which Scythia abounded. Timonax (as quoted by the Greek Scholiast) writes, in his first book concerning Scythia, that there were fifty different tribes belonging to that country. The Sigunni and Graucenii were of the number. The former took their

name from a kind of spear used by them. The Sindi were the people in whose region the Ister divided itself. Hellanicus, in his first book concerning nations, says, that as you sail into the Bosporus, the Sindi occur; and above them the Mæotæ, or Mæotic Scythians.—(Gr. Scho.) There were, in fact, two countries of the name of Scythia—the Western or Euxine, and the Eastern or country of the Massagetæ. Western Scythia was a member of Europe; Eastern, of Asia.

475. *The wild Sigynian, &c.*] Herodotus speaks thus of the country, Euterp. 19. ' With respect to the more northern parts of this region, and its inhabitants (Thrace), nothing has yet been decisively ascertained. What lies beyond the Ister is a vast and almost endless space. The whole of this (as far as I am able to learn) is inhabited by the Sigynæ, a people who in dress resemble the Medes; their horses are low in stature and of a feeble make, but their hair grows to the length of five digits. They are not able to carry a man; but, yoked to a carriage, are remakable for swiftness: for which reason, carriages are here very common. The confines of this people extend almost to the Eneti, on the Adriatic. They call themselves a colony of the Medes.'

479. *Angurus.*] A mountain near the river Ister. Timagetus mentions it, in his work on ports and harbours.—Gr. Scho.

480. *Cauliac rock.*] This was a rock in Scythia, near the Ister, of which Polemo speaks in his origin of Italian and Sicilian colonies. It is said by the poet, that the Ister divides into its two arms at Mount Angurus; one going to the Euxine, the other to the Adriatic sea.—Gr. Scho.

485. *Chronian deep.*] The Adriatic sea. It was called Chronian because of the supposition that

Chronus or Saturn passed from Greece into Italy, which bordered on the Adriatic sea. Hence Italy is called, by Virgil, Saturnian: *Salve magna parens rerum Saturnia tellus.* This fable is mentioned by Ennius, in his Annals: *Saturnus quem Celu, genuit;* and by L. Accius, in his Annals, as quoted by Macrobius. The near situation of Italy to the west of Greece naturally led the Greeks to transfer Chronus to Italy. Anciently, also, it was believed, that the west was nearer to the infernal regions, and therefore to Tartarus, whither Saturn was thrust down.—So Virgil, Æneis, lib. viii. ver. 319. On account of this flight of Saturn, the Adriatic sea is called the 'bosom of Rhea,' by Æschylus, in his Prometheus, ver. 836. See professor Heyne's fifth essay on the seventeenth book of the Æneis.

491. *Dian.*] In the original, Artemis Bryteis, or rather Brygeis; from the Bryges or Brygii, a people of Illyria, who are mentioned in a subsequent part of this book. See ver. 471, or Bryges, *quasi* Phryges. See a preceding note on the Phrygians.

505. *Treaty.*] The Minyæ, finding themselves so much outnumbered by the Colchians, and fearing that they might be overpowered and cut off by them, resorted to artifice to supply what they wanted in force: or, at least, to produce some advantage by delay. They, therefore, entered into a negotiation with their opponents, tending to a compromise; the terms of which were to be, that Medea should remain, for a time, in the hands of certain arbitrators, who were to determine whether she should be restored to her parents, or remain with Jason: and that, in the meanwhile, the Argonauts should retain the possession of the golden fleece. It seems to be pro-

bable that the Argonauts, having gained their object by the assistance of Medea, did not wish to be encumbered with her; or, at least, did not desire to expose themselves to any dangers on her account, and therefore seriously thought of giving her up, until they were turned from their purpose by her spirit and eloquence. This part of the original is very obscure and unsatisfactory. It does not appear who, on the part of the Argonauts, entered into the negotiation mentioned by the poet. Perhaps Jason himself secretly wished to leave Medea behind. The poet also has forgot to mention who were the arbitrators, whose decision was to be conclusive as to the destiny of Medea. They were, most probably, some princes of the neighbourhood. Apollodorus here differs from our poet.

523. *She mark'd, &c.*] Our poet was certainly much indebted for the impassioned and eloquent passage which succeeds to the Medea of Euripides, which contains some of the most pathetic and beautiful sentiments imaginable on the subject of a wife being deserted by her husband. Virgil has imitated the expostulatory address of Medea to Jason; Æneis, lib. iv. ver. 305. There is the same passion in both. It seems also, that Catullus had this passage of our author in view in his fine poem of the Epithalamium of Peleus and Thetis, where he introduces Ariadne complaining:

Siccine me patriis abductam perfide ab oris
Perfide, &c.

And particularly in the line following, which seems to be a transcript from Apollonius:

At non hæc quondam blanda promissa dedisti.

The passages in Virgil are so universally known, that it were idle to transcribe them here; the reader, who turns to them, will see how closely the Latin poet follows his Grecian master.

Medea was one of those dramatic characters which Horace considered as fully known and ascertained by tradition: *Sit Medea ferox invictaque.* Our author has well adhered to the outline of this delineation. In every situation she exhibits a fierce and indomitable mind. At the same time, she is not divested of feminine softness, and the graces of her sex. This shows great art and happiness, the hand of a master in the portrait.

610. *To hurl the brand.*] The same idea occurs to Dido, in the fourth Æneid, *Implessemque foros flammis:* and a little after, *Memet super ipsa dedissem.*

633. *This treaty shall confound.*] According to the account given of it by Jason, the artifice of the treaty consisted in the deceiving Absyrtus with the prospect of obtaining what he sought in a peaceable manner, and inducing him to wait until his numerous forces should disband of themselves; after which, it seems to have been the plan of the Argonauts and their leader, to fall upon him when they found his numbers greatly diminished by the departure of his followers. The speech of Jason is perfectly in character; calm, artful, and plausible.

656. *Heralds.*] These must have been heralds sent from the Colchians, for the purpose of reclaiming Medea: ' If I can induce these men (says the princess), by my artful representations, to cooperate in my views, they may be made the instruments of inducing Absyrtus to come and put himself into our power.'

658. *By thine hand to fall.*] There is something, perhaps, that shocks probability and decorum in

X 2

the ferocity of the sentiments attributed here to Medea.—Yet the Lady Macbeth of Shakspeare is equally fierce and sanguinary.

666. *Lemnian queen.*] Hypsipyle. She was daughter to Thoas, king of Lemnos, who was the son of Bacchus and Ariadne. We have seen, in the first book, how the life of this prince was preserved by the piety of his daughter.

678. *Nyseian god.*] Bacchus was so called from Nysa, a city of Arabia, where he was nursed. There was also another city of the same name in India, founded by Bacchus. One of the two tops of Mount Parnassus, which was consecrated to Bacchus, was likewise called Nysa.

681. *From Gnossus.*] This was a city of Crete, whence Theseus bore away Ariadne, the daughter of Minos, king of the island. There is something ingenious and happily ominous of the future fate of Medea, in the making Jason present her with gifts which he had received from Hypsipyle, whom he abandoned; and which had formerly belonged to Ariadne, who had been deserted by Theseus.

682. *Dia's shore.*] This was the same with the island of Naxus. Callimachus recognises this appellation, which was more ancient than that of Naxus.

696. *Hurl'd spells.*] Thus Milton, in his mask of Comus,

> ———— I hurl
> My dazzling spells into the spungy air,
> Of power to cheat the eyes with blear illusion.

699. *Pernicious love.*] Thus we have 'Ουλος ερως. And, in Virgil, Æneid iv.

> Improbe amor, quid non mortalia peotora cogis?

And again,

> Quid non mortalia pectora cogis, auri sacra
> Fames?

705. *O Muse, relate.*] The poet here invokes the muse to relate the subsequent transaction, in order to show how apprehensive he was, that the unnatural atrocity of Medea might appear incredible to posterity; and might, therefore, require the sanction of divine testimony. Apollonius is not here like some writers, who think it incumbent on them to make their heroes and heroines always in the right, and to find or invent some plausible pretence for every thing they do. He does not attempt to conceal or palliate the turpitude of the conduct of Medea and Jason, but speaks of them with the proper abhorrence that their crime deserved.

731. *Wily sister.*] See the description of the character of Pandora in Hesiod.

738. *Veil.*] The circumstance of Medea's covering her face with her veil, that she might not see the death of her brother, though she was the very person who had suggested the idea of murdering him, had instigated Jason to commit the deed, and even delivered the victim into his hands, reminds one of the momentary and abortive remorse of Lady Macbeth:

> ———— Had he not resembled
> My father as he slept, myself had don't?

The circumstance of the veil might have been suggested to the poet by the device of Timanthes the painter, who, representing the sacrifice of Iphigenia, and finding himself unable to depict the feelings of Agamemnon, threw a veil over the face of the monarch; and made him cover his eyes, that he might not behold the sacrifice of his child.

758. *Fury.*] The origin of the Furies was very extraordinary, and worthy of their nature and functions. When Chronus, the son of Uranus, at the instigation of his mother Terra, dismembered his father, the Furies were produced from the drops of blood which fell on the ground at that time. Æschylus, however, makes them the daughters of Night. Epimenides, or rather Empedocles, assigns Chronus as their father in these lines :

> Of him was golden Venus radiant hair'd,
> Of him the' eternal Fates, and last dread birth, -
> The Furies, ranging earth to punish crimes.

761. *First fruits.*] As of victims slain at the altar, from which certain parts were taken in the first instance. The ancients were possessed with such a weak superstition, that they believed if any person were treacherously slain, the murderer might escape the punishment due to his guilt, and still the terrors of his own conscience, if he were to cut off certain extremities of the dead body, and suspend them under his armpits. We find this custom alluded to in the Electra of Sophocles.—See Gr. Scho. and Hælzlinus.

771. *Entomb'd his bones.*] There was a city built at the place where the bones of Absyrtus were buried, called after him Absyrtus. It is mentioned by Apollodorus Eustathius in his comment on Dionysius Periegetes, and by Strabo, lib. vii.

792. *Peleus thus.*] This speech of Peleus is well suited to his character, which was a happy mixture of prudence and daring. The Argonauts were even yet apprehensive of the Colchians, and doubtful whether they should put to sea, until they were determined by his arguments.

806. *Electris.*] This was an island near the

mouth of the river Po, in the Adriatic gulf.—
See subsequent notes.

815. *Dispersed they roam.*] Some of these Col-
chians settled in the region where Absyrtus was
treacherously killed, and lay interred, and were
called from him Absyrtensians. Others of them
settled in Illyria, in the district of Enchelyes,
near the Ceraunian mountains.—(Gr. Scho.) The
Ceraunian mountains were high hills, on the bor-
ders of Epirus, near Valona, reaching even to
the sea, where the Ionian sea is separated from
the Adriatic. They are now called Monti di
Chimera. Heyne observes, that it is said by
Apollonius that the Colchians, who settled at
the Ceraunian mountains, migrated from the con-
tinent to an island opposite. Now there is no
island opposite and contiguous to the Ceraunian
mountains of Epirus. There were indeed, in
Illyricum, Ceraunian mountains, which are men-
tioned both by Pliny and Ptolemy, and there
are a multitude of islands opposite to Illyricum.
The recollection of this may throw some light on
the passage of Apollonius before us.

824. *Cadmus, Harmonia.*] Harmonia was a
princess of Samothrace, the daughter of Corytus,
by Electra, the daughter of Atlas. Her brothers
were Jasius and Dardanus. The former suc-
ceeded his father in the kingdom of Samothrace,
whence he removed to Phrygia, and left the
government of Samothrace to his brother Dar-
danus. Harmonia married Cadmus, whom her
brother had initiated in the mysteries of religion.
According to other fables, Cadmus married Her-
mione, the daughter of Mars and Venus; or, as
others call her, Harmonia; on which occasion
the gods came to Cadmus, and assisted at his
wedding. By her he had a son, named Poly-

dorus, and four daughters, Semele, Ino, Autonoé, Agave. For the fate of these, see Ovid and Euripides.—Vide Apollodori Bibliotheca, lib. iii. cap. 4.

825. *Enchelean race.*] These people lived on the confines of Illyria; being at war with the Illyrians, their neighbours, they were commanded by the oracle to choose Cadmus as their general. He left Thebes to his son Polydorus, and went to head them. Here it is that he and his wife were feigned to have been turned into serpents; a story, to which the name of the people among whom they settled might have given occasion. Some interpret this fable to signify, that they degenerated from their pristine civility to barbarians. Here Cadmus had another son, whom he either called Illyrius, from the Illyrians, his new conquered subjects, or else that people took their name from him: Dionysius Periegetes speaks of the transformation of Cadmus and Harmonia, and of the tomb erected to their memory.

833. *Hyllean seats.*] The Hyllenses were a people of Illyria. They were so called from Hyllus, the son of Hercules. Hercules had this son by the nymph Melita.

857. *Pheacia.*] This was the ancient name of the island of Corcyra, so much celebrated by Homer and our poet; and so famous, in latter times, for the dreadful seditions which raged among its inhabitants. It is now known by the name of Corfu. It was subject, for some centuries, to the Venetians; but has lately become part of the republic of the Seven Islands.

858. *Melita.*] The nymph Melita was the daughter of Nereus, whose residence was in the Egean sea.—(See post, ver. 922.) The island of Malta seems to have been called after her.

860. *Nausithous.*] He was the son of Neptune and Peribea, and father of Alcinous.

862. *Macris.*] An island on the coast of Caria. It was anciently known by the name of Scheria.

866. *In frantic mood, &c.*] Eurystheus, son of Sthenelus, who reigned in Mycenæ, began to look on Hercules with a jealous eye, on account of his title to the crown, as being the reputed son of Amphytryon, the cousin german of Eurystheus; and fearing lest, in time, he should be dispossessed by the hero, his hatred and jealousy rose to such height, that he left no means untried to destroy him. Hercules, who was not insensible of the motives which led Eurystheus to engage him perpetually in some desperate enterprise or other, consulted the oracle on the subject; and received for answer, that it was the pleasure of the gods that he should serve and implicitly obey Eurystheus for twelve years. By this response he was thrown into a deep melancholy, which, in the end, turned into furious madness; during the paroxysms of which, among other outrageous acts, he put away his wife Megara, and murdered all his children by her, which are supposed to have been twelve; because the king imposed on him that number of labours as an expiation for their death. After this he was restored to his senses. It must have been long after these events that the Argonautic enterprise took place, since they are alluded to in the course of the narrative.

885. *Sing, ye Muses.*] Thus Milton, Paradise Lost, book i.

Say, Muse, their names then known, who first, who last,
Roused from their slumber on that fiery couch.

The poet interrogates the Muse how the Argonauts pursued their voyage after the death of

Absyrtus, and how they arrived at the sea.
This invocation of the Muse is introduced to give
a greater air of solemnity and authenticity to the
narrative. Apollonius seems to have been aware
that many would censure the long narrative of
the circuitous navigation of his heroes, as wholly
fictitious and improbable. He seems to have
known the true description of the earth, as far
as it was known then; and to have designedly
made the truth bend to poetical tradition; from
which, perhaps, he did not think himself at li-
berty to depart, in a story of so much celebrity,
and which had been treated by so many writers,
as the Argonautic expedition. It is observable,
that Apollodorus, the Athenian, a prose writer,
agrees with our poet in the most wild and ro-
mantic parts of his story, and particularly in the
gross deviations from geographical truth. This
evinces, that all the incidents of ' the Argonautic
tale divine,' were so received and settled, by ge-
neral tradition, that a departure from them would
have appeared a sort of sacrilege. The poet,
therefore, meant his invocation of the Muse as a
sort of apology for his deviation from what he
knew to be true; for his gross and monstrous
errors in points of geography. It is intended as
an intimation to his reader, that he himself did
not believe in what he narrated, but knew it to
be fictitious. After all, why should Apollonius
be more accurate than Virgil? The description
of the strait of Messina of the latter, with its
Scylla and Charybdis, is known to be a mere
poetic fiction. In truth, the narrative of the voy-
age of the Argonauts is not more improbable
than those which Homer and Virgil give of the
wanderings of their heroes in the narrow seas
branching out into the Mediterranean, for ten or

for seven years; the shortest of which periods would have been sufficient for compassing the globe of the earth repeatedly.

886. *Ausonian.*] Some critics have charged Apollonius with an anachronism, in ascribing the name of Ausonia to Italy, as if it were an appellation of the country at the time of the Argonautic expedition; whereas, it acquired this name at a subsequent period from Auson, the son of Ulysses and Calypso; but it seems to be rather severe and hypercritical to treat poets as if they were bound, like historians, to strict chronological exactness.—See Gr. Scho.

887. *Ligustic isles.*] They were three in number, lying adjacent to the coast of Italy. They were also called Stechades, from Σroιχoς, 'a rank,' because they lay all in a row. The first was called Prota, the middle Mesa, the last Hypea: names expressive of their respective positions. They are mentioned by Pliny, lib. iii. cap. 5. They are called Ligustic, from the people who inhabited them, the Ligurians; who also gave their name to that sea. They are now known by the name of the Hieres isles. They are situated near Marseilles, on the coast of Provence: *Tres stæchades a vicinis massiliensibus dictæ propter ordinem. Quas item nominant singulis vocabulis, proten, et mesen, quæ et Pomponia vocatur, tertia Hypæa.* (Pliny.) The Ligurians were anciently an Iberian tribe, and possessed all the maritime places, not only of Gaul and Italy, but also of Spain: and, therefore, even Gades, now Cadiz, is mentioned by Stephanus Byzantinus, as a Ligustic city. The Ligures are said, in Thucydides (lib. vi.), to have expelled the Sicani, an Iberian race, from Spain.

So Dionys. lib. xxii.—Diodo. Sic. lib. v.—Silius
Ital. lib. xiv. ver. 34, 35.

907. *Hyllean plain.*] That part of Illyria be-
fore mentioned, near the place where Absyrtus
was slain.

909. *Liburnian seats.*] Liburnia was the coun-
try of Croatia, having Dalmatia on the south and
east; on the west, Carniola and Istria. Some of
these people settled in Italy. Pliny speaks of
the Insulæ Liburnicæ, lib. iii. cap. 26.—*Illyrici
ora amplius mille insulis frequentatur—natura
vadosi maris estuariisque intercursantibus, &c. &c.
Nec pauciores Liburnicæ, &c. &c.*—Apollonius
here, however, seems rather to mean Austrian
Dalmatia.—See Apollodori Bibliotheca.

911. *Issa.*] This was one of the islands in the
Adriatic sea, near the coast of Liburnia.

911. *Pityea.*] This was another island, near
the Liburnian coast. It is mentioned by Homer,
who calls it Pityusa.

913. *Corcyra.*] There seems to be a good deal
of confusion in writers respecting the name of
Corcyra. Eustathius, in his comment on Diony-
sius Periegetes, tells us, that there were two
islands of the name of Corcyra: the one, at the
Ionian bay (the Adriatic), called also Pheacia;
the other, within the Ionian bay. By the for-
mer, he means Corfu, as it is now called, on the
coast of Albania. By the other, an island, an-
ciently called Melæna, and at present Curzola,
near the head of the Adriatic gulf. It is of the
latter island that the poet speaks in this place.
Besides Curzola, there are a great number of
islands, clustering near each other, on this coast:
as Brazza, Lesina, Cazzola, Meleda, and La-
gosta. It should seem, that anciently the island
of Egina also bore the name of Corcyra.

916. *Phlius.*] A town of Peloponnesus, near the mountains of Sicyon, otherwise known by the name of Arethyrea.

919. *Black Corcyra.*] Thus the island of Curzola was anciently called Melena.

922. *Melita.*] The poet does not here speak of the island of Malta, between Sicily and Africa, so famous in modern history; but of an island between Italy and Epirus, or, according to some, between Corcyra and Illyricum. It is mentioned by Pliny.

923. *Cerossus—Nymphea.*] These were others from among the many islands that stretch from Albania along the coast of Dalmatia and Croatia.

926. *Calypso.*] Our poet calls Calypso the daughter of Atlas; others make her the daughter of Oceanus and Tethys. Our poet calls the island where she dwelt Nymphea: it is called by others Ogygia. She entertained Ulysses after his shipwreck, and he remained with her six or seven years.—See Homer, Odyss.

928. *Ceraunia.*] From being often the marks of thunder-storms. High hills on the borders of Epirus, near Valona, where the Ionian sea is separated from the Adriatic, and reaching even to the shore; now Monti di Chimera.

929. *Juno.*] The goddess, says the poet, apprehending the hostile designs of Jupiter, raised a violent storm, in order that the Argonauts might escape the doom which awaited them, by desisting from their course, and arriving at the isle of Circè, called Electris; which, had they persevered in the course they then held, they would not have had occasion to visit. Thus they would have failed of obtaining expiation.

939. *Dodona's wood.*] Dodona was a city of Epirus, on the confines of Thessaly. It was fa-

mous for a fountain and a grove, consecrated to Jupiter, where was an oracle. The answers were given by the whispering of the leaves, which produced certain articulate sounds.

949. *Twins of Leda.*] Castor and Pollux were, probably, selected for this transaction, on a supposition that their prayers and intercession would be most agreeable to Jupiter, whose sons they were, by Leda, the wife of Tyndarus.

965. *Young Phaëton.*] So Ovid, Metam. lib. ii. l. 319. Phaëton was the son of Phœbus and Clymene, who espoused Merops. Having set the world on fire, he was struck with lightning by Jupiter.—This fable of Phaëton may, perhaps, be borrowed from the traditions of the fall of Lucifer.

973. *The daughters of the Sun.*] So Ovid, lib. ii. ver. 340.

974. *Enclosed in poplars.*] Ovid, who seems to have studied our poet attentively, and has frequently imitated him, says,

——— Cortex in verba novissima venit.
Inde fluunt lacrymæ ; stillataque sole rigescunt,
De ramis Electra novis : quæ lucidus amnis
Excipit, et naribus mittit gestanda Latinis.

Mat. ii. 366.

The occasion of Phaëton's demanding the chariot of the sun was his being reproached by Epaphus, the son of Jupiter and Io, as falsely deriving his birth from Apollo. Ovid fancifully pretends, that the people of Ethiopia (to which region, or to Egypt, Phaëton is supposed to have belonged) became black, in consequence of the conflagration and excessive heat produced at that time by their countryman :

Sanguine tum credunt in corpora summa vocato,
Ethiopam populos nigrum traxisse colorem.

985. *Celtic race.*] The Celtes, or Gauls, were the descendants of Gomer, according to the best authorities, as the Scythians were of Magog, his next brother: although the Celtes and Scythians have been confounded together by many ancient writers. They had some appellations, which seem evidently to allude to the name of Gomer; as Cymbrians, Cimmerians, Cammerians. All Europe, and the far greater part of Asia, were peopled by these two famous nations; the former, from the utmost parts of Spain to European Scythia eastward; the latter, from thence almost to the territories of China. The sons of Gomer migrated gradually from Asia to Europe, and passed, in regular progress, from Phrygia, their first settlement, through Thrace, Hungary, Germany, Gaul, Italy, till they had spread themselves to the utmost borders of Spain.

990. *Hyperborean climes.*] The term Hyperboreans, among the Greeks, had different significations in different ages, according to the progress of geographical knowledge. Their country seems to have been anciently a *Terra incognita,* and the name a sort of vague relative term. Herodotus places the Hyperboreans to the north of the Scythians. The situation of their country does not appear to have been precisely known to him. He thought it began about the meridian of the Tanais (now the Don), and extended indefinitely eastward, occupying the country quite to the sea, in the extreme part of the north. (Melp. 13 and 36). He says they were the only people in the world who were not always at war with their neighbours, perhaps because they had no neighbours with whom they could engage in hostilities. By the extended bounds which Herodotus gives to Europe, making it greater than

Asia, it appears that he meant to include the Hyperboreans in that division of the earth. The Hyperboreans of Herodotus must have been the people of Russia, and part of Siberia, who inhabit along the rivers Oby and Irtish. Britain, according to Diodorus Siculus, was the Hyberborean country of more ancient times; and after that, the more remote northern parts of Europe and Asia, which the Greeks knew only by report. Pliny, the historian, is more particular in his description of the Hyperboreans than any other writer. He places them beyond the Riphean mountains, at the heads of the Tanais and Jaik.—See lib. iii. cap. 12. The reader who wishes for more detailed information on this subject, will find it in Major Rennell's work on the geography of Herodotus. There were, in fact, so many inconsistent fables among the ancients respecting the country and situation of the Hyperboreans, that modern geographers have been unable to reconcile them.—(See Gesner de Navigationibus intra Columnas Herculis). Callimachus, in his Hymn to Delos, speaks of the Hyperboreans as a distinct nation, and a people of great antiquity. Pindar places them near the Atlantic isles, or islands of the Blessed, which were supposed to have been opposite to Mauritania in the Mediterranean sea, and speaks of their religious rites.—See Olymp. Ode 3, and Pythic Ode 10. The words of Pliny, in the passage mentioned above (lib. iv. cap. 12), and of P. Mela, show that they understood by Hyperboreans very different people : *Pone eos montes, ultraque Aquilonem, gens felix (si credimus), quos Hyperboreos appellavere, annoso degit evo, fabulosis celebrata miraculis. Ibi creduntur esse cardines mundi, extremique siderum ambitus, semestri luce et unâ die solis aversi ; non, ut imperiti dixere, ab equinoctio verso in autumnum semel in anno solstitio, oriuntur iis soles brumaque, semel occidunt. Regio aprica felici temperie omni afflatu noxia carens : domus iis nemora lucique, et deorum cultus viritim gregatimque : discordia ignota, et egri tu do omnis, &c.* Plin. Hist. Nat. Pomponius Mela (lib. iii. cap. 5) says, *In Asiatico litore primi Hyperborei, super Aquilonem, Ripheosque montes : sub ipso siderum cardine jacent, ubi sol, non quotidie ut nobis, sed primum verno equinoctio exortus autumnali demum occidit, et ideo sex mensibus dies, et totidem aliis, usque continua nox est, &c.* Which shows, that by Hyperborei, Mela understood the people so near the pole as to have six months day, the same night. Herodotus says (Thalia 115), that it was certain both tin and amber were brought from the extreme regions of the north; and amber, in particular, from the river Eridanus, which discharged itself into the North sea. On this name Eridanus, he observes, that it is certainly of Greek derivation, and not barbarous; and was, as he conceives, introduced by one of their poets. Larcher, observes, that the Eridanus here alluded to could not possibly be any other than the Rho-daun, which empties itself into the Vistula, near Dantzic; and on the banks of which amber is now found in large quantities.

993. *Lacerea.*] This place seems to be put for Larissa, a town of Thessaly; or, perhaps, there is some corruption of the text here. Coronis, the mother of Æsculapius, is called, by Ovid, ' Larissea Coronis,' lib. ii. ver. 542.

> Pulchrior in totâ quam Larissea Coronis
> Non fuit Æmoniâ.

· 994. *Coronis.*] Æsculapius, according to an-

cient mythology, was the son of Phœbus, and
the nymph Coronis, who was otherwise called
Arsinoe. She being too familiar with Ischis,
the son of Elatus of Thessaly, a raven spied
them together, and acquainted Apollo with it,
who slew the nymph and ripped the infant out
of her womb, whom he named Æsculapius, and
committed to the care of Chiron the centaur.
Hence, it is said, the raven's feathers, which
before were white, were changed into black,
that he might mourn for ever for the death of
Coronis.—Æsculapius, becoming supremely skil-
ful in the art of healing, restored to life Glaucus,
the son of Minos; or, according to other ac-
counts, Hippolytus, the son of Theseus; on
which account he was struck with lightning by
Jupiter. Apollo, being unable to avenge him-
self on Jupiter in person, resolved to attack the
Cyclops who had forged the thunderbolts, and
destroyed them. For this deed he was driven
from heaven by Jupiter; and forced to serve
Admetus, king of Thessaly.—Hyginus, fab. 49.
Æsculapius is said to have been the first who
discovered the art of midwifery. The reader will
find a curious story on this subject in Hyginus;
fab. 274. Æsculapius was, in time, permitted
to return from the infernal regions, and advanced
to divine honours. This fable is given at some
length by Virgil, Æn. vii. ver. 764. Pindar, in
his third Pythian Ode, strophe 13, speaks of the
fate of Coronis.

995. *Amyrus.*] A river of Thessaly, near the
birthplace of Æsculapius. It is mentioned by
Val. Flac. lib. ii. v. 11.

1009. *The Rhone.*] Cluverius, in his ancient
geography (article Italy, cap. 34), may be con-
sulted respecting the confusion of names inci-

dent to the Greek writers. The gross mistake, of saying the Rhone meets the Po, and flows (it is to be supposed jointly with the Po) with one of its branches, or arms, to the Adriatic sea, while the other disembogues itself into the Sardinian sea, is not unlike that which the poet had already made respecting the Danube, with its two supposed branches flowing from the Riphean mountains, and meeting the Euxine sea with the one branch, the Ionian with the other. Indeed, the whole geography, not of our poet alone, but of the whole set of Argonautic poets and annalists, is extremely wild and erroneous. It is remarkable that the Greek Scholiast of Apollonius, who is a very sensible, and, in general, a well informed writer, conspires with his author in this gross error; and says, ' The Rhone, a river belonging to the country of the Celtes, mixing his waters with the Eridanus, and then dividing, proceeds in two channels to the sea: with one, he flows into the Ionian gulf: with the other, into the Sardinian sea.' A strange description this of the Rhone ; which, rising from the Alps, not far from the sources of the Rhine and Danube, runs by Geneva westward through France, and discharges itself by three outlets into the Tyrrhenian sea: it traverses the great sheet of water, called the lake of Geneva ; and, near the walls of that city, unites itself with the Arve.—(See Stolberg's Travels, vol. i. p. 181.) It is probable that the first navigators and travellers were both ignorant and faithless : that their acquaintance with regions, rivers, and mountains, was but imperfect; that the information and notices which they received from the people to whom they applied, were often fallible, and calculated to mislead. Their memories also might have been treacherous on many occasions, and confounded and disguised the names of places and natural objects, ascribing to one the attributes and descriptions which belonged to others. Add to this, the little acquaintance which those early Greek voyagers must be supposed to have had with the languages and dialects of the regions they visited, which, of course, augmented the difficulty that lay in the way of their acquiring knowledge, and obtaining accounts from the foreigners on the coasts where they touched. If to these causes we join the love of the marvellous so generally incident to travellers, we shall find an abundant source of the fabulous. Thus may we account for the many geographical errors, inconsistencies, and impossibilities, in the first accounts of the Argonautic expedition; the main incidents of which, however, were so fully established and defined, by received opinion and tradition at the time when Apollonius came to write, that he did not think himself (as I have already observed) at liberty to innovate by varying them. Besides, it is to be remembered, that the Argonautic labours and wanderings had been the favourite theme of a variety of writers, both in prose and song; many of whom were very ancient, and gave a high degree of credit to the traditions which they had handed down. Now it is certain, that Apollonius was a diligent imitator of the writers who preceded him, and borrowed from them the most if not the whole of his materials. This appears from the testimony of his learned Scholiast, who was himself a writer of considerable antiquity: and this will account for our poet's having permitted so many inconsistencies, improbabilities, and errors. To this he submitted, lest he should violate the received creed of mythological tradition; and, by running counter to all the fabulous history of preceding times, consult historical and geographical truth, at the expense of poetical probability. It is evident, that the poet confounds with the Rhone other rivers of Italy; as the Ticinus and the Addua, which irrigate Piedmont and Lombardy, and fall into the Po; and some of them, as the Atiso, which fall into the lake of Garda, pretty near approach the Rhone. It is probable that he confounds the Arno, which flows by Florence and meets the Tuscan sea, with that branch of the Rhone which (according to him) passes to the Sardinian sea.

1021. *Spreading lakes.*] It seems, that by the λιμναι δυσχειμονες in the original, the poet meant the lakes of Garda, Lago Maggiore, and Como, which fully answer the description of the text; as they are subject to sudden gusts of wind, which render their navigation extremely dangerous. See the different travels in Italy which mention them. Virgil speaks of these lakes, and the storms which agitate them.—Georgic ii. ver. 159.

1022. *Celtic land.*] He must mean here the northern part of Italy, the Milanese and Piedmont, formerly called Cisalpine Gaul; and the regions of the Alps, now the Cispadane territory.

1024. *A sunken rock.*] Such is the interpretation of Rotmar, an ancient translator, who has rendered Apollonius into Latin hexameters. The Oxford editor, adopting the version of Hælzlinus, translates the word ἀπορρωξ, by *brachium*, an arm or creek of the river; and this sense seems to be adopted by Mr. Fawkes, who says:

For through a creek to ocean's depths convey'd,
To sure destruction had the hero stray'd.

Certainly, the original Greek word means either a branch of a river, or an abrupt craggy rock. In my apprehension, the latter meaning is more agreeable to the context and course of the poet's narrative.

1031. *Hercynian mount.*] Here again the poet, who could not at any rate be expected to have very accurate notions of the northern regions of Europe or Asia (as they were very imperfectly known to the ancient Greeks in general, as is observed by Major Rennell and other writers), seems to pursue his fanciful system of ideal geography; and to make use of names at random, with little attention to reality; and in this he is followed implicitly by his scholiast. He speaks of the Hercynian mountain or rock. No such mountain is known. The Hercynian wood was anciently a very great forest in Germany. It is described by Cæsar in his Commentaries, B. Gal. lib. vi. c. 24. Great part of it has been cut down since the time of Cæsar, yet still the greatest woods which remain in Germany seem to be parts of it. It is now known by the name of the Schwartzwalde, or the Black Forest. It will readily occur to the reader, that the poet had nothing to do with the Hercynian wood, or any thing belonging to it, as it was not situated near the place where the Argonauts are supposed to have encountered this difficulty.

1042. *Nations of the Celts.*] Must mean the people of the Milanese and Piedmont, where the Po and the rivers that join it wander.

1054. *Saving aid:*] Horace recognises the protecting power extended to mariners by Castor and Pollux, lib. i. ode 3. And again, same book, ode 12. But this salutary and kindly influence they were supposed to possess then only when

they appeared conjointly. Thus Pliny writes;
lib. xi. cap. 37.—*Castorum stellas, cum simul
videntur salutares crede, cum solitariæ graves et
noxias esse.*

1057. *Ethalia.*] The island of Ilva or Elba, near
Leghorn, so much celebrated in the last war,
where those mottled pebbles, such as are men-
tioned by the poet, are yet found. These peb-
bles, as Aristotle observes, are vulgarly supposed
to bear still the marks of the sweat which dropped
from the Argonauts.—Lucas Holstenius says,
' When I was obliged, by fear of pirates, about
twelve years ago, to take refuge in the isle of
Elba, and remained some days at Porto Ferrajo,
the chief town, I observed with surprise that the
stones were all spotted, as if something liquid
had fallen on them in drops.' The fact is, that
the island of Elba abounds in mines of iron, and
the stones bear the marks of this quality in the
soil ; and, from the great predominance of ferru-
ginous particles, are stained with a sort of ochrous
spots.

1059. *With pebbles on the shore.*] The passage,
in the original, is somewhat obscure and ambi-
guous. It may either mean, that the Argonauts
made use of those Ψηφοι, or pebbles, as Σλιγγισ-
ματα, or strigils, for the purpose of chafing and
cleansing their skins, or that, as they rubbed and
cleansed their skins, the sweat dropped on the
stones of the shore, ψηφισιν, and discoloured them.
If this latter sense should be considered, the fol-
lowing couplet may be substituted in the transla-
tion.

> They cleansed their well worn sides from briny dew,
> Which, falling, stain'd the beach with kindred hue.

Aristotle, in his work Περι Θαυμασιων ακυσματον,

alludes to this circumstance, and thus furnishes an argument in favour of the reality and authenticity of the Argonautic expedition. He says, that among other monuments of the Argonautic expedition, there are found on the beach, at Elba, spotted stones. The island of Elba is a rock of ferruginous earth, the crystallized parts of which represent all the colours of the prism.—Denon.

1067. *Ausonian deep.*] Here taken for the Tyrrhenian sea, or *Mare inferum ;* so called, in opposition to the Adriatic, on the other side of Italy, which was called *Mare superum.* The name Ausonia was derived from the Ausones, or Ausonians, who seem to have been aboriginal inhabitants of the country ; and to have lived near Circeii, or along the river Siris, in the country which was afterwards called the territory of the Latins : although, in time, the name of Ausonia extended to Campania and all the lower part of Italy, and was sometimes employed to denote the country in general.—See Heyne, Exc. iv. A. vii.

1070. *Circè held her court.*] We have the fullest description of Circè, and her habitation, in the tenth Odyssey of Homer. This beautiful fable seems to have struck the imagination of all poets, ancient and modern, most forcibly. Our poet, who had his mind strongly possessed with the romantic accounts which Homer gave of the wanderings of Ulysses, and has endeavoured to emulate them in the voyages of his Argonauts, has not omitted to embellish his poem with the introduction of this celebrated and interesting personage ; and has done it both ingeniously and very naturally. Horace notices the celebrity of Circè, and her enchantments : *Sirenum voces, et Circes pocula nôsti.* Virgil, finding his hero on the shores of Italy, near the promontory of Circeii, is led to pay his respects to the enchantress, *en passant*, and does it with great taste and beauty. *Vid.* Æneis, lib. vii. ver. 15.   The description of Circe, her magic, and her enchanted island, have been imitated by Tasso, in his loves of Rinaldo and Armida; by the Cavalier Marino, in his account of the gardens where Venus entertained Adonis; and by Spenser, in his description of the bower of bliss, in the Faerie Queene, book ii. can. xii. st. 42.

> Thence passing forth, they shortly do arrive
> Whereat the bower of bliss was situate;
> A place pick'd out by choice, of best alive,
> That nature's work by art can imitate, &c.

What is very remarkable, and would lead one to suppose that the English bard must have had our Greek poet immediately in his view, is, that he has introduced the story of Jason and Medea, as being portrayed in sculpture on the ivory gate of the bower : ut sup. st. 44.   Circè, it seems, was the daughter of Sol and the nymph Persis : she poisoned her husband, the king of Scythia, that she might reign alone; and also several of her subjects.   For these causes she was expelled from the kingdom, and emigrated to Italy; where she resided at a promontory, which from her borrowed the name of Circeii.   Here she continued to exercise her magic and destructive arts; and transformed Picus, king of the Latins, near whose territory she resided, into a woodpecker; and Scylla, the daughter of Phorcus, into a marine monster.   The fables, both of the Sirens and Circè, which are very properly joined together by Horace, have a fine allegorical meaning; and denote the alluring blandishments of pleasure, and the inordinate indulgences of sensual appetites;

which draw men to destruction, or transform and degrade them into beasts.

There appears to be some doubt respecting the place of residence of Circè, and whether it was an island, or on the main land. Certainly, the place which yet bears the name of Circè at this day joins the continent.—Virgil, however, makes her place of residence an island; and introduces Helenus apprizing Æneas, that *Eææque insula Circes lustranda*. In this he follows Homer, who places Circè in an island. To this Pliny alludes, lib. iii. cap. 5 and 9 : *Circeii insula quondam immenso quidem mari circumdata, ut creditur Homero, at nunc planitie.* Varro too, as quoted by Servius in his comments on the passages of the third and seventh Æneid where Circè is mentioned, is said to have stated, that ' the place called after Circè had been formerly an island, before the salt marshes were dried up, which divided it from the continent.' This is not surprising, if we consider the ancient state of Italy when it was in great part covered with wood, before it came to be highly cultivated by the Romans; and if we consider, that even at this day there are many lakes in the neighbourhood of the place alluded to which overflow in the winter season, and that the Pontine marshes take their rise from thence. And therefore it is that Strabo, in his fifth book, reckons Circeii among the unhealthy places, where pestilential morasses were formed by stagnant inundations of the sea. It is a very extraordinary thing, to be sure, that the ancients should have conducted Circè, the sister of Æëtes, king of Colchis, a region bordering on the Black sea, from Æa, the capital of that country, to an island situated on the coast of Italy ! We can only account for it, from the profound ignorance of the ancient Greeks as to geographical subjects. Before the time of the Trojan war, the boundaries of the western regions, and the face of the country in that quarter, were altogether unknown to them. Before the time of Homer, they had only heard of this part of the world by wild and fabulous stories. Behind Sicily they imagined that a vast ocean was drawn around, and extended without interruption even to the north pole. The fable was very ancient respecting Circè, the daughter of the sun, and of her being visited by the Argonauts; who, whether they were asserted to have been conveyed on the Tanaïs or the Ister, were still believed to have returned home by that fabulous northern sea invented in remote antiquity. In process of time this part of the globe, so little known to the Greeks, began to be visited by their ships; and thus they gradually acquired a more certain and genuine knowledge respecting Italy, Gaul, and Spain. Circeii was a situation very proper for this enchantress, who was supposed to deal in poisons, and know the power of herbs; for Strabo observes of it, that it abounded in plants and herbs. Mount Circeum is said to abound in deadly poisons, and Theophrastus, in his History of Plants (lib. v. c. 9.), says, that the promontory of Circeum was thickly covered with trees, and especially with myrtles; of which a certain low species, that was in much request for making crowns or wreaths, sprung on the tomb of Elpenor, one of the companions of Ulysses. (See the first Essay of Professor Heyne on the seventh Æneid.) The fable of Circè seems to have been derived by Homer from some older poet, who meant to describe the allurements of pleasure by the way of apologue. The names are obviously of Greek invention. Æa is the Greek name of the earth; Æëtes is the progeny of the earth; her parents are the god of day and a nymph of ocean.

1073. *In visions of the night.*] The judicious introduction of visions often has a fine effect, and may be rendered one of the most powerful and affecting pieces of machinery in poetry. Visions prepare the reader to expect certain incidents, and a particular mode of speaking and acting. If the conduct and sentiments of the actors and speakers should be rather incredible and extraordinary, the introduction of a vision serves to reconcile the mind to it, and to render it more probable; as including in it something of overruling influence and supernatural agency. This machinery also gives an opportunity of introducing a variety of wild and picturesque imagery, by the way of episodical ornament.—Apollonius, who is certainly in many respects a very judicious and scientific poet, has made an artful use of this engine. In a former part of this poem, a melancholy vision has a powerful effect on the mind of Medea; and the present dream is well imagined, to fill the breast of Circè with alarm, and send her, in consequence, with her attendants, to the shore to meet the Argonauts.

1085. *With pious rites, &c.*] The custom of performing ablutions to avert evil, after frightful and ill omened dreams, prevailed very generally among the ancients. Thus, Silius Ital. lib. viii. and Aristophanes Ranæ, 1379.

1098. *Her first rude work.*] So Milton, Paradise Lost:

The grassy clods now calved.

The description in the original is very fanciful and ingenious.

1118. *The vestal hearth.*] The behaviour of Ulysses was similar on his arrival at the palace of Alcinoüs. He took his station at the hearth. So, when Coriolanus took refuge in the house of Tullus Aufidius, the Volscian chief, he seated himself on the hearth, as a suppliant. The rights of suppliants, as well as the laws of hospitality, were most religiously observed among the ancients : the suppliant was peculiarly under the protection of Jupiter, who thence obtained the appellation of Ιχησιος, the god of suppliants. Jupiter was also worshiped under the title of Φυξιος, or the god who protected fugitives. Those who had the misfortune to commit homicide were permitted to save themselves by flight ; and enabled, by certain religious rites and oblations, to expiate the guilt they had incurred. The same spirit is recognised in the Jewish law, which made a provision for the slayer who killed his neighbour ignorantly, and not of malice prepense; and appointed three cities of refuge, to which he might flee, ' lest the avenger of blood (the kindred of the deceased) might pursue him while his heart was hot.'—See the nineteenth chapter of Deuteronomy.

1121. *Stung with reproaches.*] The pensive and contrite demeanour of Jason and Medea is finely imagined, and truly natural. Apollonius was not one of those indiscreet poets who delighted, like the German playwrights, in depicting objects that outrage nature, ' monsters redeemed by no virtue.'

1133. *The atoning sacrifices.*] The passage which succeeds, in the original, is one of those which very much vex and annoy translators. The minute descriptions of ancient manners and religious ceremonies cannot easily be transferred from a dead to a living language, and yet they are often the most curious parts of ancient classics. In the passage before us, for instance, it is not easy to tell in smooth verse, and without falling into the low and mean, that Circè offered up a sucking pig (which was the victim used in these rites of atonement and purification), and that she washed the hands of the suppliants in its blood.

1162. *Listen'd.*] Circè was anxious to hear Medea speak; as, at first glance, she had suspected that she might be her kinswoman, from observing in her eyes that peculiar fire and lustre which distinguished the descendants of the god of day.

1174. *Some events, &c.*] There is great delicacy, and a feminine attention to decorum, in Medea's saying that she fled from the wrath of her father with her cousins, the sons of Phryxus, instead of owning that she fled with Jason. Her reserve and caution on this occasion, and her desire to pass over in silence the death of her brother, are very beautiful and natural. Medea, though ferocious, artful, and a slave to her unruly passions, is not devoid of virtuous feelings; in particular, she shows a strong sense of feminine delicacy, a regard to character, and a wish to preserve decent appearances. Thus the poet judiciously forbears to outstep the modesty of nature, by an unqualified exhibition of depravity.

1176. *In vain.*] The behaviour of Circè is very noble, and finely marked. Her superior penetration, reading the guilt and weakness of Medea through her attempts at concealment, and this mixed with compassion for her sex; the superior

dignity of Circè: all these form an admirable con-
trast to the conscious guilt and humiliation of
Medea.

1185. *Ties of kindred.*] Circè was the daugh-
ter of the sun, and sister of Æëtes, according to
our poet.

1190. *Hence with that partner, &c.*] There is
much dignity and propriety in the whole conduct
of Circè on this embarrassing occasion. She felt
for the affliction of Æëtes, and saw the criminality
of Medea in all its deformity; but she could not
think of violating the sacred laws of hospitality,
or the rights of suppliants; neither could she
forget that the unhappy Medea was also her
relation.

1208. *For Juno sought to learn, &c.*] Juno was
anxious to know the precise time when the Argo-
nauts should renew their voyage, that she might
exert herself to protect them, and facilitate their
progress.

1217. *Vulcan's forges.*] Agathocles, in his re-
cords or memorials respecting the forges of Vul-
can, relates that there are two islands on the
coast of Sicily; one of which is called Hiera,
the other Strongyle, which day and night emit
flames. One of these islands is called Lipara,
according to others. The same writer again, in
his seventh book, says, ' There are islands on
the coast of Sicily; two of them are volcanic:—
the one is called the island of Eolus, the other of
Vulcan. In which latter there is said to spring
a river of fire.'—Gr. Scho.

1218. *Deafening hammers sound.*] These islands
are also called the Eolian islands, on account of
the intimate and natural connexion between air
and flame. The Greek Scholiast says, that the
peculiar residence of Vulcan is in Lipari and

Strongyle (these are two of the islands of Eolus), on which account a violent noise and crackling of fire was heard in them. It was an ancient tradition, that any person who chose might bring unwrought iron and leave it on the shore of these islands, together with money, as the price of manufacturing it; and that, if he came the next day, he was sure to find in the place of it a sword, or whatever other thing he wished to have forged for him. Pytheas relates the same story in his, ' Circuit of the Earth,' and adds, that the sea all around those islands is on fire.

1223. *Progeny of air.*] This is strictly and philosophically just; because the winds are produced by currents of air, or rather are currents of air.

1230. *The nymph.*] Virgil evidently had this machinery of our poet in view in the first Æneid. But he has improved very much on his original, by resorting to other sources, and combining an imitation from Homer, lib. i. ver. 51. Again, Æneis, lib. v. ver. 606:

—— Irim de cœlo misit Saturnia Juno
Iliacam ad classem ventosque aspirat eunti.

1241. *Stormy winds.*] Homer speaks of Eolus in the same manner with our poet and Virgil:

Κεινον γαρ ταμιην ανεμων ποιησε Κρονιων.

Baron Stolberg, in his travels, gives the following account of the Eolian or Lipari islands, vol. ii. p. 518: ' As these islands, which rise out of the sea like mountains with their steep shores, are seen to a great distance, and as you turn towards them (like the wandering rocks of Homer, in face of Scylla) always appear to have a different situation; the great poet, profiting by these circumstances, called the island of Eolus the swimming island. Lipari, like its companions, is high; and, like theirs, the declivity of the shores have the colour of iron; at least, when seen, as they were by us, at a distance. The island of Lipari was formerly volcanic. The following is the account which Diodorus gives of it:

'The wind bursts forth with great rushing and noise from the caverns of Strongyle (Stromboli) of Hiera Hephæsta, consecrated to Vulcan, and now called the volcano. They cast out sand and hot stones, so that some believe that they have a subterranean passage, and are connected with Ætna, and that they mutually vomit fire.

'Liparus, son of the Italian king, Auson, driven away by his brother, first peopled and cultivated the Eolian islands; and after him Lipara (Lipari) took its name. Æolus, the son of Hippotas, came there, and married Cyane, the daughter of Liparus. He was king of Lipara, and aided his wife's father, who sighed after Italy, to conquer Sorento. Ulysses visited this Æolus, who was an upright man, and was called the friend of the gods. The invention of sails is ascribed to him. By observing the tokens which the fire afforded (the ascending smoke, that appeared fiery by night), he could prognosticate concerning the winds to the inhabitants; from which the fable arose, that he was lord of the winds. Æolus had six sons, one of whom reigned in the country of Rhegium: the five others in Sicily. The fame of their father, and their own mild and just behaviour, induced the Sicani and the Siculi, who had always before been at variance, to obey them. The family reigned long, and till it was extinct; and the Siculi afterwards selected their own princes. The Sicani waged civil wars.'

The fiction that Æolus ruled the winds, and the

account of his being able to foretell the change of
the wind by the prognostics of fire, on which this
fiction is founded, were occasioned by the op-
portunities he had of observing the wind, which
changes sooner in high regions than in the low;
and mariners, to this day, predict the change of
the wind from the smoke that rises out of the vol-
canic islands, and from the vapours that ascend
from the others.

Rucellai has given a fine description of the
Cyclops, in his beautiful and classical poem, ' Le
Api :'

Come ne la focina i gran Cyclopi,
Che fanno le saette horrende, &c.

1254. *Wandering isles.*] The rocky islands,
named the Cyanean, were also called Πλαγκτας,
or ' erratic,' by the Greeks. Dionysius Periegetes
speaks of those wandering rocks.   See Heinsius
on Ovid, Metam. lib. vii. ver. 162.

1260. *Scylla.*] So Virgil, Æneis, lib. iii. ver.
420.

1264. *Thy proud virtue.*] This was not alto-
gether the case, according to ancient mythology.
It was rather the prudence of Jove himself than
the reserve of Thetis, that prevented the progress
of this amour.   It had been foretold, that if Ju-
piter should proceed to gratify his passion for
Thetis, the offspring would be a son who should
dethrone him, as he had dethroned his father
Saturn.   Ovid, in his Metam. lib. xi. ver. 221,
ascribes this prophetic warning to Proteus.

1276. *Themis.*] She was one of the daughters
of Uranus and Terra, the sisters of the Titans,
who were called Titanides.   The names of the
other sisters were Tethys, Rhea, Mnemosyne,
Phœbe, Dione, Thea.—See Apollodorus, Ath.

lib. i. c. 2, where he speaks of the birth of Pallas; and see note on this subject, on book iii. near the beginning.

1283. *First of mortals.*] Peleus. Aristophanes speaks of the temperance of Peleus in his comedy of the Clouds. Peleus, on this account (his prudence and temperance) received the sword.'— There is a noble poem of Catullus on the nuptials of Peleus and Thetis.

1287. *Sustain'd the nuptial light.*] That is to say, I acted as your mother, on the occasion of your marriage ceremony, in sustaining the nuptial torch. For it was the office of the mothers of the brides to bear these torches. This custom is mentioned by Euripides in his Phœnissæ. ' I did not light the flame of a legitimate fire, for thy nuptials, as suits a happy mother.' Juno dwells on her performing this office, to show her particular regard and tenderness towards Thetis, and to engage that goddess to a return of gratitude. Juno, at any rate, was the goddess who peculiarly presided over marriage rites, whence she was called ' *Pronuba* Juno.'

1294. *Naiads.*] He means Chariclo and Philyra, by whom Achilles was nursed in the cave of Chiron. The former was the mother, the latter the wife, of the centaur.—Gr. Scho.

1296. *Doom'd to wed.*] Anaxagoras says, that, in reality, all these fables respecting Achilles were invented by the people of Sparta, to do honour to that hero. Some relate, that the gods, sympathizing with his mother Thetis, raised Achilles to immortality. Ibycus was the first who related that Achilles, arriving at the Elysian fields, married Medea. In this fable he has been followed by Simonides (*vide* Gr. Scho.), and many others of the ancient mythologists.

1298. *And Peleus too.*] There is something dramatic here. The author of the Egimius, in his second book, says, that Thetis, being desirous to know whether her sons by Peleus were mortal or immortal, threw some of them into caldrons of boiling water, and others into the fire; and that many of them being destroyed in this manner, Peleus became enraged, and prevented Achilles from being plunged in the fatal caldron. Sophocles, in his play called 'The Lovers of Achilles,' says, that Thetis, being bitterly reproached by Peleus, deserted him. Staphylus, in his third book respecting Thessaly, relates, that Chiron, being a person of great wisdom, and skilful in astronomy, was desirous of rendering Peleus very illustrious and famous; for which purpose he sent for the daughter of Actor the myrmidon, and caused reports to be generally circulated, that Peleus was about to intermarry with Thetis, the marine goddess, under the sanction of Jupiter, who was to bestow her on him as a bride, and that the gods would come, with rain and storm, to the nuptials. Having spread these reports, he watched the time when he knew by certain prognostics there would be a vast deal of wind, and fixed the solemnization of the nuptials for this period; and Peleus having espoused Philomela, the daughter of Actor, the fame of his being married to Thetis became general.—Gr. Scho.

1315. *Charybdis and Scylla.*] The rocks opposed to each other in the narrow and dangerous strait between Italy and Sicily, called the Faro of Messina. Scylla was on the side of Italy; Charybdis on that of Sicily, adjoining Cape Pelorus. The Greek Scholiast says, that the fable of Scylla arose from the circumstances of the promontory of Scylla, when viewed at a distance, having some imaginary resemblance to a woman's head; and there being a number of vast and terrible rocks beneath, that were full of hollow places and deep caverns, the resorts of monsters of the sea. The vessels which, endeavouring to avoid the rocks of Scylla, approached too near the whirlpool of Charybdis, were sucked in by it, and swallowed up; and those which strove to avoid the dangers of Charybdis, being driven on the rocks of Scylla, were dashed to pieces and destroyed. When the vessels were wrecked, the dogs of the sea, and other destructive monsters, used to issue from their retreats, and devour the unfortunate mariners. It seems that Scylla, according to the descriptions of the poets, had dogs with ravening mouths projecting from her sides and breast, which used to seize on the sailors who approached her; a fable which originated in the circumstance of the seals, and other monsters of the deep, emerging from the recesses beneath the promontory. Acusilaus relates that Scylla was the daughter of Phorcus and Hecaté. Homer says, that the mother of Scylla was named Cratais.—Odyss. λ. Apollonius seems to follow their accounts, and reconcile them by adding, that Hecaté was named Cratais. The author of the ' Μεγαλαι εοαι' says, that Scylla was the daughter of Phorbas and Hecaté. Stesichorus, in his Scylla, says that she was the daughter of Lamia. (Thus far the Greek Scholiast.) Milton, Paradise Lost, book ii. ver. 659, alludes to these descriptions :

> ———— Far less abhorr'd than these
> Vex'd Scylla, bathing in the sea that parts
> Calabria from the hoarse Triuacrian shore.

Homer, in his Odyssey, book xii. ver. 73—97,

gives the description of Scylla. It is thus trans-
lated by Pope:

> High in the air the rock its summit shrouds
> In brooding tempests and in rolling clouds;
> Loud storms around, and mists eternal rise,
> Beat its bleak brow, and intercept the skies.
> When all the broad expansion, bright with day,
> Glows with the' autumnal or the summer ray:
> The summer and the autumn glow in vain;
> The sky for ever lours, for ever clouds remain.
> Impervious to the step of man it stands,
> Though borne by twenty feet, though arm'd with twenty
> hands, &c.

The poet, desirous of creating a bold fable out of
these rocks, was obliged to give them a terrific
form. That figurative sense which he has so
frequently employed, and which so few of his
commentators have understood, he employs here,
that he may envelope his object in clouds. This
rock, in reality, is not so high as to be covered
with clouds on a clear day; but its form is strik-
ing, and inspires terror: at present the rock is not
pointed, for a castle has been built upon it; but,
even now, had a man twenty hands and twenty
feet, as Homer says, he would not be able to
climb it. It rises like a round tower; the breadth
of which, compared to its height, may justify the
epithet deformed; and, towards the sea, it pre-
sents a sharp three-forked cliff. In this cliff we
find the three rows of teeth of Homer. The
neighbouring cliffs too presented themselves to
the creative fancy of the poet. The fiction of
the sea dog, the dolphin, and the still more huge
monsters which she makes her prey, is founded
on an admirable knowledge of the nature of the
sea: for it abounds in dolphins, and a large kind
of fish which the Italians call *cane del mare*. It
even occasionally happens that a kind of whale,

of the species the French call *cachelot*, is stranded on those shores.

There have been frequent contests concerning Charybdis, which, as described by Homer, is no longer to be found. He could not mean the lower rocks; for his description has placed Charybdis opposite to Scylla. These countries, ever subject to the grand phenomena of nature, may have suffered great changes from earthquakes. Is not even the opinion of several ancient and modern philosophers probable, which maintains that Sicily was anciently separated from Italy by an earthquake? It was the supposition of Cluverius, that, according to the relation of Homer, which placed Charybdis opposite to Scylla, it must have been at the promontory of Pelorus, now called Capo di Faro: but as he could not find it there, he supposed the whirlpool, which is opposite the lighthouse of Messina, to be the true Charybdis, and accuses Homer of an error. But how came he not to find the real whirlpool of Homer, which is known to every fisherman of Scylla, of Capo di Faro, and Messina, and forms itself between Capo di Faro and Scylla? The current runs from the northeast to the straits of Faro. There is a regular ebb and flow of the tide every six hours; and when a strong wind sets in to oppose either the ebb or the flow, a whirlpool still rises before the promontory.

This ebb and flow has been ascribed by some to a subterraneous passage, said to exist between Mount Ætna and the sea. By Aristotle it is ascribed, like other ebbs and flows, to the influence of the moon; and this opinion is confirmed by the regularity of the six hour tide. It is certain, that, in the time of Homer, the tides,

which were common to but few places of the
Mediterranean, were very imperfectly understood.
He therefore says, that three times a day Cha-
rybdis engulfed the waters, and three times a day
vomited them up again.

The navigator of a small packet boat, if unac-
quainted with these seas, might probably meet
with the misfortune against which Circé cautions
Ulysses, when she warns him, while avoiding
Scylla and her projecting cliffs, ' Not to ap-
proach the whirlpool of Charybdis.' Earth-
quakes, or some other natural cause, have now
operated a material change; and this strait is by
no means so formidable to mariners as in ancient
times; even men of war may now pass through it.

1329. *And raging fires.*] The subterranean fires
boiled up from the depths near this dangerous
pass of Scylla and Charybdis, so that the sea was
heated by them; as Metrodorus says in his first
book concerning history. Theophrastus, in his
historical monuments, says, the crackling and
noise of flames are heard from the Eolian islands
to the distance of a thousand stadia; and that a
sound, resembling thunder, is heard from them, in
the neighbourhood of Taurominium.—Gr. Scho.

1368. *But beware.*] This injunction was given
to her husband by Thetis from a motive of re-
serve and delicacy. It was natural for her to
think, that a principle of vanity might dispose
Peleus to point her out to his companions among
the Nereids; a circumstance which would be
highly offensive to her feelings, as she knew
they were all to appear naked.

1382. *O'er flaming lamps, &c.*] The reader will
find a fable resembling this in the Persian tales:
where a prince is married to a beautiful and
accomplished princess of the race of the Genii.

One of their children is thrown into a great fire,
and immediately disappears : another is, imme-
diately after its birth, given to a great bitch, who
carries it off in her mouth. The husband, like
Peleus, breaks out into an agony of passion.
This produces a separation from his wife, and a
series of misfortunes to the prince. The princess,
however, is induced, in process of time, to relent,
and return to her husband, with their children
now full grown, and, completely adorned with
beauty and accomplishments; and it then ap-
pears, that she had taken the method above men-
tion of sending away these children, that they
might be educated among the Genii. This fable
is also applied to Ceres, when she undertook to
bring up Triptolemus; in order to render him
immortal, she fed him all day with celestial food,
and covered him at night with burning embers.
His father, Elusinus, observing this, expressed
his fears and anxiety for his child. The goddess,
in displeasure, struck the father dead; but con-
ferred immortality on Triptolemus.

1411. *They soon a fair and florid.*] I have
followed the Oxford editor in his translation of
the Greek word ανθεμοεσσαν, in the text, which
he renders *floridam.* But the Greek Scholiast
seems to make this word the proper name of the
island. For he says, ‘The poet has followed
Hesiod, in calling this island of the Sirens by the
name of Anthemoessa.’

1412. *Sirens.*] Stolberg, vol. ii. p. 104, says,
‘ It was generally believed among the ancients,
that Surrentum, now Sorento, derived its name
from the Sirens. I cannot conceive how the
naked rocks that project from the promontory of
Massa, or those smaller cliffs that face Sorento,
could have been supposed the island of the me-

lodious Sirens; but he likewise tells us, they
sang in flowery meadows. That the charming
island of Homer lay between the promontory of
Circè and the gulfs of Sicily is certain; but I
should rather seek it in the vicinity of these gulfs.
We find, that after Ulysses and his companions
had passed the island, they heard the thunder,
and saw the smoking billows of Scylla:

> Now all at once tremendous scenes unfold,
> Thunder'd the deeps, the smoking billows roll'd.
> POPE, *Odyss.* Book xii. ver. 240.

' The cliffs situated on the bay of Salerno, on
the further side of the Cape of Sorento, called
" Le Galle," are commonly supposed to be the
island of the Sirens. Mount Erix overlooked
Drepanus, celebrated for a temple of Venus.
This city was much renowned for the beauty of
its female inhabitants: hence perhaps the fable
of the Sirens; and the truth of Butes being
allured by the Sirens might be, that, attracted by
the beauty of the women, he remained behind
the Argonauts.'
The city, formerly Lilybeum, is now called
Marsala. The Butes mentioned in the text is
said to have had a son by Venus, who was
named Eryx, and from whom the mountain of
that name was called. In reality, Eryx was the
son of Butes, and Lycaste, a famous courtesan,
who for her beauty was denominated Venus.
The names of the Sirens were, Thelxinoè, or
Thelxiopè, Molpè, and Aglaophonos. The fable
of the Sirens is variously moralized. Plato sup-
poses them to have been the goddesses of har-
mony, who tuned the spheres; a beautiful and
poetical notion, which has been adopted by
Milton :

———— Then listen I
To the celestial Sirens' harmony,
That sit upon the nine infolded spheres,
And sing to those that hold the vital shears,
And turn the adamantine spindle round, &c.

Pausanias will have it, that they were the goddesses of eloquence and persuasion in all their branches. Others suppose, that by the Sirens are meant the allurements of sensual pleasure; and that their number is fixed at three, with a reference to the three grosser senses, of smelling, tasting, and feeling. Certainly this is one of the most agreeable fables in Greek mythology; and one which has made a greater impression on the imagination, and furnished more learned allusion, and matter of more poetical embellishments, than perhaps any other. The reader will find some similitude to it in the fictions and traditions of the beautiful and animated poetry of the east. Spenser has availed himself of the fables respecting the Sirens in his fine description of the mermaids, that sing to tempt Sir Guyon; book ii. canto xii. stanzas 30—33. Among others, whom Ceres sent in quest of Proserpine, were the Sirens. On which occasion she gave them wings. It is observable, that Spenser meant to refine on the ancient mythology, in making his mermaids five in number, evidently in correspondence with the whole number of the senses. Though I doubt whether the ancients were wrong in omitting sight and hearing, as being productive of pleasures more spiritual and less degrading than the other three, from the number of their Sirens. The passage of Spenser to which I allude is not inferior to any in that exquisite poet. Orpheus, in his Argonautics, gives us the substance of the song, with which, he says, he overpowered the seductive strain of the Sirens.

1436. *He swept with mastery.*] The line in the original, which expresses this idea, is a most happy instance of the sound echoing to the sense, and shows the consummate skill of our poet in versification. It is verse 907 of the original:

Κραιπνον ευτροχαλοιο μελος καναχησιν αοιδης.

All the feet in this verse but the last are dactyls, and the words are all such as accord with the sense. They express the sonorous crash of a bold and hurried descant; the energetic and rapid numbers of the masculine strains, which the bard of Thrace employed to counteract and overpower the seducing songs of the Sirens. On the contrary, the preceding lines, which describe the songs of the Sirens, are not less expressive of languor and seductive softness. The word Κρεγμω, used by the poet, is particularly expressive of the strong and energetic manner in which Orpheus played, or rather smote the lyre.

1450. *Queen of love.*] Venus protected Butes in a double right; both as having some influence over the sea, from whence she sprung, and as considering Butes, who was the victim of soft indulgence, as a peculiar object of her favour. Another similar fable has sprung from this; it is related by Diodorus, in his fourth book, concerning Eryx, the son of Butes, who became the husband of Venus. Eryx is the name of a mountain between Drepanum and Panormus.

1453. *Lilybeum rears.*] Dionysius Periegetes (De Situ Orb.) speaks of the three promontories of Sicily.

1463. *The flame of Vulcan.*] See the note on a preceding line. Pindar, Callimachus, and Virgil (in his third Æneid), seem to have vied with each other, in sublime and magnificent descriptions of the eruption of volcanic fires, and the labours of Vulcan and the Cyclops at their forges. The verses of Callimachus, describing the roaring of the flames and the noise of the hammers of the gigantic workmen, are a noble instance of the power of versification, in making the sound an echo to the sense. See Hymn to Delos; and Pindar's first Pythian Ode, decade 5.

Stolberg says, vol. i. p. 453: 'The promontory of Circè, now called Monte Circello, has likewise been called by the inhabitants Monte Felice. And even those to whom the name of Circè is as little known as the name of the poet, who rendered the enchantress immortal, have yet their narratives to detail concerning the great sorceress who once inhabited this mountain. 'Near this (he says) he observed, that suddenly a Will of the Wisp rose over a marsh, which the traveller concluded to be the beginning of the Pontine marsh. I had never seen one (says he) so bright before: it frequently rose very high, danced to a great distance, and always returned back to its former place. Appearances of this kind must have impressed the minds of the rude and ignorant with awe, and disposed them to suppose the neighbouring regions the haunts of sorcery, and the residence of spirits and demons.'

Stolberg's Travels, vol. ii. p. 197: 'The rock of Homer has a fantastic and terrifying form. We took boat, and went to it; as soon as we arrived, let us hear the description of the great poet, and wonder with how much penetration he observed, and how much there was of reality in his daring imagery.

'Circè warned Ulysses against the Planetæ, the erratic or wandering rocks. Immediately in the front of the rock of Scylla craggy cliffs ad-

vance out of the sea, against which the foaming
waves more or less continually dash. The eye is
deceived, or might be induced to ascribe the
motion of the sea to the cliffs. A similar acci-
dent happens in the Baltic, where people, as I
have often experienced, mistake the stones,
which the sea now washes, and now leaves
bare, for swimming seadogs. Homer may have
made the voyage on board a Phœnician or Gre-
cian vessel; or rather, no doubt, a Phœnician;
and still it is probable, that the mariners of his
age were ignorant enough of these coasts ac-
tually to imagine that the cliffs floated. Pliny
himself, that great naturalist, believed that the
rocky islands of the Lago di Bolsena floated.'

1468. *Around the vessel now, &c.*] Virgil has
imitated this passage in the first Æneid: in the
passage which describes the seanymphs extri-
cating the Trojan vessels from the rocks and
Syrtes. Camoëns was so particularly struck
with this passage, that he has imitated it in his
second and fifth books.

1500. *Their labours Vulcan, &c.*] This is beau-
tifully and fancifully imagined. I cannot for-
bear remarking here what I have already fre-
quently observed, the graphic talent of Apollo-
nius. What a fine subject for painting is here
furnished! the whole sea animated; the Nereids
swimming in different groups and various atti-
tudes, supporting the ship over the rocks. Vul-
can propped on the handle of his hammer, and
looking forward to view their labour from the top
of a high promontory. Juno gazing down from
heaven, and, in a transport of solicitude and fear
for the safety of the vessel, throwing her arms
round Minerva. This preceding passage of Apol-
lonius is imitated by Camoëns, book ii.

1508. *Such was the delay.*] There seems to be

some doubt what was the portion of time in-
tended by the poet in this passage. The gene-
rally received interpretation is, that he meant
the half of the artificial day, Νυχθημερε, or the
space of a vernal day, twelve hours. On the
one hand it may be objected, that the poet gives
but a despicable idea of the energy and exertions
of the goddess and the nymphs, in supposing
that they consumed so much time in extricating
the vessel from its dangerous situation; on the
other side it may be replied, that Apollonius
wished to impress on his readers the arduous
nature of the task. However, the passage will
bear the meaning of a space of three hours, one
fourth part of a vernal day; or perhaps even of
one hour out of twelve, of which the vernal day
consists, when days and nights are equal. This
version is confirmed by resorting to the subse-
quent line, 1513, where it is said, the Argonauts
sailed past the pastures of the sun in the course
of the day; which seems to intimate, that the re-
sidue of the day was thus employed. (Hælzlinus.)

1522. *Of the flocks and herds of the sun.*] Some
later writers have placed these flocks and herds
of the sun at Mylæ, on the western shore, on ac-
count of the extraordinary fertility of the lands
there.—(Vide Cluver. Sicil. 115. p. 307.) The
origin of the name Trinacia, or Thrinacia, is
doubtful; that of Trinacria is later. Some have
sought for Thrinacia in Ortygia, as Martorellus:
I Fenici I primi abitatori di Napoli. Rather ac-
cording to the guidance of fancy than reality.
Respecting the flocks and herds of the sun, there
was an ancient and very elegant fable or alle-
gory, prior even to the time of Homer, concern-
ing the lunar year consisting of 350 days; which
some mythologists had ingeniously feigned to be

fed as the flocks and herds of the sun. Their
generation was said never to fail, but to be ever-
lastingly renewed. Their colour was pure white,
and their horns of gold, in allusion to the bright-
ness of the sun. Nymphs, the daughters of the
sun, were assigned to them as their guardians;
and the station where they were fed was as-
signed to them in some sea, at that time little
known, and very far to the west; by which was
meant Sicily, then called Thrinacia, Trinacia,
and after Trinacria. The first idea of this beau-
tiful fiction might have been suggested by the
numerous consecrated flocks and herds which
were fed in many places, and dedicated to the
indigenous and tutelary deities of the soil.—See
Heyne not. in Apollod. 214.

1523. *A silver crook.*] The word in the original,
χαιον, signifies a staff curved at one end, which
shepherds use.

1524. *Shining brass.*] In the original *orichal-
cose.* Horace takes notice of this metallic sub-
stance, *Tibia non ut nunc orchalco vincta.* The
Greek Scholiast says, this was a species of brass
which took its name from a certain man named
Orius, the son of Euretus. Aristotle, in his
Τελεται, denies both the etymology of the name
and the existence of the thing. Others say, that
this is a rash and hasty assertion, and that there
is really a metal so called. Stesichorus and
Bacchilides mention it; and Aristophanes, the
grammarian, takes notice of it. Some, as So-
crates and Theopompus (in his twenty-fifth book),
say, that Orichalcus was the name of a statuary.
—See Gr. Scho. on ver. 973.

1534. *Beyond the Ionian bay.*] By the πορθ-
μος ιονιος, in this place, the poet means the en-
trance into the Adriatic gulf, before which the

island of Corfu lies. This island had various names anciently; among others that of Ceraunia. The fable of the sickle of Saturn, with which he dismembered his father Cœlus, being here deposited, seems to have arisen from the falcated form of the island. Corcyra was at first called Drepané, a name borrowed from Δρεπανη, or Δρεπανονα, 'sickle;' either because (as has been mentioned) the sickle of Saturn was there deposited, or from Ceres, who, for a time, inhabited this island, and having first taught the Titans to sow and reap corn, obtained a sickle from Vulcan in return. She afterwards was fabled to have concealed this sickle in the maritime parts of the island, which conformed to the shape of it. Ceres is reported to have made this island her place of residence, out of affection to Macris, the nurse of Bacchus. The Pheacians, who inhabited this island, were said to be of divine origin. After the name of Drepané, Corcyra obtained that of Scheria. The origin of this name is assigned by Aristotle, in his 'Polity of the Corcyreans.' This name, also, is deduced from the interference of Ceres. It is said that she, being very apprehensive that Drepané, in a course of years, might become a continent, by the alluvions of rivers, entreated Neptune to turn the course of the rivers in question; and the god having complied with her request, the island, instead of Drepané, began to be called Scheria; from two Greek verbs, σχειν, 'to restrain,' and ρειν, 'to flow.' The island was also called Macris, from the nymph who nursed Bacchus: Corcyra from a nymph of that name, the daughter of Asopus.—Gr. Scho.

1536. *With spacious harbours.*] The word, in the original, αμφιλαφης, intimates, that this island afforded excellent ports on both sides; the projecting necks of land, on which the city of Corfu and the town of Pagiopoli are situated, run out parallel to each other; and have, on each side of them, deeply indented bays; so that the epithet 'Αμφιλαφης, or ' capacious,' applies with peculiar propriety to the port of Corcyra. Callimachus, speaking of the harbour of this island, describes it as capacious, and αμφιδυμος, affording an approach on either hand. Apollonius, in his Periplus of Europe, speaks of the haven of the Pheacians.—See Gr. Scho.

1543. *Bounteous Ceres.*] It appears that Corcyra must anciently have been a great corn country, and of uncommon fertility, since Ceres had so great a share in the fabulous traditions and antiquities of the island. The Pheacians were great lovers of pleasure and good cheer, to which they were naturally led by the fertility of the soil, and the benignity of the climate. This disposition of theirs is noticed by Horace : *Pheax reverti*, to return sleek and pampered. The inhabitants of Corcyra are celebrated by Callimachus, Hymn to Delos, for their hospitality.

1547. *Pheacians mild.*] Acusilaus says, in his third book, that the drops of blood which fell from Cœlus or Uranus, when he was mutilated by his son Saturn, (' who, from his own and Rhea's son, like measure found'), impregnating the ground, became the origin of the race of the Pheacians : and Alceus agrees with Acusilaus in saying, that the Pheacians have their origin from the drops of blood of Uranus. Homer says, that the Pheacians were domestic with the gods, on account of their descent from Neptune; which is a poetical mode of intimating, that they were famous for commerce and navigation. (See

Gr. Scho. v. 992.) The love of the Pheacians
for sensual indulgence was so remarkable, that
to live like a Pheacian became proverbial, to de-
note a *bon vivant*. The reader, who wishes to
know more of the hospitality of this people, par-
ticularly of Alcinoüs and his subjects, and their
fondness for the good things of this life, may
consult Homer's Odyssey. At the time of the
Trojan war, and perhaps even of the Argonautic
expedition, if we believe the accouuts of Homer
and the theories of some who make even the
Argonautic enterprise a commercial speculation,
some trade was carried on. It must, however,
have been very confined, as money was not then
in use; nor was any coined until long after the
Trojan war. The commerce of those times was
therefore limited to an exchange of commodities.
The Greeks purchased wine at Lemnos; and
gave in exchange, brass, iron, hides, oxen, and
slaves. The convenience of their ports, and the
fertility of their soil, especially in corn, must
have given the Pheacians a great share in what-
ever commerce subsisted at that time; and this
will account for their opulence and luxury, be-
yond the manners and situation of other cotem-
porary nations, and also for their free and unre-
served communication with strangers.

1559. *Colchian myriads.*] Part of the Colchi-
ans, as has been already related, proceeded
through the Ister, led by Absyrtus; and came
upon the Argonauts at the Brygean islands.
The body of Colchians, whom the Greeks now
encountered at the island of Corcyra, were those
who had passed through the Cyanean rocks.—
Gr. Scho.

1588. *Be witness, Hecaté, &c.*] There is a
great attention to the observation of manners

and characters here. The swearing by Hecaté was peculiarly proper in Medea, on account of her being a Colchian, and addicted to magic rites, over which Hecaté presided; besides, Medea was priestess of Hecaté.

1599. *The dearest treasure of our sex.*] It is part of the character and description of Medea to possess words at will, and a knack of talking in a most plausible and persuasive manner. The poet has never been inattentive to this circumstance. The topics of the present address to Areté are particularly well chosen and affecting. Her palliation of her frailty, and her solicitude to convince the queen that she had preserved her chastity inviolate, are highly feminine and characteristic.

1626. *Furies to the suppliant, &c.*] That is to say, the avenging powers which await to protect suppliants, and avenge any wrongs or outrages which are committed against them. The person who was capable of violating the rights of hospitality, and injuring the suppliant and the stranger, was held to be execrable and obnoxious to divine vengeance.

1670. *O spouse beloved.*] The speech of Areté to her husband is very artful and insinuating; the time is very opportune, and the motives of self-interest are judiciously selected to influence the mind of Alcinoüs. Areté was a woman of superior talents, and possessed great influence. Homer represents her as administering justice.

1696. *The fair Antiopé.*] Antiopé, the daughter of Nycteus, was seduced by Jupiter, under the form of a satyr: flying from the rage of her father Nycteus, she took refuge in Sicyon with Epopeus, and having brought forth Amphion and Zethus, exposed them on Mount Citheron. Nycteus died of grief; but, before his death, gave it in charge to his brother Lycus to bring back his daughter. Lycus led an army into Sicyon, and killed Epopeus; then, carrying away Antiopé captive, he delivered her into the custody of ‣Dircé, her stepmother, who consigned her over to her children to be tormented by them. Amphion and Zethus were brought up by a shepherd, and having attained to man's estate, they released their mother, and destroyed Dircé, by tying her to a wild horse. Having sent for Lycus, under the pretext of delivering Antiopé to him, they were about to kill him; but Hermes prevented them, and ordered Lycus to yield up the sovereignty to them.—(Gr. Scho.) Ovid, Metam. lib. vi. l. 110, adverts to this fable.

1609. *Danaé.*] Pherecydes, in his twelfth book, says, that Acrisius married Eurydicé, the daughter of Lacedæmon. Danaé was the produce of this marriage. Acrisius having consulted the oracle, to know whether he should have a son, the Pythian god answered, that he himself should not have a son; but that his daughter would bear one, who was fated to destroy him. Acrisius, on his return to Argos, caused a brazen chamber to be constructed in the court of his palace; where he shut up Danaé with her nurse, and kept her confined and closely watched, to prevent her having a son. Jove, being enamoured of the virgin, gained admission to her in a shower of gold, which glided through the roof, and was received by Danaé in her bosom. The offspring of this intercourse was Perseus. Danaé, with the assistance of her nurse, nourished him privately, and eluded the vigilance of Acrisius until he was three or four years old. Then Acrisius, hearing the voice of the infant playing, called Danaé and the nurse before him, and killed the latter on the spot. Having led his daughter to the altar of Jupiter Hercius, he interrogated her, without witnesses, respecting the father of the infant. She ascribed him to Jove; but the father, disbelieving this story, caused a coffer to be made, in which he shut up Danaé and her infant, and ordered them to be cast into the sea. They were wafted to the isle of Seriphus. Dictys, the son of Peristhenes, being there fishing, with a net drew them to land; and, at the entreaties of Danaé, opened the coffer. He conducted them to his house, and took care of them, as if they were his own kindred. Dictys and Polydectes were, it seems, the sons of Androthoé, the daughter of Castor, and Peristhenes, the son of Damastor, the son of Nauplius, the son of Neptune and Amymoné; as Pherecydes relates in his first book. When Perseus was now grown up to manhood, the king of Seriphus fell in love with Danaé, and would have offered violence to her, but was prevented by her son. In order, therefore, to get rid of him, Polydectes sends Perseus to Africa to obtain the head of the famous gorgon, Medusa. To his surprise and mortification, he saw the young hero return crowned with a twofold success, having obtained Medusa's head, and also having rescued Andromeda, the daughter of Cepheus and Cassiope, king and queen of Ethiopia, from being devoured by a sea monster to which she was exposed. In the interim, the mother of Perseus and Dictys had been forced to take refuge from the violence of Polydectes. Perseus turned the tyrant into stone, by the gorgon's head, together with many of his people, and invested Dictys with the sovereignty over the survivors. After this, he sailed to Argos with the Cyclops, his mother,

and Andromeda. He did not find Acrisius there
on his arrival. The monarch had retired to La-
rissa, in Thessaly, and the country of the Pelas-
gians, through fear of his grandson. Not find-
ing Acrisius, Perseus leaves Danaé with her
mother Eurydicé, together with Andromeda and
the Cyclops, and hastens to Larissa. There,
having made himself known to Acrisius, he per-
suades him to return with him to Argos. As
they were on the point of setting out, it happened
that Tantalus, the king of that country, caused
funeral games to be celebrated in honour of his
deceased father. Perseus being present at these
games, in company with Acrisius, contended at
the discus (the pentathlon it seems was not then
known, but each game was distinct and separate),
and the disk happening to fall on the foot of his
grandfather, wounded him in such a manner,
that he died at Larissa. In consequence of this
unfortunate accident, Perseus retired from Ar-
gos. See a subsequent note respecting the head
of Gorgon. Horace alludes to the fable of
Danaé, in his Odes, lib. iii. Ode 16. Some
verses of Simonides are preserved, on the pa-
thetic subject of Danaé with her infant being
committed to the waves ; which are distinguished
by a beautiful and affecting simplicity. They
are supposed to be addressed by the unhappy
mother to her infant.—See No. vii. of the remains
of Simonides.—Brunk's Analecta, vol. i. p. 121.
Vide Ovid, Metam. lib. iv. ver. 610.

1702. *Echetus.*] Echetus is mentioned by Ho-
mer as one of the most cruel of the human race ;
and branded with the appellation of ' Echetus,
the scourge of humankind.' Offenders are threat-
ened with the punishment of being delivered up

to this monster of inhumanity, both in the Iliad and Odyssey, as the most dreadful doom that could befall an unhappy wretch. There seems to be some small anachronism in this place; Echetus was still alive, according to Homer, not only in the time of the Trojan war, but even many years after, at the return of Ulysses : and yet, so long before as the time of the Argonautic expedition, he is described by Areté as the injurious Echetus, already notorious to the world by his cruel treatment of his daughter. The Greek Scholiast informs us, that the story of Echetus is to be found in a work of Lysippus, the Epirot, which is entitled ' Catalogue of impious Men.'

1718. *I will not veil my purpose.*] There seems to be a vast deal of equity and good sense, and, indeed, a strict conformity with natural law, in this determination of Alcinoüs. It is most likely that Alcinoüs in his heart believed that Medea was not married; and wished to suggest to his wife the necessity of hastening her nuptials, without appearing in the transaction himself :—while his wife was flattered by attributing the whole arrangement of the business to her own address and dexterity, and supposing that she had even overreached and circumvented her husband.

1744. *Bay of Hyllus.*] This was a harbour belonging to the island of Corcyra. It took its name from Hyllus, the son of Hercules, and the nymph Melita.

1754. *Pheacian cave.*] This cave had been the habitation of the nymph Macris, who gave her name to Corcyra ; and here she had nursed Bacchus. This cave, it seems, had two entrances : and hence (from δις and θυρα) the god obtained the name of Dithyrites, and that species of poetry which was employed in the hymns composed in honour of Bacchus was called Dithyrambus.— (Gr. Scho.) Milton speaks of the cave,

——————— Where old Cham,
Whom Gentiles Ammon call, and Libyan Jove,
Hid Amalthea, and her florid son
Young Bacchus, from his stepdame Rhea's eye.

1768. *Queen of Jove.*] Juno, through that resentment which she felt against all those who were privy to the illicit amours of Jupiter, had expelled the nymph Macris from the island of Euboea; an isle which was peculiarly sacred to Juno, because she had received Bacchus from the hands of Hermes, and nursed him.

1784. *Fear and modesty.*] These rustic nymphs, on account of the beauty of the fleece, were desirous of approaching and handling it; but were restrained by shame and delicacy, on account of the rites of love to which it was so soon to be subservient.—See Gr. Scho.

1787. *Egeüs' sacred stream.*] The Egeüs was a river of Corcyra; the god of the stream was father of the nymph Melita, who bore Hyllus to Hercules, who gave his name to a race of people on the continent of Epirus, and to a harbour of Corcyra. Panyasis, in his account of Lydia, says that Hercules had two sons, who were both called Hyllus, from Hyllus, a river of Lydia, which is said to have contributed to his cure on his return.—Gr. Scho.

Authors differ respecting the place where the nuptials of Jason and Medea were celebrated. Timæus agrees with our author in fixing the place at Corcyra. Dionysius, the Milesian, in the second book of his Argonautics, says, that their nuptials were celebrated at Byzantium. Antimachus, in his Lydia, says, that Jason and Medea indulged their mutual passion near the river Phasis; and this is most probable.—See Gr. Scho.

1793. *Retains the name.*] Apollonius here, according to his practice, displays his knowledge of antiquities. The Greek Scholiast informs us, that other writers took notice of this cave bearing the name of Medea.

1810. *Race of hapless man.*] This sentiment is imitated by Ovid, lib. vii. ver. 454.

1823. *Around the point of Macris.*] He speaks of the peninsula, or projecting neck of land, on which the chief city of the Pheacians then stood, and where stands at present Corfu, the capital of the island. Apollonius (says the Greek Scholiast) describes it in his Periplus of Europe. Others seem to think, that the poet here speaks of a Chersonese running out from the main land of Epirus, opposite to Corcyra, which was called Macridia; probably on account of its being peopled by a colony from Euboea, which was anciently called Macris.—See the Greek Scholiast. Probably this was the place where Buthrotum was situated, mentioned by Strabo in his seventh book.—Greek Scho.

1826. *Sceptre.*] The sceptre was the symbolical ensign of royalty. It was nothing more than a staff more or less ornamented. It was borne by the sovereigns of those ancient times, and even by their delegates when they proceeded to solemn acts, such as concluding treaties, or pronouncing judgments. The sceptre of the ancient sovereigns of Russia was a simple staff. Such is still the sceptre of the little despots of Moldavia and Wallachia. The throne was a seat of stone, on which the monarch sat. The judges were at his side on benches of the same kind.

1876. *Origin from Bacchus.*] The Bacchiades

of Corinth, who took their name from Bacchius, the son of the god Bacchus. They were the most illustrious family in Corinth: and were expelled on account of the death of Actæon. The story runs thus: Melissus, having rendered important services to the Corinthians, who were in danger of being destroyed by Phidon, king of the Argives, was advanced to high honours among them on this account. The Bacchiadæ, coming to his house by night, attempted to carry off his son Actæon by force; but were resisted by the parents of the youth. A scuffle ensued, in which Actæon was unfortunately killed. Melissus, standing on the altar, denounced the most dreadful curses against the Corinthians, unless they avenged the death of his son: this was at the commencement of the Isthmian games. After he had spoken in this manner, he threw himself down headlong from a precipice which lay before him. The Corinthians, cautious of leaving the death of Actæon unpunished, and, at the same time, being urged by the commands of an oracle, expelled the Bacchiadæ. Chersocrates, one of the Bacchiadæ, founded the city of Corcyra, having expelled the Colchians; who retired to the continent, and settled there near the Ceraunian mountains.—Gr. Scho.

1877. *Ephyra.*] Corinth was thus called from Ephyra, the daughter of Epimetheus. Eumelus says, that Ephyra was the daughter of Oceanus and Tethys, and wife of Epimetheus.—Gr. Scho.

1879. *Bacchiadæ.*] The story told by the scholiast, concerning the Bacchiadæ, does not agree with the most authentic historical relations. After the line of Sisiphus was extinct, the kings, who descended from Aletes, affected to call themselves Heraclidæ, Aletes being descended from

Hercules. This name they after changed to Bacchiades, from Bacchius, the fifth in descent from Aletes. They held the kingdom for a long time, until the family grew so numerous, and the people so weary of regal government, that they entirely dissolved it by common consent, in the reign of Telestes their last king. This prince becoming odious to his subjects, two of his kinsmen formed a conspiracy against him. After his death, two hundred of the principal Bacchiadæ seized on the government, and shared the administration of affairs among themselves, electing a supreme out of their own body, whom they called Prytanis. Corinth continued under this aristocracy for about two hundred and forty years; when Cypselus, one of the Bacchiadæ, by the mother's side, but not in the paternal line (being encouraged to the attempt by an oracle), possessed himself of the sovereign authority, and became king.

1878. *After times.*] Timæus says, that Chersicrates was expelled from Corinth, and founded the colony in question, upwards of six hundred years after the time of the Trojan war.

1885. *Nestæan seats, &c.*] Scylax, in his Periplus, says, that the Nestæi were a people of Illyria. From their country to the bay of Manius is (according to him) one day's sail. Eratosthenes says, in his geography, ' After the Illyrians come the Nestæi.'—(Gr. Scho.) Oricos was a maritime town of Epirus, nearly opposite the port of Brundusium, in Italy, now called Brindisi.

1889. *Altar by Medea.*] Timonax, in the first book of his Sicelics, says that Jason married Medea in Colchis, with the consent of Æëtes; and that he saw in his voyage about the Euxine sea, certain gardens, which are called the gardens of Jason; at the place where that hero is said to have landed. He adds, that gymnastic exercises, and the throwing of the discus, are still kept up there in honour of the Argonauts; and that the bridal chamber of Medea, where the nuptials were consummated, was preserved; and also a temple near the city, erected by Jason; together with many other temples consecrated by him. But Timæus says, that Medea and Jason were married in Corcyra; and, speaking of sacrifices, asserts, that, in his time, sacrifice was performed annually in the temple of Apollo, where Medea originally sacrificed; and that monuments, erected to commemorate her marriage, remained at the shore not far from the city, and were called the monuments of the Nymphs and Nereids.—Gr. Scho.

1890. *Nomian Phœbus.*] Apollo was so called from the Greek Νομος, ' a law;' as presiding over law and justice. This altar was erected by Medea, to perpetuate the memory of the righteous doom pronounced by Alcinoüs, which she supposed to be inspired by Apollo Nomius.

1908. *Ambracia.*] A famous city of Thesprotia, in Epirus, near the river Acheron, formerly called Epuia and Paralia. Here was kept the court of king Pyrrhus. After Augustus had conquered Mark Anthony, he called this city Nicopolis, in honour of his victory. Its port was particularly famous.—*Vide* Mela, lib. ii. c. 3. and Livy, lib. xxxviii. c. 3.

1909. *Hallow'd seats.*] It is doubtful whether the seat of the Curetes here meant is not Acarnania; to which place the Curetes are said to have emigrated when they were expelled from Etolia. Strabo has a long but unsatisfactory passage on this subject in his tenth book.—Oxf.

Edit.) See also Diod. Sic. lib. v. c. 64, *et seq*. The Curetes are supposed to have had their first origin from Crete.—Virgil, Georgic, lib. iv. ver. 151 :

> Curetum sonitus crepitantiaque æra secutæ
> Dictæo cœli regem pavere sub antro.

1910. *Echinades*.] These were five small islands in the Ionian sea, near the mouth of the river Acheloüs, and not far from the gulf of Lepanto.

1912. *Land of Pelops*.] So Ovid : *Pelopeia Pittheus me misit in arva*. He means Phrygia, where Tantalus, the father of Pelops, reigned.

1917. *Syrtes*. There were two Syrtes on the coast of Libya ; the greater and the lesser. They are mentioned by most of the ancient writers. Milton's description, Paradise Lost, book ii. ver. 939, corresponds with that of Apollonius :

> Quench'd in a boggy Syrtis, neither sea
> Nor good dry land ; nigh founder'd on he fares,
> Treading the crude consistence, half on foot,
> Half flying ; behoves him now both sail and oar.

Major Rennell speaks thus of the Syrtes, in his excellent work on the geography of Herodotus, p. 646, *et seq*. (by whom they are mentioned in his Melpomene, 169) : ' The Syrtes, which were the terror of ancient mariners, are two wide shallow gulfs which penetrate very far within the northern coast of Africa, between Carthage and Cyrene, in a part where it already retires very far back, to form the middle bason or widest part of the Mediterranean sea. The north and east winds of course exert their full force on these shores, which are exposed to them. At the same time, that not only certain parts of those shores are formed of moveable sand, but the gulfs themselves are also thickly sown with shallows of the same kind; which, yielding to the force of the waves, are subject to variations in their form and positions. To this must be added, the operation of the winds, in checking or accelerating the motions of the tides; which are, therefore, reducible to no rules.

'The two Syrtes are more than two hundred German miles asunder, and are distinguished by the terms greater and lesser; of which it would appear, Herodotus knew only the former, by the name of Syrtis; the latter, by that of the lake Tritonis. Not but that both were known, and had obtained the above distinctive names, in the time of Scylax, whom we may conceive to have written before the time of Herodotus. It is remarkable, that Herodotus is silent respecting the properties of the Syrtis, which he mentions by name; whilst he speaks of the dangers of the other in a pointed manner. We are not, however, to infer from this silence, that he was ignorant of the dangers of the greater Syrtis. The greater Syrtis bordered on the west of the province of Cyrenaica; and penetrated to the depth of about one hundred miles within the two capes that formed its mouth or the opening, which were that of Boreum on the east, Cephalus or Tricorium on the west. In front it was opposed to the opening of the Adriatic sea; and the Mediterranean, in this part, expanding to the breadth of near ten degrees, exposed this gulf to the violence of the northerly winds. Scylax reckons it a passage of three days and nights across its mouth. It is not, however, pretended that the whole extent of this space was equally dangerous, or that there were dangers in every part.

'The lesser Syrtis lay opposite to the islands of Sicily and Malta. It appears to be no more

c c 2

than forty or fifty German miles in breadth, but penetrates to about seventy-five within the continent.   We have the word of Scylax, that it was the most dangerous of the two.   The islands Cercina and Cercinitis bounded its entrance to the north; Meninx, or that of the Lotophagi, on the south.   It was here that Jason is said (by Herodotus) to have been in imminent danger of shipwreck, previous to his setting out on the Argonautic expedition.—Melp. 179.

‘ There are several short descriptions of the Syrtes on record; that of Lucan is the most pointed, and, making allowances for the colouring of a poet, not very different from that given by Edrisi in later times; or, indeed, what may be collected from Strabo :

> When Nature's hand the first formation tried,
> When seas from lands she did at first divide,
> The Syrts, not quite of sea nor land bereft,
> A mingled mass, uncertain still she left.
> For nor the land with sea is quite o'erspread,
> Nor sink the waters deep their oozy bed,
> Nor earth defends her shore, nor lifts aloft its head.
> The site with neither and with each complies,
> Doubtful and inaccessible it lies ;
> Or 'tis a sea with shallows bank'd around,
> Or 'tis a broken land with waters drown'd;
> Here shores advanced o'er Neptune's rule we find,
> And there an inland ocean lags behind. ‣
> Thus Nature's purpose, by herself destroy'd,
> Is useless to herself and unemploy'd,
> And part of her creation still is void.
> Perhaps, when first the world and time began,
> Here swelling tides and plenteous waters ran ;
> But long confining on the burning zone,
> The sinking seas have felt the neighbouring sun.
> Still by degrees we see how they decay,
> And scarce resist the thirsty god of day.
> Perhaps, in different ages 'twill be found,
> When future suns have run the burning round,
> The Syrtes shall be dry and solid ground.—

Small are the depths the scanty waves retain,
And earth grows daily on the yielding main.'—
Rowe's Lucan.

This description, as Major Rennell observes, has a boldness peculiar to itself.

'The dangers of the two Syrtes were different. Those of the greater being produced by the quicksands, both on the shore and in the offing (and it is of these Apollonius speaks), and which were rendered more formidable by their great extent. The dangers of the lesser Syrtis arose, more particularly, from the variations and uncertainty of the tides on a flat, shelvy coast. In effect, Pliny supplies no description at all of the Syrtes : he only says, they are horribly dangerous (lib. iv. c. 5). Neither does Solinus ; but both of them seem to consider the irregularity of the tides as the sole or chief cause of danger. Strabo imputes the danger, not only to the tides, but to the flatness and ooziness of the bottom; and observes, that ships, whilst navigating this part, keep as wide as possible of the indraught of the gulfs.' Major Rennell observes, that the Goodwin Sands of England possess much the same properties as the shallows and coast of the greater Syrtis. The lesser Syrtis is now called the gulf of Kabes : from this cape (Capoudia) says Dr. Shaw, all along to the island of Jerba (*i. e.* of the Lotophagi) we have a succession of little flat islands, banks of sand, oozy bottoms, or small depths of water. The inhabitants make no small advantage of these shallows, by wading a mile or two from the shore, and fixing, as they go, hurdles of reeds, which enclose a number of fish. Dr. Shaw was informed, that frequently at the island of Jerba, on the south side of the Syrtes, the sea rose twice a day above its usual height.

1928. *Winds conspiring, &c.*] The description of this shoal and inaccessible lee shore, with a raging north wind beating on it, is exactly conformable to the description given by the different writers quoted in Major Rennell's work.

1930. *Tides resistless.*] It has been supposed that there are no tides in the Mediterranean; it is ascertained, however, that this is a vulgar error, by various relations, both ancient and modern. Apollonius, in speaking here of the violent and dangerous effect of the tides, is strictly correct and conformable to truth. The whole extract from Major Rennell, above given, will be found to reflect considerable light on this part of the poem of Apollonius.

1939. *No path, no haunt of shepherds.*] Sallust agrees perfectly with our poet, in his description of a part of Libya, in the Jugurthine war. Collins, in his second oriental eclogue, entitled 'Hassan, or the Camel Driver,' has employed the same ideas to great advantage.

1946. *Better the dangers known.*] Virgil has imitated this passage, Æneis, lib. i. ver. 93.

1957. *Sad Ancæus.* The speech of Ancæus is much in character. His observations are sensible, and show the care and attention of an experienced mariner.

2014. *The parent bird.*] This simile is perfectly original, and highly beautiful and expressive. The fears, the tenderness, and unavailing cries of the Pheacian virgins (who found themselves sent, from the ease, the plenty, and indulgence of a palace, in Pheacia, their native country, to perish by hunger in that Libyan desert), are well expressed by the helpless state of the young and unfledged birds falling out of the parent nest in a rock in the absence of the mother. The virgins here mentioned are those whom Areté sent with Medea to attend her. This simile is copied by Virgil, Æneis, lib. xii. ver. 475, in some degree:

Pabula parva legens, nidisque loquacibus escas.

2033. *Heroines.*] These nymphs of Cyrene are also called Heroides in an epigram of Callimachus, which is found in the first volume of Spanheim's edition of Callimachus, p. 368. The word in the original of Apollonius is, by synalæphe, ἡρωσσαι, for ἡρωισσαι.

2044. *The shading veil.*] The veil is properly an ornament of women; the circumstance of Jason having a veil thrown over his head, as he lay upon the ground, shows how much he was dejected and unmanned by his sufferings and sorrows.

2055. *A local reign.*] These rustic and pastoral deities were properly said to obtain local dignity and influence in Libya, or Cyrenaica, where the pastoral life and manners prevailed. Near this was the most fertile part of Libya.

2062. *Tender parent.*] The nymphs here speak in an obscure and oracular manner. The careful parent, darkly mentioned by them, appears, in the sequel, to be meant for a description of the ship Argo; which had borne the Argonauts in her hold, as in a womb, through the various perils of the voyage. There is a similar double meaning, and withdrawing of the obvious truth, in the prophecy of the harpy Celæno, in Virgil; where she tells the Trojans that they should be reduced to eat their tables. Æneis, lib. iii. ver. 255:

Non ante datam cingetis mænibus urbem
Quam vos dira fames nostræque injuria cædis
Ambesas subigat malis absumere mensas.

Many instances of similar obscure predictions

occur in ancient histories. Such was the answer of the oracle to Cresus respecting Cyrus—Herodotus, Clio :

> When o'er the Medes a mule shall bear the sway,
> Then, Lydian, tremble ; and on Hermus' bank
> Prepare thy flight, nor dread a coward's name.

Cyrus was called a mule, because he was half Mede, half Persian, by birth. Of this nature was the oracle which cautioned Epaminondas to beware of what the Greeks called the ' Pelagus;' which he understanding to mean the sea, which is called in Greek Πελαγος, forbore to go in any ship or galley. Whereas it was the Mantinean wood of that name of which the oracle bid him beware. Much after the same manner is the Carthaginian general said to have been deceived, when he was told by an oracle that he should be buried in Libya ; whence he concluded, that after he had beaten the Romans, he should return and die in his own country; whereas the oracle meant the town of Libyssa, which the Nicomedians called Libya. When the elder Brutus went with the Tarquins, his kinsmen, to consult the oracle of Delphi, they were told, that he who should first kiss his mother, on their return, should obtain the chief authority at Rome. Brutus, who alone apprehended the true meaning of the oracle, fell down, as if by accident, and kissed the ground, the common mother of all. Such is the language in the prediction of the witches in Macbeth, when they assure him he shall never be conquered ' Till Birnam wood do come to Dunsinane;' and again tell him,

> Fear not, Macbeth—no man of woman born
> Has power to hurt thee,

We have another instance in history of a puzzling

oracle. The Lacedæmonians proved unsuccessful in a war against the Arcadians; and were told by the oracle, they should continue to be so till they brought back the bones of Orestes, the son of Agamemnon. Where to find them was the difficulty. They again consulted the oracle, and were answered:

> In the Arcadian plain lies Tegea,
> Where two impetuous winds are forced to blow;
> Form resists form, mischief on mischief strikes:
> Here mother earth keeps Agamemnon's son;
> Carry him off, and be victorious.

The solution of the enigma was accidentally found out by Liches, a Spartan; who, being one day at Tegea, observed a smith working at his forge; who told him, that in sinking a well, he had found a coffin seven cubits long; and having had the curiosity to open it, to see if the body answered the length of the coffin, he had found it exactly fitting, and laid it again where he found it. Liches, comparing the place he was in, and the answer of the oracle, conceived, that by the two winds were meant the smith's bellows; by the contending forms, the hammer and anvil; and by the double mischief, the ills which are caused by iron. He had himself banished, for some pretended crime, the better to elude suspicion; he repaired to Tegea; and having, with some difficulty, hired the smith's enclosures, dug up the bones privately and conveyed them to Sparta.

2066. *Achæan shore.*] By this he means Thessaly or Hellas; but it is better to understand Thessaly, the inhabitants of which are called Achei.

2068. *The nymphs evanish'd.*] The appearance of these rural divinities, and their address to Jason, with their sudden vanishing, evidently

seem to have furnished Virgil with the idea of
the scene between Venus and her son, in the
first Æneid, ver. 315.

2080. *Forward he rush'd, and loudly call'd, &c.*]
Is it too fanciful to suppose, that the picture here
given by Apollonius, of Jason calling aloud and
rousing his companions who lay extended on the
sands, despairing and confounded, furnished Mil-
ton with his first idea of Satan calling to the
fallen spirits, who lay stretched and confounded
on the oblivious lake? The arch fiend, like Jason,
rouses himself by an effort :

> Forthwith upright he rears, from off the pool,
> His mighty stature.

With equal loudness he calls to his companions :

> He call'd so loud, that all the hollow deeps
> Of hell resounded.———

And the Argonauts and angels of darkness, in like
manner, at the call of their respective leaders,

> Came flocking where he stood on the bare strand.

The words ' bare strand' actually seem to refer
to the present state of the Argonauts.

2085. *The tawny lion.*] There is a noble
amplification in this passage. The roar of the
lion is supposed to be so loud and tremendous
that even the places which lay low and secure
shook. There is a peculiar appositeness in this
simile. The call of the hero, though it sounded
loud and dreadful to strangers, was the call of
friendship to his companions, and welcome to
their ears; in the same manner the roar of the
lion was the voice of savage love; and though
terrible to the shepherd, it was pleasing and ac-
ceptable to the females.

2112. *And to your mother.*] It is usual with

the ancient poets, when any command or pre-
diction of a divinity, or any person of very supe-
rior rank (as, for instance, of a king, or other
person having supreme authority), is to be pro-
pounded, to recite it over again word for word.
The reader who is conversant with Homer will
recollect a multitude of instances of this kind in
his writings. The nymphs here spoken of were
indigenous or local deities, peculiar to Libya.
They are supposed by the poet to have been ad-
vanced to this high station for the attention paid
by them to Pallas when she first rose to exist-
ence. The Greek Scholiast says, that Stesi-
chorus was the first who pretended that Minerva
sprung armed from the head of Jove. The nymphs
are called Ἀυδήεσσαι, affable, or admitting of a
communication with man, because they were a
kind of protecting geniuses, who were in the
habit of revealing themselves, and conversing
with mortals. Milton speaks thus of Raphael.
He calls him ' Raphael, the affable angel.'

2127. *Of joy and grief.*] Sorrow, to think they
could not develope the meaning of the oracle or
injunction of the Libyan heroines; joy, to think
that their condition was not altogether hopeless.
A situation like that described by Milton, Para-
dise Lost, book ii. ver. 224 :

> For happy though but ill, for ill not worst.

2129. *A courser.*] So Virgil, Æneis, lib. iii.
ver. 537 :

> Quatuor hic primum omen equos in gramine vidi.

I perhaps deceive myself; but there seems to me
to be something in the sound of this line of Vir-
gil, expressive of the trampling and prancing of
horses. The taking an omen of good fortune

from the appearance of these horses, palpably was suggested to Virgil by the horse which is here introduced by our poet. It is curious to remark these coincidences, even in minute things, since they show how constantly Virgil had the poet of Alexandria in his thoughts.

2142. *Vessel.*] The poet has here, in a very sublime and poetical manner, embellished and related a simple and common transaction; namely, that the Argonauts hauled their vessel ashore, and carried it over some part of the land, to avoid the dangers of the Syrtes. This does not seem to be a thing altogether so incredible as at first view might be apprehended. The ships, in those early times, were small and light, mere barks; and the lading of the Argo could not have been very ponderous.

2155. *So has the Muse.*] Here again we find the poet resorts to the authority of the Muses, as a sanction for what he narrates; and tells the reader, that he only repeats what he had received from them. This proceeds from a consciousness, that what he was about to tell must appear incredible. Thus Ariosto, whenever he is about to relate some extravagant fiction, always refers his reader to the authority of Archbishop Turpin, the early historiographer of romance; and assures him, that he only repeats what he had learned from *Il buon Turpino.*

2160. *And thus they sang.*] Virgil, perhaps, may be censured for having related that the lock of Dido was cut off by Iris, and that the ships of Æneas were turned into seanymphs. Apollonius is much more modest and more cautious of violating credibility. Apprehensive that it might seem improbable that the Argonauts, without the assistance of any deity, and merely by their own strength and exertion, βιη και αρετη, should have been able to carry their ship during so many days; he takes care to ascribe this piece of history to the Muses.—See Mr. Upton's note in the Oxford edition.

2164. *Twelve times did Phœbus.*] This circumstance, of making them carry their bark twelve days' journey, agrees well enough with what Major Rennell says of the distance between the greater and lesser Syrtis : if by the lesser Syrtis we understand the lake of Tritonis.

2173. *The lake of Pallas.*] For more particular considerations on the lake Tritonis, see the note in a subsequent passage.

2178. *Burning thirst.*] The waters of the lake Tritonis were quite salt, and could afford them no relief. The soil about them was also so impregnated with salt, that the springs are brackish. The same is the case in the deserts of Egypt.

2182. *The serpent Ladon.*] The dragon which guarded the Hesperian fruit was called Ladon. Pisander supposed him to be the offspring of the earth. Hesiod says, that he sprung from Typhon. Agretas, in the third book of his Lybics, asserts, that what were commonly supposed to be apples were not fruit, but certain flocks of sheep, of surprising beauty, which were called ' golden,' on account of their great value (this mistake might have arisen from the ambiguity of the word μηλα); and that these flocks were guarded by a very savage and ferocious shepherd, who, from his fierce and cruel disposition, was called a dragon. Pherecydes, in his tenth book of the ' Marriage of Juno,' says, that the land in islands of the ocean produced golden apples, or apple-trees bearing golden fruit, which were guarded by a dragon sprung from Typhon, who had a hun-

dred heads, and uttered all manner of sounds
and voices: and that the nymphs, the daughters
of Jove and Themis, who resided in a cave near
Eridanus, suggested to Hercules, who was in
deep perplexity on the subject, the idea of inquir-
ing from Venus where the golden apples were
to be found. Hercules, by their advice, seized
Nereus forcibly, who at first transformed himself
into water, then into fire; but at last, returning
to his original form, revealed to Hercules the
place where the apples were to be found. Her-
cules, in consequence of this information, pro-
ceeded in quest of his object; and, having arrived
at Tartessus in Spain, passed over from thence
to Libya. There his first exploit was to kill An-
tæus, a savage and injurious person, sprung from
Neptune. After this, he penetrated to the Nile
and Memphis, and to the dominions of Busiris,
who was also the son of Neptune. Him too the
hero slew, with Iphidamas his son, Chalbes his
herald, and his attendants, at the altar of Jove,
where they had been used to sacrifice strangers.
Having arrived at Thebes, he proceeded through
the mountains into the region beyond Libya, in
the deserts of which he killed many wild beasts
with his bow and arrows. Having purged Libya
of the monsters which infested it, he descended
towards the sea which lies beyond it; and having
received a golden cup from the sun, he passes
over in it to Perga, sailing through the sea
beyond Libya, and through the ocean. Having
arrived where Prometheus was bound, and being
seen by him, he takes pity on his sufferings and
supplications. He kills the vulture, and frees
him. Prometheus, in return for his kindness,
advises him not to go in person for the golden
apples; but to repair to Atlas, and order him to

go for them, while he himself should support the heavens in the place of Atlas, during his absence on this mission, to obtain these apples from the Hesperides. Fortified with this advice, Hercules proceeds to Atlas, explains to him the nature of his labour, and directs him to go and procure for him three of the apples. Atlas, having rested the heavens upon the shoulders of Hercules, hastens to the Hesperides; and, having received from them the apples, returns and finds Hercules supporting the heavens. Instead of giving the precious fruit to the hero, as he had promised, he proposed that Hercules should continue to support his burden, while he himself should proceed with the apples, and deliver them. Hercules seemed to assent to this proposition, but contrived, by stratagem, to return the burden to him who had so long sustained it. He desired Atlas to resume his charge for a moment, until he (Hercules) should prepare a cap for his head (a *ruse*, which had been suggested by Prometheus). Atlas, not suspecting the scheme, laid down the apples on the ground, and received the heavens on his head and shoulders. Hercules immediately possessed himself of the apples, and bidding Atlas farewell, hastened to Mycenæ, and delivered his prize to Eurystheus. Such is the entertaining fairy tale of the good old scholiast. —Vid. Gr. Scho.

Spanhemius, in his notes on the hymn to Ceres, of Callimachus, ver. 11., employs much pains and learning on the explication of this fable of the dragon and the golden fruit. It is most probable, that these golden apples were citrons and oranges, produced in the islands on the coast of Africa. Malta, we know, is still celebrated for its admirable oranges. This fruit, when first known, was considered as a great curiosity among the Greeks. Citrons and oranges were called *Mali Punica.* They were used in the mysteries of Bacchus, according to a line of Orpheus, which is quoted by Clemens Alexandrinus. Spanheim observes, that there is an antique medallion which is in the collection of the king of France; it represents Hercules taking these apples from the tree of the Hesperides. It is said by some that Atlas (having laid down the burden of the heavens which he had long sustained) agreed with the Hesperides for the possession of these apples. It is supposed by many, that all this fable of the apples and the serpent, may be a faint shadow, derived by tradition from the scripture account of the fall of man.

2185. *Soil of Atlas.*] Africa, where, according to the ancients, Atlas reigned. Thus Virgil, Æneis, lib. iv. ver. 481:

Ultimus Æthiopum locus est, ubi maximus Atlas.

2186. *Hesperian maids.*] So called, either from the appearance of evening, or from their residing in Hesperia. The Hesperides were the daughters of Phorcus and Ceto. From one of these nymphs the island borrowed its name, which was inhabited by Geryoneus; who owned the dog Orthus, the brother of Cerberus, and whom Hercules killed. Some say, that this dog was the property of Atlas.—Gr. Scho.—Virgil, Æneis, lib. vii. ver. 661, alludes to this exploit of Hercules, mentioned by the scholiast:

———— Postquam Laurentia victor,
Geryone exstincto, Tirynthius attigit arva,
Tyrrhenoque boves in flumine lavit Iberas.

Servius, in his note on this passage, mentions the dog Orthus. Geryon and his dog are likewise celebrated by Pindar, first Isthmian Ode. The scholiast, in commenting on this passage, mentions the dog Orthus. And one of the annotators on Pindar remarks, that there is an enallagè of the number in the preceding lines; since, in fact, Geryon had but one dog. This dog is also noticed by Hesiod, in Theog. ver. 309. According to other accounts of the Hesperides, they were the daughters of Hesperus, the brother of Atlas, and shepherdesses by profession. Hermes carried off their sheep, which, for their exquisite beauty, were called ' golden' (as has been already said), and killed the shepherd.

2210. *Whether you join, &c.*] The hero addresses the nymphs in this strain of uncertainty, because there were various classes and descriptions of these divinities. Some were Uraniæ, or celestial nymphs; others Epigææ, or terrestrial; some Potamiæ, or river nymphs; others Limnææ, or nymphs of the lakes: some Thalassiæ, or nymphs of the sea. In short, the general denomination of nymphs was subdivided into several tribes or families, as Mnesimachus says, in his Diacosmi.—Gr. Scho.

2216. *Some rock disclose.*] We find the goddess Rhea in the same manner praying for water, in the first hymn of Callimachus ' *ad Jovem.*' All the land, according to the poet, being at that time destitute of springs. One cannot forbear remarking the striking resemblance between the passage now cited and the description in scripture of Moses in the wilderness, striking the rock with his staff and causing water to flow, to satisfy the thirst of the Israelites. It is, indeed, one of those passages which may lead us to think that the Alexandrine poets had access to the inspired authors of holy writ, in the translation of the seventy interpreters. The passage is in Exodus xvii. ver. 6. ' Behold, I will stand before thee there upon the rock in Horeb; and thou shalt smite the rock, and there shall come water out of it, that the people may drink: and Moses did so in the sight of the elders of Israel.' And in the Psalms: ' He smote the stony rock, so that the waters gushed out, and the streams flowed withal.'

2231. *Soon in trees, &c.*] Hespera, Erytheis, Eglé—these were the names of the nymphs. This passage is very poetical and original. It is one of the prettiest and most fanciful transformations that can be found in any poet, ancient or modern. The compassionate nymphs, desirous to recreate the senses of the weary Argonauts, first cover the ground with grass; then cause taller herbs to spring; then transform themselves into various trees: but not like the Hamadryads, who had each of them a permanent union of connexion and vital existence with some particular tree. At last these nymphs pass from the semblance of trees to their original and proper nymphlike appearance.

2262. *Lake of Pallas.*] The lake Tritonis. It is mentioned by Lucan, lib. ix. ver. 347. Herodotus speaks thus of the lake Tritonis; Melp. 178, 179, 180: ' Towards the sea, the Machlyes border on the Lotophagi. They extend as far as a great stream called the Triton, which enters into an extensive lake named Tritonis, in which is the island of Phía. An oracular declaration they had said had foretold, that some Lacedæmonians should settle themselves here.

' The particulars are these: when Jason had constructed the Argo, at the foot of Mount Pelion, he carried on board a hecatomb for sacrifice, and a brazen tripod. He sailed round the Peloponnese, with the intention to visit Delphi. As he approached Malea, a north wind drove him to the African coast; and, before he could discover land, he got amongst the shallows of the lake Tritonis: not being able to extricate himself from this situation, a Triton is said to have appeared to him, and to have promised him a secure and easy passage, provided he would give him the tripod. To this Jason assented; and the Triton, having fulfilled his engagement, placed the tripod on the bank, from whence he communicated to Jason, and his companions, what was afterwards to happen. Amongst other things, he said, that whenever a descendant of the Argonauts should take away this tripod, there would be a hundred Grecian cities near the lake of Tritonis. The Grecians, hearing this prediction, concealed the tripod.

'The Machlyes have an annual festival, in honour of Minerva, in which the young women, dividing themselves into two bands, engage each other with stones and clubs. These rites, they say, were instituted by their forefathers, in veneration of her whom we call Minerva; and if any die, in consequence of wounds received in this contest, they say that she was no virgin. Before the close of the fight they observe this custom: she, who, by common consent, appears to have fought the best, has a Corinthian helmet placed on her head, is clothed in Grecian armour, and carried in a chariot round the lake. How the virgins were decorated in this solemnity before they had any knowledge of the Greeks, I am not able to say; probably they might use Egyptian arms. We may venture to affirm, that the Greeks borrowed from Egypt the shield and the helmet.

It is pretended that Minerva was the daughter of Neptune, and the divinity of the lake; and that, from some trifling disagreement with her father, she put herself under the protection of Jupiter, who adopted her as his daughter.'

Scylax, as quoted by Major Rennell, says, ' In this Syrtis (the lesser one) is the island and river of Triton, and the temple of Minerva Tritonia. The mouth or opening of the lake is small; and in it, on the reflux of the sea, is seen an island. When the island is covered, that is, when the tide is up, ships may enter the lake. The lake is large, being about 1000 stadia in circumference; it is surrounded by Libyan nations, and has cities on its western border, and also fertile and productive lands.' Scylax calls the whole gulf of Kabes, the great lake of Tritonis; in which the lesser Syrtis, called likewise Cercinnitica, is also included as a part of it. Hence it would appear, that in the times of Scylax and Herodotus it was the custom to call the whole Syrtis and lake, collectively, the lake or gulf of Tritonis : although in the times of Strabo, Pliny, Polybius, and Ptolemy, the word Syrtis was applied separately to the bay or gulf; Tritonis to the lake. ' We must, therefore (says Major Rennell), regard the lake Tritonis of Herodotus as the lesser Syrtis and lake of Lowdeah united; and must conclude that he either knew, or took for granted, that the dangerous gulf, into which Jason's ship was driven, together with the water which received the river Triton, and also contained the island of the same name, were one and the same.' Dr. Shaw was clearly of opinion, that the lake Lowdeah was the Tritonis; but seems to have had no suspicion of its having ever communicated with the outer gulf. If we may suppose an ancient communication, now closed up by sand gradually thrown up by the surge of the sea, we may naturally suppose that a great part of the lake itself has been filled up by the same operation. The lake itself is, at present, as salt as the sea; which may arise, either from the sea water oozing through the sand, or from the salt rivulets which flow into it, from a soil strongly impregnated with that mineral; or even from the salt, washed down by dews, and occasional showers, from the neighbouring mountains of Had-deffa. Major Rennell supposes the rivulet of El Hammah to have been the river Tritonis. At present this rivulet, composed of several hot springs, which furnish a number of baths (whence its name El Hammah), runs several miles towards the lake, and there loses itself in the sand.

Pliny says, lib. v. c. 4: ' Near to them (the Philænian altars) the great lake, denominated from the river Triton, receives into it that river. But Callimachus calls it Pallantias, and places it on this side the lesser Syrtis, though many place it between both.'

From the Africans on the borders of this lake (says Herodotus) the Greeks borrowed the vest, and the ægis, with which they decorated the shrine of Minerva: the vests, however, of the African Minervas are made of skin, and the fringe hanging from the ægis is not composed of serpents, but leather. In every other respect the dress is the same. It appears by the very name, that the robe of the statues of Minerva was borrowed from Africa. The women of this country wear below their garments goat skins without the hair, fringed and stained of a red colour: from which part of dress the word *ægis* of the Greeks is unquestionably derived.—(Melp.

c. 189.) We find, in conformity with this description of Herodotus, our poet, in the preceding passage, has dressed the Heroines or Libyan nymphs. Dyed goat skins were anciently in much request, and formed a considerable article of commerce. In allusion to this custom, Isaiah has, ' Who is this that cometh from Edom, with dyed garments from Bosrah?'

2274. *As swarming ants.*] Virgil has imitated this simile, Æneis, lib. iv. ver. 402.

2286. *E'en absent, godlike chief.*] There is something very interesting and pleasing here in the art of the poet, who thus brings back Hercules to the view of the reader, and makes him, even in his absence, contribute to the success of the Argonautic expedition, by his proving the means of preserving the band of his friends from perishing of thirst.

2304. *And fifth with them.*] The four first heroes were eminently fitted for the task they undertook, by their qualifications and endowments, as the reader will see by resorting to the description of their characters in the catalogue of the Argonauts, book i. As to Canthus, the poet says he was impelled by fate; because he had already mentioned, in his first book, that he was ordained to perish immature. There is something very interesting in the spirit and friendship of Canthus, who thus resolved to proceed with intrepidity, and demand of Hercules, formidable as he was, an account of his friend.

2314. *Mysia's soil.*] Polyphemus, being left behind in Mysia, founded the city of Cius, which took its name from the river which flowed round it. He fell in battle with the Chalybes, as Nymphodorus relates. His having founded Cius is mentioned by Charis in the first book of his chronology.   Cius is now a village, called Ghemlek by the Turks.

2329. *Through gray beginnings.*] This simile is imitated by Virgil, Æneis, lib. vi. ver. 453.   Lynceus, it appears, though he could see Hercules, yet perceived, at the same time, that it would be but labour in vain to attempt to follow him; he was so distant.   The endowment of Lynceus seems to have resembled very much the second sight of the Scotch.

2351. *Lycorean.*] This has the same import as Delphic.   For the people of Delphis were anciently called Lycoreans, from a certain village named Lycorea.   This epithet is recognised by Callimachus, in his hymn to Apollo, ver. 119. And in the Orphic hymn to Apollo, Λυκωρευ φοιβε.   See the learned annotations of Spanhemius on the passage of Callimachus now mentioned.

2353. *Acacallis.*] Alexander, in the first book of his Cretics, says, that both Hermes and Apollo had an intercourse with Acacallis.   To the latter she bore a son, called Naxus, who communicated his name to one of the Greek islands; to Hermes, a son named Cydon, from whom the city of Cydonia in Crete took its name.—Gr. Scho.

2358. *Amphithemis.*] The meaning of the poet is, that he was called by both names.   It seems to be doubtful whether the Garamantes, a Libyan tribe, were called after this son of Phœbus, or he obtained the name of Garamas from the people in question.—Gr. Scho.

2363. *Nasamon.*] This was the name of a Libyan tribe, not far from the lake Tritonis.— Lucan, lib. ix. speaks of this people:

Quas Nasamon, gens dura colit, qui proxima ponto.

2363. *Caphareus.*] Much dependence should not be placed on the similitude of names; but one cannot forbear remarking a very striking one with respect to this name of Caphareus. There is, at this day, in the southern part of Africa, a country called Caffraria; and a nation, who are called Caffres, or Coffres. Such a coincidence of names in the same continent, though, certainly, in very distant regions, is somewhat extraordinary.

2392. *Perseus.*] Hence the passages of Ovid, Metam. lib. iv. ver. 615. and Milton, P. Lost, book x. ver. 526.

2394. *Gorgon—falchion.*] Polydectes, king of Seriphos, fearing the resentment of Perseus, planned a scheme for his destruction; and having invited the neighbouring princes to an entertainment, where an introductory present was required from each guest, he required a horse from each of the other guests, but Perseus was required to bring the head of Medusa, one of the Gorgons. The day after the banquet, the guests brought horses; and Perseus brought one, like the rest; but Polydectes refused to receive the horse of Perseus, and insisted on his producing the head of Medusa; and threatened, if he should fail to do so, to make his mother answerable. Perseus departed in affliction, lamenting his fate, to the extremity of the island. Here Hermes appeared to him, and having learned the cause of his lamentation, encouraged him; and, by the counsel of Minerva, conducted him to the old women, the daughters of Phorcus, Pemphredo, or Pephredo, Ento, and Jaino. These three sisters, had but one eye and one tooth among them, which they used alternately. Perseus contrived to carry away the precious eye and tooth. He confessed to the

sisters that he had them in his possession, but
refused to restore them, unless the old women
would point out to him the nymphs who kept the
helmet of Orcus, which had the power of render-
ing the wearer invisible, the winged sandals, and
the scrip. They agreed to point them out, on
condition of regaining their eye and tooth. Per-
seus, proceeding to the nymphs, obtained what he
sought, by the intercession of Hermes. He binds
the sandals under his feet, and suspends the scrip
over his shoulders. In this manner he flies over
the ocean, accompanied by Hermes and Pallas;
and, finding the Gorgons sleeping, his divine
companions instruct him how he might cut off the
head he sought, with his face averted. They
showed him in a mirror Medusa, who alone of the
Gorgons was mortal. He having approached her
cut off her head without looking at her, with a
curved falchion given him by Mercury, and depo-
sited it in his scrip. After which he fled away
with all speed. The Gorgons, perceiving what
was done, pursued him; but were unable to dis-
cover Perseus, on account of the helmet of
Orcus. Perseus, on his reaching Seriphos, re-
pairs to Polydectes; and desires him to assem-
ble the people, that he may show them the head
of the Gorgon, well knowing that all who behold
it must be turned to stone. Polydectes, having
collected his people, desires Perseus to show the
fatal head. He, with face averted, takes it from
the scrip; and all the beholders become stone.
Minerva, having received the head of Medusa
from Perseus, placed it in her ægis; bestowed
the scrip and winged sandals on Mercury; and
returned the helmet of Orcus to the Nymphs.
Such is the tale related by Pherecydes in his
second book. Others say, that Perseus, having

cut off the head of Medusa, flew over Libya, where wild beasts, serpents, and other monsters sprung up from the blood that dropped from the head: on which account, Libya abounds in those dreadful creatures.—Gr. Sch.—See Apollodorus, lib. ii. c. 14.—Hesiod, Theog. ver. 270.—Hygin. in prefatione.—Lucan, Pharsalia, lib. ix. ver. 696, gives an account of the various serpents with which the soil abounded.   And see Milton, Par. Lost, book x. ver. 521.   See also Herodotus (Melp. 191), who says, that on the west of the river Triton, the country is infested with wild beasts, and abounds in serpents of enormous size.

2421. *The subtle poison.*] Lucan, lib. ix. ver. 770, has described the appearances in the body of a soldier dying of the poison of a serpent, with great variety of circumstances, and strength of colouring.

2424. *Brazen, &c.*] Anciently, from the scarcity of iron, not only arms and warlike engines, but instruments of husbandry, were made of brass. We find that this was formerly the case in Ireland; where spear-heads, and other weapons of brass, some of them of great size, have frequently been found in the earth.

2427. *Heap the' incumbent clay.*] The practice of raising barrows, or sepulchral mounds, over the dead was not peculiar to the Celtic tribes, but was almost universal in the earlier ages. Homer mentions it as usual among the Greeks and Trojans.   And it appears, by the relations of Chandler, and other travellers who have visited the Troade, that the barrows of many of the heroes who fell on both sides, during the Trojan war, remain at this day.   Xenophon says, that the same custom prevailed among the

Persians. It also obtained among the ancient
Germans; and we know, from the vast number
of barrows of the most remote antiquity which
are every where to be seen in Ireland, that the
use of them was general throughout that island.

2428. *The mourning warriors, &c.*] The origin
of funeral games is not known. Pliny says they
existed before the time of Theseus. Homer,
whose poems are a treasure of ancient learning,
in describing the obsequies of Patroclus, has
enumerated all the usual funeral ceremonials.—
Il. xxiii. Electra, in the play of Sophocles which
bears her name, alludes to this custom, which
prevailed among the relations and friends of the
deceased, of cutting their hair, and placing it, as
an offering, on the tomb of the defunct. Briseis,
in Homer, cuts off her hair, and consigns it, as
an oblation to the memory of Patroclus. When
the hair was thus cut off, in honour of the dead,
it was done in a circular form, something like a
monkish tonsure. Ovid takes notice of this cus-
tom: *Scissæ cum veste capillos.*—Virgil mentions
funeral rites similar to those described by our
poet, in his eleventh Æneid, ver. 188. The
widow of General Le Clerc is said to have
revived this ancient practice, by cutting off her
hair, and placing it on the dead body of her
husband.

2454. *Triton.*] The ancients really believed in
the existence of Tritons. See the story in Hero-
dotus, which reflects some light on this passage.
The historian makes the interview of Jason with
Triton anterior to the arrival of the hero in Col-
chis. Pindar, in his fourth Pythian ode, ad-
dressed to Arcesilaus of Cyrene, in which he
has given a complete history of the Argonautic

enterprise, introduces Triton as appearing in a human form.

2456. *A verdant sod.*] This sod was offered to the Argonauts by the deity, in token of his devotion to their service. Earth was one of the symbols given by the ancients, and also by the moderns, under the feudal law, in token of fealty and allegiance. Thus, we find Cyrus sending to the Scythians to demand earth and water as an acknowledgment of their submission to his dominion : and the ambassadors of Xerxes made a similar demand of the Athenians.

2472. *Eurypylus.*] He was king of Cyrene, and son of Neptune and Celæno, the daughter of Atlas. Phylarchus, in his seventh book, calls him Eurytus, and says that his brother was named Lycaon. Acesander, in his first book concerning Cyrene, the daughter of Hypseus, says, that after him (Eurypylus) Cyrene, the daughter of Hypseus, reigned over Libya. This Eurypylus is mentioned by Callimachus, Βωι σινιν Ευρυπυλοιο.—Gr. Scho. And see Pindar, Pyth. iv.

2474. *Euphemus.*] Euphemus is made the first to receive the sod from the hand of Eurypylus, because he was of the same blood ; being himself the son of Neptune and Europa, the daughter of Tityus.—See Pindar, Pyth. iv.—Gr. Scho.

2476. *Where Apis.*] The text has *Atthis*, but the Greek Scholiast approves of *Apis*, as the better reading. Apis, it seems, is the name of the island which lay near Crete, or in the sea of Minos, Μινωιον πελαγος. A name derived from the famous sovereign and lawgiver of Crete, who obtained the sovereignty over this sea and all the adjacent isles. After this the sea in question bore the name of Cretan sea. Thus Horace has, *In mare Creticum.* After this, it was called the Egyptian sea.

2493. *Near a deep outlet.*] It seems that the outlet here mentioned was the communication of the lake Tritonis with the lesser Syrtis, or gulf of Kabes; mentioned in the extract of Major Rennell, given in a preceding note. It appears, that it was difficult to find this communication among the shoals.

2506. *Till boldly swelling.*] He advises them to keep the shore in view, until they should make a certain cape or promontory, from whence they might take a departure, and stand over to Crete. This was consonant to the timid practice of ancient navigators. The cape or headland here meant is the promontory of Phycus, now cape Rasato.

2550. *A tail enormous.*] The word in the original, αλκαιη, properly signifies the tail of a lion; and is derived from αλκη, *robur,* from the force with which he lashes his sides. Callimachus improperly applies it to the tails of flies.—(See Gr. Scho.) The simile of the lunar crescent, to express both the form and brightness of the vast fins in which the tail of the Triton ended, is very apposite.

2560. *Argo's name.*] The port of Argous, near the lake of Triton and lesser Syrtis. Notwithstanding the dreadful accounts given by the ancients of the Syrtes, there were ports in them, and they were not unfrequented by mariners.— See Rennell.

2572. *Southern blasts.*] The Argonauts were glad of the ceasing of the west, and the rising of the south-west wind: because, as Libya lay to the south-west of Greece, the latter wind was favourable to their course homeward. The worst wind which could have blown for them would have been the north; which, indeed, is peculiarly dangerous in the neighbourhood of the Syrtes. —See the preceding extract from Major Rennell.

2574. *Hesper.*] Hesper is called, in the original, 'Αστηρ αυλιος, or the 'bedward star,' from αυλιζεσθαι, to retire to lodgings, or resting places. The natural effect of the close of day. —Gr. Scho.

2584. *Carpathus.*] This island is one of the Sporades, and lies near Cos.—It is mentioned by Homer, and it is called at this day, Scarpanto.

2588. *Brazen Talus.*] *Hæc verba felicissime transtulit,* Val. Flac. lib. x.—'Valerius Flaccus has most happily translated this passage in his tenth book.' Such is the note of the Oxford Editor. The lines quoted by him are these:

> Ferreus arce procul scopuli Dycteide terrâ,
> Hos prohibet sævo ore Talos suspendere funes,
> Et legere hospitium, &c.

It is truly surprising that the Oxford Editor, Mr. Shaw, should speak of the Latin passage here mentioned, as proceeding from Valerius Flaccus, or have quoted a tenth book of that poet: since it is a matter of notoriety, that Valerius Flaccus did not produce any tenth book. Had Mr. Shaw taken the trouble of only consulting the preface to Burman's edition of Val. Flaccus, he would there have seen, that the Latin poet left his Argonautics imperfect; and that his work was continued, chiefly from Apollonius Rhodius, by a modern Italian poet, Pius Bononiensis, who also edited the Argonautics of Valerius Flaccus. The continuation first appeared in that edition, which is now become rare; and has since been

adopted in other editions of V. Flaccus. Plato,
in his dialogue on law, entitled Minos, explains
the fable of Talus. He says, that Rhadaman-
thus and Talus were the assistants of Minos in
administering justice: that Rhadamanthus pre-
sided over the capital, Talus over the rest of
Crete. The latter used, thrice in a year, to take
a circuit through the villages and districts of the
island, to see if the laws were duly observed;
which laws he carried about with him, inscribed
on tablets of brass; from hence he obtained the
name of ' brazen.' It is conjectured, that the
story of the bursting of the vein above the ankle
of Talus, by which he died, arose from a mode
of punishing criminals practised by him, which
was the opening of a vein above the ankle,
whereby they bled to death. Eustathius (not.
Odyss. ver. 302) says, that Talus was made by
Vulcan, and presented to Minos, that he might
guard Crete and Europa.—His mode of punish-
ing those who invaded his precincts was to leap
into the fire, and, when he was throughly heated,
to clasp the offender in his arms. Hence came
the expression of a Sardonian laugh. Suidas, on
the phrase, ' Sardonic laugh,' ascribes this story
to Simonides. Talus, it seems, by the context,
before his arrival in Crete, had resided in Sar-
dinia; whence he seems to have brought colo-
nists to Minos. See Bacon on the Wisdom of
the Ancients, for the allegorical sense of their
fables.

2640. *In rage she grew.*] See Virgil, Æneis,
lib. vii. ver. 445. See also the description of
Erichtho in Lucan.

2698. *Melantian rocks.*] The Melantii were
two rocks, so called from one Melas, who pos-
sessed the adjacent region. They were near the

island of Thera, of which more in a subsequent note.

2703. *Sporades.*] These were certain islands of the Archipelago, about twelve in number; some of them inhabited, others not. They had the name of Sporades, from their being scattered here and there; or, as if sown in the deep, from σπειρω, *semino.* The little island, to which Apollonius alludes, was near Thera, now Santorin, and took its name of Anaphé, from ἀναφαινω, ' to reveal.'

2706. *Hippuris.*] Was an island, which also lay near Thera. The commentaries of Spanhemius on Callimachus—Hymn to Delos, deserve to be consulted, for an illustration of this passage. See also the travels of Olivier, vol ii. and the concluding note.

2726. *Loud bursts of laughter.*] This passage is highly natural and characteristic. The light and thoughtless disposition of these young girls, easily moved to laughter, and made to forget the dangers and difficulties of their situation by trivial circumstances, is well imagined and described.

2739. *Mirthful sallies.*] Callimachus, who perhaps, through the influence of his Egyptian origin and education, is passionately fond of introducing the epithets of deities, and the details of religious rites and ceremonies, says, in allusion to this custom, in his Hymn to Delos, ver. 324:

Κιρζοντι και 'Απολλωνι γιλασον.

It is observed by Spanhemius on this passage, that among the ancients, many of their sacrifices were performed not only with festivity, but even with laughter, mutual taunts, and a sort of licensed ribaldry and grossness. Such were the

Saturnalia among the Romans; such the rites of
Apollo in Delos, mentioned by Callimachus in
his Hymn to that island; such were the rites of
Apollo Ægletes in Achaia, mentioned by Pausa-
nias. The same license of jesting prevailed in
other sacrifices of Ceres, the Thesmophoria, as
may be seen in Apollodorus, lib. i. c. 6. And in
Callimachus, Hymn to Ceres, ver. 18.

2743. *Vows to Maia's son.*] Euphemus is here
said to have prayed to Mercury, because he was
the god who presided over dreams.—Gr. Sch.

2746. *That sod.*] Euphemus, it seems, from
the time he had received the sod from Triton, had
preserved it in his bosom, as a charm or pledge
of good fortune.

2750. *A beauteous maid.*] There is something
in this passage of Apollonius very like that in the
Paradise Lost of Milton, where Adam, in a
vision, sees the Creator forming Eve:

Under his forming hand a creature grew.

2761. *Nurse of thy progeny.*] Euphemus inha-
bited the territory of Laconia, near the seashore.
But Sesamus, one of his descendants, emigrated
and colonized Thera. From him descended Aris-
totle, who led a colony to Cyrene, as Pindar
relates in his Pythian Odes; and as it is more
particularly mentioned by Theochrestus, in the
first book of his Cyrene. They mention, that
Thera rose, and grew in the sea, from the sod
which was cast into it. Pindar says, it was
melted and mixed with the waves, near the island
now called Thera, through the carelessness of
the attendants. Apollonius states, that the sod
was cast into the sea designedly, with the con-
currence of Jason.—Gr. Scho.

2786. *Lemnos held.*] Some of the Argonauts,

on their return, settled at Lemnos.—Being after-
wards expelled by the Pelasgians, who came
from the coasts of Italy, they repaired to Sparta;
where they were received.—See subsequent note.

2790. *Theras from Autesion.*] Theras was of
the race of Œdipus, being the son of Autesion,
the son of Thersander, the son of Polynices.—
Gr. Scho.

2792. *Thera.*] Olivier, an elegant French tra-
veller, says (in his second volume, p. 234), nothing
can be more frightful than the violent convulsion
which has taken place all along the coast of
Thera, Therasia, and Aspronisi. Nothing more
astonishing than the formation of the roadstead,
and of the three islands, which have issued from
the bottom of the sea at known periods. The
coast of Santorin, nearly a hundred toises in ele-
vation in some places, presents itself like a per-
pendicular mountain, formed of various strata,
and of different banks of volcanic substances.

Santorin, according to Pliny, received the
name of Calista, or 'handsome island,' after
having issued from the bosom of the waters; it
afterwards bore that of Thera, from the name of
one of its kings: the name which it bears at pre-
sent is formed of that of St. Irene, to whom the
island was dedicated under the emperors of the
east. It is not to be doubted, that if we con-
sider what Santorin must have been at its second
period, because it is still so at this day, it must
have been one of the finest and most fertile
islands of the Archipelago. Its circular form, a
soil entirely susceptible of culture, which rose by
degrees from the borders of the sea, in form of
a calotte flattened at the top, Mounts St. Stephen
and Elias, situated at one of the extremities,
covered perhaps with verdure and wood: every

thing concurred to render Santorin, if not a very beautiful island, at least one of the most agreeable of the Archipelago.

In the Annals of the World, by Brietius, we find, that thirty years before the Ionic emigration, Theras, son of Autesion, and nephew of Polynices, caused a colony of Minyæ to be conveyed to Calista, in order to augment the number of the inhabitants. The Minyæ were descendants of the Argonauts, who had followed Jason into Colchis: and who, on their return, had stopped at Lemnos, and had there established themselves. The descendants of those heroes, driven some time after from Lemnos by the Pelasgi, took refuge in Sparta, where they were kindly received. Lands were given to them, and they were married to girls of the country. But as these strangers, ever restless and ambitious, were in the sequel convicted of endeavours to seize on the sovereign authority, they were apprehended and condemned to death. Love inspired one of their women with a trick, which succeeded. Having obtained permission to see their husbands previous to the execution of the sentence, they changed clothes with them; by means of which disguise the husbands escaped in the dark, and fled to Mount Täygetus: then it was that Theras demanded, obtained, and conducted them to Calista, which from that time was called Thera. —(See Herodotus.) Santorin, in proportion to its extent, is the richest and most populous of all the islands of the Archipelago. This intelligent traveller says: ' After having visited, with the greatest attention, Thera, Therasia, and Aspronisi, and convinced ourselves that these three islands, at a remote epoch, must have formed but one, and that there has taken place a

sudden and violent depression, which has divided
them, it remained for us to see, whether the three
islands of the road presented an organization
different from the other three.   We employed a
whole day in this examination, and had reason
to be satisfied, that even had not history told us
any thing on the subject, these islands carry with
them the stamp of the period of their formation.'
It appears that all these islands were of volcanic
origin.   Brietius says, 'That in the year 47,
there arose on a sudden, from the bottom of the
sea, near Thera, a small island, which had not
before been seen.'—Briet. Ann. Mund. tom. ii.
p. 63.   Justin says (lib. iii. c. 4),   'That there
was seen to issue, after an earthquake, an island,
between Thera and Therasia, which was called
sacred, and was dedicated to Pluto.'   (This was
in the year 196 before Christ.)

Dion Cassius mentions the sudden appearance
of a small island, near that of Thera, during the
reign of Claudius.   Syncellus mentions it to have
happened in the forty-sixth year after Christ, and
places it between Thera and Therasia.   But it
appears that some time after there arose another
island called Thia, which disappeared afterwards,
or was united to the sacred island.   Mention is
made of it in Pliny, in Theophanes, and in Brie-
tius.   The words of Pliny are : *Et in nostro evo,
Thia juxta eandem Hieram nata.*   Lib. iv. c. 12.

Nothing remarkable happened afterwards, till
1427, when a fresh explosion produced another
great and very distinguishable increase to the
island of Hiera: mention of which is made in
some Latin verses, engraved on a marble at
Scarva, near the temple of the Jesuits.   In 1573
was formed, after a fresh explosion which lasted
for some time, the little Kammenie; such as we

see it at the present day. Father Richard, a
Jesuit, says, that in his time there were several
old men in Santorin, who had seen that island
formed in the middle of the sea; and that they
had, on that account, named it *Micra Caimene*,
' little burnt island.'

When Tournefort visited Santorin, at the be-
ginning of the last century, the new Kammenie
was not yet in existence: it was not till some
years after, from 1707 to 1711, that it issued by
degrees from the bottom of the sea, after various
earthquakes. Every increase that the island
received was announced by a dreadful noise, and
followed by a white smoke, thick and infectious.
The whole was terminated by a shower of frag-
ments of basaltes, pumice-stones, and ashes,
which were spread to a great distance. The de-
tails of this memorable event are reported at
length, either in the journals of the times, or in a
Latin pamphlet made on the spot by a Jesuit.

If the reader reflects on the changes which
Santorin has experienced, through the effects of
a volcano, which acts on it from a very remote
period, he will remark in them four principal
eras, distinct from each other. At the first, the
island was united to Mounts St. Stephen and
Elias, as far as the environs of Pergos and Me-
saria; the only places which were not volca-
nized. The second was, the formation of the
rest of the island, as far as Therasia and Aspro-
nisi. The roadstead did not then exist, and the
island was as large again, of a rounded or oblong
form. The ground rose in the form of a calotte,
more or less irregular at its summit, commanded
at one of the extremities by Mounts St. Stephen
and Elias. The third period was, the sudden
and extraordinary depression which took place

in the middle of the island, whence has resulted the roadstead. The fourth and last period, is the formation of three islands, which have successively issued from the bottom of the sea. Perhaps, there will one day be formed others; perhaps, all these islands will be united to each other, and all the space which the roadstead occupies will be filled up. It is impossible to foresee all the changes which may take place, as long as the volcano which exists at Santorin shall remain in activity. The reader will see a curious article, called 'Account of the submarine Volcanoes of Santorin and the Azores;' extracted from Dallas's translation of the Natural History of Volcanoes, in Dodsley's Annual Register for 1801.

2822. *Aulis.*] This was a city of Bœotia, lying opposite to Eubœa. It was here the Grecian armament under Agamemnon lay wind-bound.

2823. *Locrian cities.*] The cities of the Locri Opuntii. The Opuntii had their names from Opus, the son of Jupiter and Protogenia.——Opus was also the name of a river of Locris. It appears that the Argo passed through the Euripus, between Eubœa and the main land.

2824. *Pagasæ.*] A bay and harbour of Thessaly, whence the Argonauts sailed, and to which they returned.

THE END.

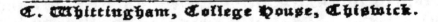
C. Whittingham, College House, Chiswick.

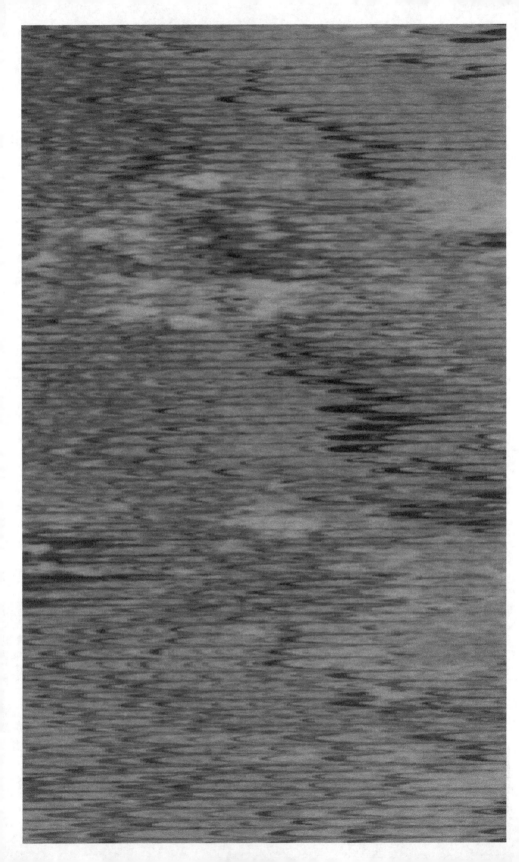

Check Out More Titles From HardPress Classics Series In this collection we are offering thousands of classic and hard to find books. This series spans a vast array of subjects – so you are bound to find something of interest to enjoy reading and learning about.

Subjects:
Architecture
Art
Biography & Autobiography
Body, Mind &Spirit
Children & Young Adult
Dramas
Education
Fiction
History
Language Arts & Disciplines
Law
Literary Collections
Music
Poetry
Psychology
Science
…and many more.

Visit us at www.hardpress.net

CPSIA information can be obtained
at www.ICGtesting.com
Printed in the USA
BVHW081817220819
556561BV00020B/4545/P